T0357863

GOOD GAME, NO REMATCH

GOOD GAME, NO REMATCH:

A LIFE MADE OF VIDEO GAMES

MIKE DRUCKER

HANOVER
SQUARE
PRESS

HANOVER
SQUARE
PRESS™

Recycling programs
for this product may
not exist in your area.

ISBN-13: 978-1-335-01269-2

Good Game, No Rematch

Hanover Square Press
22 Adelaide St. West, 41st Floor
Toronto, Ontario M5H 4E3, Canada
HanoverSqPress.com

Printed in U.S.A.

For mom, dad, Tiffany, and Daniel. This is all your fault.

GOOD GAME, NO REMATCH

TABLE OF CONTENTS

SECTION 1:

YOUR SAD ELECTRIC SON

FALLING IN LOVE
WITH A PLUMBER

I would love to say that I was born with a controller in my hands, but that would've ultimately meant a horrifying injury for my mother. Plus, how did the controller even get in there? Was it supposed to be there? Did it get stuck? How would I have even known how to hold it? It's a metaphor that begs a lot of questions.

I was three when we got a Nintendo Entertainment System for my sister's birthday. It's one of my first core memories, along with being way too hot at a carnival, and being terrified of *Who Framed Roger Rabbit*. I don't remember many of *my* birthdays from childhood, but I'll always remember my sister's seventh.

Nintendo is now an elder statesman in the video game ecosystem. But in the '80s, especially in North America, video games were in a bad place. While it had dominated the market in the late '70s and early '80s with hits like *Adventure* and *Pitfall*, Atari began to overplay its hand and rush awful, pretty much unfinished material out the door. Fans had faced an avalanche of terrible games that nobody bought. Case in point, the famous story of *E.T.: The Extra-Terrestrial* for the Atari, a game so terrible that hundreds of copies were literally thrown into a garbage dump. It was either that or just chuck the game's box at people and hope someone took it home. There was a moment between the decline of Atari and the rise of Nintendo that some people thought video games were just a passing fad. While computers like the Sinclair ZX Spectrum had better luck in Europe with games, the market was still rough. By the time we got a Nintendo, owning an Atari was almost quaint.

The Nintendo Entertainment System is what saved games—or at least saved console games as we knew them. Otherwise, I'm sure obtuse World War II simulators would probably still be coming out on PC. I would still play them and I would still be bad at them.

When we finally got our hands on an NES, Nintendo's slogan was "Now you're playing with power!" which feels more like a warning you give a child who's about to put a butter knife into an electrical outlet. While the NES's counterpart in Japan, the Famicom, had bright red and gold colors with a plastic sheen that screamed *TOY*, Nintendo went the opposite direction in the West. Their system looked like a VCR. A fancy VCR that would rarely work until you blew into the cartridge, no matter how many times Nintendo warned us not to do that exact thing.

As I said, our family got the original Nintendo for my sister's birthday, but we *definitely* both wanted it. By the time we got around to acquiring the system—three years after its release—we had seen endless television commercials, print ads, and merchandise. One commercial had a group of cool kids stunned as their TV broke open and R.O.B. the Robot came out! Holy shit! R.O.B. (Robotic Operating Buddy) was a part of Nintendo's strategy to make their system seem high-tech. *Seem* is important here since R.O.B. the Robot never amounted to anything. There were only two official games made for the toy. Two. Even then, it played those games with the energy of a retired fax machine.

While I hadn't played a Nintendo game yet—again, I was three—my sister had. What she described sounded like a dream: pipes, mushrooms, secret warp zones. And there was *another* game—on the same cartridge!—where you hunted ducks with a plastic gray gun called the Zapper. I was little, I was impressionable, and this sounded like toys where the toys played *back*.

It's important to note that we *knew* we were getting an NES. My parents had told us that—mostly so my sister didn't ask for anything else. But we still had to get through the birthday itself. We went out for a special breakfast: no Nintendo yet. We waited for Grandma and Grandpa: no Nintendo yet. We had cake: no Nintendo yet. They made us wait until that night before giving us the present. Then the screaming began. In a good way.

The box was cool as hell, especially the sci-fi-style packaging, which looked less like your parents had bought a plastic device from Sears and more like something fell off the back of the space shuttle. Inside the box was the console, controllers, and a cartridge that contained *Super Mario Bros.* and *Duck Hunt*. While *Duck Hunt* and *Mario* were available on their own, around 1986 they started selling the two on a single cartridge bundled with the console in what they called the "Action Set."

And the aforementioned Zapper light gun. Forgot that part. Big, shooty games have existed longer than video games. You can still play them at carnivals. It made sense to translate that attraction into something for home audiences. Especially since Nintendo literally made an analog hunting game called *Duck Hunt* in the '70s.[1] You could say that we as a society were wildly less concerned about putting a toy gun in a kid's hands. The gun itself was a futuristic silver and white, which they later changed to bright orange because someone realized that maybe that first one wasn't the greatest idea. It was a different time then.

Anyway, I was a three-year-old with a toy gun, and I knew above all else that *Duck Hunt* would be my obsession and NOT *Mario*. My dad set up the system, and there were two titles on the screen, not that I could read. I simply knew one had some random dude that looked like my dad's friends, and one had a duck. I wanted the ducks!

Yet I still remember the joy on my dad's and sister's faces when they played *Super Mario Bros.* for the first time. I watched as they flew through the air and collected coins and jumped on strange monsters. I remember my dad happily shouting, "We're going for a trip!" the first time Mario entered the pipe to World 1-2. Suddenly, the landscape changed. Mario was in a darker, more ominous area. The music had gone from fun

---

1 It worked by projecting images onto a wall that you'd shoot, and then it would sense if your shot overlapped the projected image. It actually seems pretty awesome.

and upbeat to sinister and rumbly. The Mushroom Kingdom was a land of mystery and magic.

But the whole time I was like, "Okay, this is nice, but when do we get back to the ducks?"

I was being pulled into the world of video games, and I already had bad opinions. Fake fans like things. Real fans hate everything. Remember that. Humanity built an entire internet on that philosophy.

Once my dad and my sister got a Game Over—or, more likely, got bored and hungry—the pleasure of the Nintendo Entertainment System was unceremoniously handed over to me. When I began crying because I was (need I remind you) three, my sister came back and reset it for me and put on *Duck Hunt*. God bless you, Tiffany. You sacrificed half of your childhood to scald your mouth on Kid Cuisines while babysitting us. May this positive mention of you in a book carry you through both good times and bad. And please get a new console. It's weird that you only have a PlayStation 3.

But finally, I had *Duck Hunt*. I was holding the Zapper in my shaking hands. This was it. This was the day I became a man. When the first duck flew on the screen, I knew what I had to do. Unfortunately, my body was still learning what movement was, so every shot missed. I quickly came face-to-face with that fucking, laughing *Duck Hunt* dog. Ostensibly, the dog should be helping you. Instead, it does absolutely nothing of note except laugh at you with a big, stupid grin and a weird 8-bit wiggle sound every time you miss a duck. He might be the first instance of a video game outright bullying the player. I mean, I know we all hate him, but that dude is such an asshole. He presents the ducks proudly when you do well but laughs when you don't? That's not what a friend does. It's what a family does.

Eventually, I switched to the mode where you shoot at clay discs rather than at ducks. There was no dog in this mode, which I was discovering was vitally important to my self-esteem. On the other hand, this mode was even harder, so I sucked even more. Just a frustrated little boy weeping while waving a gun at a TV. Nobody checked on me. At three, I was already known as someone who would burst into tears if you asked me if I was going to burst into tears. And I'll be real honest; I'm still that guy.

I began to inch closer to the screen. I was so bad at this game that I instinctively figured out how to cheat at it. A couple steps forward and suddenly I could start hitting those clay discs a little more accurately. Even closer and that dog wasn't laughing so much anymore, was he? Finally, I had the tip of the Zapper pressed against the glass of the screen and shot everything as if I was a Mafia hit man with terrible vision.

And oh, did I love it! The game didn't know I was basically cheating. It was an 8-bit system that could barely handle Mega Man walking between screens. But here I was, a hunting god. For a moment, I was Artemis herself! Ducks fell. Entire species were exterminated. I was blowing up so many goddamn discs there was a national clay shortage. When I asked my parents to look at me—look at what I can do!—they asked if I was supposed to be that close to the screen. I said, "I think so," and they didn't bother me again. The important thing is I was doing something that would keep me from talking.

The problem with being the God of the Hunt, of course, is that it gets boring pretty quick. Within a few days, shooting ducks with my Zapper against the screen just wasn't fun anymore. It was definitely my fault that it wasn't fun anymore, but how would I know that? The game gave me a job: kill. It's not my fault you don't like my methods.

I was left with one option: *Mario.* Sure, I asked my parents if we could get another shooting game, but they weren't doing "great" with "money" at "that time," so even renting a game when we just got two new ones wasn't in the cards.

So, finally, I tried *Super Mario Bros.* I'd seen my dad and sister play enough to know the basics. Run across the screen from left to right. Get a mushroom that makes you big. Grab a flower and you can spit fire. Jump on the turtles. Lava is bad. That last one is actually a pretty good life lesson.

Here's what I did not know: *Super Mario Bros.* is fucking great. You've got some good design sense when your game is intuitive for a tiny, whiny child. I wasn't even a smart three-year-old. I used to think that if I was hungry, I could swallow air to feel better. There is no genius in here. Only regrets.

Playing *Mario* was different than watching *Mario.* Mario's Mushroom Kingdom is itself already a place of wonder with its riffs on *Alice in Wonderland.* Everything was magical. Stars made you invincible. You could walk and jump and break bricks with your fist, despite it clearly looking in the game like Mario was breaking the bricks with his head. There's a water stage with lovely music as you swim by enemy fish. Even the aboveground stages would change their look, going from day to night, going from grassy green to snowy white. Moving through progressively harder castles to find Princess Toadstool made it all epic: it really did feel like a *kingdom* that you were exploring. Even if every time Toad told me that the princess was in another castle, I thought, "I really hate this kingdom. Why does this kingdom need eight castles? I'm not even sure if it has eight people."

As you may have read in the history books, the Mushroom Kingdom was run by Princess Toadstool. Her name's since been changed to her Japanese version, "Peach." Personally, I feel Princess Toadstool has a little more pizzazz, but nobody asked me. Despite the crude graphics and Princess Toadstool looking like Sloth from *The Goonies*, the game took hold in my mind. I convinced myself it was all real.

Video games, as a medium, let you interact with the art directly. They create a space in which you have power and belong. It's not a difficult jump for a little kid to conclude that these spaces mean something and could even be visited with enough imagination. All I had to do was figure out all the game's secrets.

And the great part of being a three-year-old, outside of never hearing the term "student debt," was that my imagination was just beginning to explode. By sheer chance, Mario—and soon, Link, Mega Man, Samus, and the sexy *Tetris* L-Block— had hit my brain the moment it started making stories. With my parents working day and night, often with multiple jobs, I had a lot of time alone. Video games helped fill that void. If my siblings didn't want to play with me, I'd just go to the Mushroom Kingdom and hang out. I'm not saying the games babysat me—that was my reluctant sister—but they did give me a place to be myself and pass the time. My real world was drab. My parents screamed at each other. I had trouble making friends. It was nice to escape.

But my *Mario* obsession was just beginning, and it perfectly coincided with the rise of *Mario* as a cultural phenomenon. There were toys. Bedsheets. School folders. Large stickers you could put on your wall that promised not to ruin said wall. McDonald's Happy Meals. Even nightly news programs covered the popularity of the plumber. *Super Mario Bros.* sold about 40 million copies for the NES—that's *not* including rereleases and ports for other systems. It was the bestselling game for decades. I know we all know it was big, but it had an *impact* that arguably wasn't seen again until *Pokémon*.

Of the initial wave of merch and media, my absolute favorite was *The Super Mario Bros. Super Show!*, a cartoon bookended with live-action sequences starring professional wrestler Captain Lou Albano as Mario himself. In one episode, a fake Cher shows up to hang out with the Mario Brothers. In a different Mario cartoon, Princess Toadstool visited Earth to see Milli Vanilli. I'm not making that up. Those are events that happened in the Mario Universe Alternate Timeline, which is a term I just made up.

I embraced all of it. I wore Mario shirts. I had a Mario backpack. A Mario lunch box. A Mario cereal, shared with Link from *The Legend of Zelda*, which was the coolest thing any child has ever seen before or since. No matter what you've experienced, it is not as good as that cereal. This was my Beatlemania. Remember those wall stickers I mentioned? Yeah, I got them for Christmas and absolutely ruined the wall in my room by shuffling them around as much as possible. I also fell off the top bunk trying to put a Goomba up on the popcorn ceiling.

Parents with more time and resources on their hands might have seen this as a problem. But my family wasn't outdoorsy, and a product that kept their loudest child silent was a god-send. *Super Mario Bros. 2* came out shortly after we got the NES, which only made things better. *Super Mario Bros. 2* is a weird game. Nintendo had already made a direct sequel to *Super Mario Bros.*—one that looked pretty much exactly like the first entry in the series. But the developers thought it was too hard for those cowards in the Western audience, so they reskinned a different game and packaged that as *Super Mario Bros. 2* for the rest of us. It's a cute game, even if the controls are a bit floatier than the rest of the series. But hey, you can play as Toad and Princess Toadstool, which oddly was still a rare feature for a while after that.

The thing is, because I was so on board with video games, I kind of assumed everyone else was, too. And let me tell you, they were not. But the good news is that I found this out by humiliating myself in front of a crush.

There were identical twins in my class, Caroline and Cora. I was in elementary school, and *Super Mario Bros. 3* had just come out. While *Super Mario Bros. 2* was considered lovely, if odd, *Super Mario Bros. 3* was a return to form with the marketing blitz to match. Fred Savage starred in a movie-length commercial for Nintendo called "The Wizard," which showed off the game as if it was the most important invention of our time, which it clearly was. One television ad featured children shouting "Mario" across the globe. So obviously, with *Mario 3* being *such a big game*, Caroline and Cora would know everything about it.

I was years from the horrors of puberty, but I did know in my primal heart that I wanted to impress them. While a lot of folks go the traditional route of impressing someone by accomplishing things and living their best life, I did something far worse and far more embarrassing: I made my own Super Mario costume.

I cut up and donned a red cardboard box for the outfit and a red hat my dad must've bought me at some sporting event or other. Then I cut out a piece of my dad's black socks for a mustache and, like a genius, used Elmer's glue to stick it to my face directly below the nose.

And as the final touch, the thing that made it really special, I added a raccoon tail. Because, as we all know, Mario has a raccoon tail in *Super Mario 3*. I almost wrote "Tanooki Tail," but then I realized that Raccoon Mario and Tanooki Mario are not the same Mario. You can see why this was already a bad idea. But I couldn't! So I took another piece of cardboard, used crayons to draw a yellow-and-black tail—looking far more like a bee's dirty ass than a mammal's tail—and taped it to myself. Scotch tape didn't work on this one, so I did the next best thing: duct tape. I duct-taped a tail to my butt.

To summarize: my Mario costume was a cardboard outfit, a red sports-team hat, a mustache of sock glued to my face, and a floppy tail with creases. One look in the mirror and I recognized that this was going to be the day that I… Actually, I've got no idea what I expected to happen if it went well. Maybe Cora would hug me with tears in her eyes and say, "You're dressed as Mario, a character I'm both familiar with and love as much as you." Then Caroline would say, "You seem happy. I won't ignore you anymore." Then we'd hug. And then Caroline and Cora would ask if I wanted to "Do the Mario," and I'd say, "Of course," and we'd sing the opening theme from *The Super Mario Bros. Super Show!*

That song, by the way, is truly a banger. Unfortunately, I don't think Caroline and Cora would have agreed based on their response. Which, I want to be clear, was the normal person response.

I walked across the neighborhood to where I thought their house was. This was a bit of a gamble, since the houses in my neighborhood looked the same and mistakes happen. It's terrifying to knock on the wrong door when you're six and have a man in his underwear open up and ask what you're selling.

Fortunately, the blonde woman who opened the door at least appeared similar to Caroline and Cora. Their mom looked me up and down, and then with the deepest of sympathies asked, "Are you okay?" I affirmed that I was but I would love to talk to Caroline and Cora if they were home. "Oh, are you one of their friends?"

"We're in the same class together!" Which is kind of a dodgy answer. With the same confused look on her face that I'd soon see on her children, the woman asked me to wait and closed the door.

When the door opened, there were Caroline and Cora. The angels of Maplewood Elementary School's first-grade class. Both were absolutely baffled by what they were seeing in front of them. I must have looked like a child that had got caught in a pile of garbage before trying to hang out with kids to maybe score a Capri-Sun. Cora politely asked me what I was wearing. This was my first clue that things were not going to plan. I took a breath.

"I'm Mario!"

"Who?"

"Super Mario!"

"Oh! From the game!" A saddened politeness…from someone who was literally my age and in my grade. Cora sort of knew who Mario was, while Caroline had seen the cartoon a few times. Neither had played it, but this was progress. Maybe I'd spend a few hours explaining games in the way that every girl likes having a guy talk at them.

This interaction did not last long.

I explained that, in *Super Mario Bros. 3*, Mario can pick up a dead brown leaf and become a flying raccoon. After the longest silence in Earth's history, I asked Cora if she wanted to hang out. Caroline said "no" on her sister's behalf.

The good news is I wasn't really aware of the concept of rejection yet. And honestly, the fact that they were nice at all during what must have been a very weird experience for them is a compliment. I may have confused them. But I didn't terrify them. Although maybe I should have clocked that wearing a plumber-with-a-tail costume in the middle of the day wasn't necessarily going to impress anybody, including fans of Mario. Fortunately, Caroline and Cora took the polite tact of pretending this never happened.

Still, Mario was my guy. Maybe it was the fact that the main character was a little fat plumber and I was a little fat kid with nascent body issues. When I was younger, almost every superhero and action star had to have massive muscles and six-packs and big guns and catchphrases. Here, instead, was a friendly, chubby man with a blue-collar job. I knew I'd never look like GI Joe, but I could *definitely* end up looking like Mario. He was one of us.

Clearly, as I grew in age, wisdom, and birthday presents, I began to obsess over new little pixel people. Mega Man still holds a huge spot in my heart, and it's probably no coincidence that I was drawn to another chunky, silly character. Mega Man is a robot, so his blue-collar job is just "robot." Like Mario, Mega Man was an action hero that seemed to eat too many burgers. Oh, later on, Mega Man X would thin our boy up,[2] but at what cost? At. What. Cost?

But it was Mario that pulled me in. It's wild to think how much that one gift changed the direction of my life. Or, considering I was basically a large toddler, that gift *started* the direction of my life. The path from my sister's seventh birthday to me writing this book is a straight line through video game land. In short, video games informed how I move through the world—even if that meant trying to impress somebody with the most embarrassing costume ever made by human hands.

---

2 Yes, X is canonically a different robot than Mega Man. Please save your angry letters.

NOW YOU'RE PLAYING WITH PORTABLE POWER

The tagline was "Now you're playing with portable power!" And it clicked right away, baby. Nintendo was now in its cool-kid phase. We were still a year or two out from Sega releasing ads that essentially said Nintendo was a pussy and you were a loser for liking it. You have to remember, we were all so much dumber. Video game ads can be embarrassing these days, but they were fucking humiliating in the past. There was an entire rap song about *The Legend of Zelda*, and that was one of the *better* commercials.

But when it came out in 1989, the Game Boy was *the future*. At least, it seemed that way. With its blocky rectangular body, white-gray exterior, and red buttons, it was designed to look and feel like the original Nintendo Entertainment System. This included the box, which featured glowing hands holding a shining system in one of those vast but empty 1980s cyberspace landscapes. All the mighty technology of a home console—*on the go*. Forget the fact that it was the size of a brick and had a vomit-green screen that was barely visible. Nobody in my school cared about that. We just knew three things: this was a Nintendo we could take on road trips; this was a Nintendo we could sneak into class; and, again, the boxes and ads featured crackling electricity, which was pretty cool. Electricity equals computer!

God, we were nincompoops.

Still, we all needed one. When one of your friends got a Game Boy, they would hand it to you with sorrow and fear in their eyes, as if they were a scientist handing an infant a canister of nitroglycerin. Inevitably, your friend would mumble an assertive but nervous "Can I have that back?" I'm sure if I dropped a friend's Game Boy, my parents would not have found the pieces of my body spread across Broward County.

Nintendo also knew how to squeeze their biggest suckers, because, as part of the promotion, they released a special comic book in which a tiny Super Mario entered the real world after being summoned by children and flying out on a Game Boy. Why? Because a weird, creepy adult shoplifted a Game Boy from his retail job and used it to summon all the enemies from *Super Mario Land*, of course! I kid you not when I say that this story literally involves a dinner at the World Trade Center and characters hijacking a plane. Don't worry: the hijackers only crash into Walt Disney World. I actually own this comic in mint condition. It's graded 9.8, which is pretty amazing. It's only worth about $100, which is less amazing.

While it was a portal in the comics, the Game Boy became a full-on character in the Saturday morning cartoon *Captain N: The Game Master*. Don't worry if you haven't heard of it, because nobody has. It was a short-lived show on NBC in which a teenager from the real world and his dog are sucked into Video Land, an amalgamation of all the popular Nintendo games circa 1989. Or at least, the games that the show could get permission to use. It's kind of hilarious to watch now, because while the show was able to *get* characters from different franchises, they didn't know what to *do* with them. Personalities are completely changed. The vampire hunter Simon Belmont from *Castlevania* goes from laconic and serious to being vain and brainless. Mega Man goes from being a brave blue robot boy to a weird green dude with the voice of an eighty-year-old smoker. And the angelic Pit from *Kid Icarus*, well, they just renamed him Kid Icarus. Why not? Companies didn't have style guides to rely on, and fans didn't have forums to voice their grumpiness.

When Game Boy joined the team, he had this bright, childish personality that was ostensibly supposed to connect the cartoon on the screen to the demands on our birthday and holiday lists. Game Boy was a kid, just like us! Unfortunately, the character was actually just kind of annoying. As with every other element of the show, it was vastly clear that none of the adults at the wheel knew what the fuck was going on. Having worked in TV now for most of my adult life, my best guess was that the producers were shown, like, five pictures of an actual Game Boy before it came out and were told, "This heavy slab of plastic is one of our leads now."

None of us could resist the promise of an actual portable system. Nor was this our first encounter with one. A few years before the NES, Nintendo released a series of toys called Game & Watch, which were basically handheld systems with the power of a calculator. They used little, still LCD images of heroes, enemies, and items that would appear on-screen in chunky jumps to seem like they were animated. I had a *Zelda* wristwatch before I had a Game Boy, complete with an obtuse, abstract game where Link explores a dungeon. And that's not to mention the Tiger Electronics games, which were themselves essentially Game & Watch games with branding from popular IP like *Jurassic Park* or *Sonic the Hedgehog*. Were they fun? Absolutely not! But without a Game Boy, they were mostly all we had for car rides. This was really, for a lot of us, the first time we'd have a screen we could carry around. And not for nothing, I like to think that this was the first brave step into the nightmare hellhole that we live in today.

That all said, my family was not in a great financial position during this era. Neither of my parents had a college degree, and they'd had their kids relatively early in their twenties. My dad worked for car dealerships he loved but sometimes had health issues. My mom worked multiple jobs from retail to customer service. A lot of school supplies and holiday gifts were bought with the help of employee discounts. Every time we had to go on one of my parents' boss's fucking boats for some d-bag party, I'd just marvel at how much money these people had while listening to them talk in their loudest voices about which Miami Dolphins cheerleaders were hot.

When my parents argued, it was almost always over money. Sometimes that anger spilled over onto us. Having kids was expensive. Owning a house was expensive. Forcing your sons to be in Cub Scouts was expensive. We didn't grow up in poverty, but throughout my childhood, things were always in a state I'd euphemistically describe as "iffy."

In other words, while I desperately wanted a Game Boy,

I didn't see one in my near future. Oh, I asked for it! Oh, my parents knew I wanted it! But in their minds, we'd just got a Nintendo a couple years earlier and that was expensive enough, which is fair. It didn't help that they could see straight through the techno-advertising: "Wait, it's in black-and-white? And it takes four batteries? And you can barely see the screen?! *No!*" My dad compared it to listening to music on a tin can attached to a string rather than using a stereo system. I compared it to having a Game Boy, and I really wanted one.

Still, even as a little kid, I understood my parents' money situation. The JC Penney corporation should be held criminally responsible for the amount of yelling I had to overhear about credit card debt. I understood why a Game Boy wasn't happening anytime soon. I wasn't mad about that. I was a depressed child, but I kind of put the math together that if my parents bought me a Game Boy, they'd probably be even more mad at each other about money, which would mean I would have to once again blast *Tiny Toons Adventures* to avoid the next goddamn back-and-forth.

So when my birthday came around, I didn't expect much. I don't even know what I expected. What do you get a kid when they're six? A ball? I feel like a hoop and a ball. I also wasn't old enough to think that my birthday was the most important day of the year and everyone had to worship me and lavish me with expensive products. That wouldn't come until my late twenties.

Whether I had a birthday party or not that year, I don't know. I do know I attended at least two friends' birthday parties at McDonald's, which, at the time, was the height of luxury. I'm not sure when it happened, but at some point in recent history, McDonald's birthday parties went from "Aw, this is fun!" to a troubling sign that the kid's family wasn't doing too hot. Then again, read the above paragraphs. Who knows. Our local McDonald's had a little plastic column of flowing water bubbles, which, to me, meant it was a classy joint.

Regardless, when we were kids we'd often have a regular birthday, and then that weekend, my father's parents—the grandparents who lived near us in Florida—would drive down from whatever Boca Raton snowbird condo they were living in and take us out to lunch anywhere we wanted to eat as long as it was Chili's.

Don't get me wrong: we were very glad and grateful that we had our dad's parents. Our mom's mom was amazing, but she lived far away and died while we were relatively young. My mom's dad left the picture when she was a little kid, so we never met him at all. When we found out he'd died, our collective reaction was to take a second and then ask if anyone was hungry and wanted to get dinner. So due to circumstances and geography, we mostly only had Grandma Lori and Grandpa Shelly. Both were social butterflies with strong interests in pastel colors (which are great) and golf (which is golf).

The good news is Lori and Shelly *loved* spending time with us. The bad news is by *us*, I mean my sister and my brother. They found me kind of annoying, and I get why. I was a boy, so my grandma thought I should hang out with my grandpa. Sadly, I didn't like golf, so that mostly meant standing outside in the humid Florida sun while he tried to explain the difference between irons and woods. I know they loved me, but I think they were also befuddled by me. I couldn't swing a golf club, but I could name a lot of dinosaurs.

This got even worse at family holidays like Thanksgiving or Passover. My mother raised me Catholic, but my father's family practices what I'd call "Holiday Judaism." The Druckers are proud of their heritage, but they also loved a good Christmas ham, and Passover seders often involved my grandpa mumbling "Let's skip along a bit" five or six times.

Meanwhile, I existed in a liminal space. After the meal, all the women would go to the kitchen and clean. I wasn't allowed in there. All the men would go to the family room and watch football. I did not want to be in there. So I'd quietly sit on a fifty-year-old couch looking at glass animals and counting down the hours until I was able to play *Mario* or *Dragon Warrior* or not have to listen to my uncle talk about the stock market and why this time—this time!—it was gonna be big, baby! As a bonus, I'd often be scolded *as a little child* for not investing my money yet. Being a kid couldn't have been more fun!

I loved my grandparents. I still love my grandparents. I dream about them sometimes. However, I did not expect them to be the people who would get me a Game Boy. They weren't fans of the Nintendo Entertainment System, I'll tell you that for free. Whenever they visited and saw us playing, they'd demand we shut it off and put on "Real TV." Real TV never meant something fun or an action movie or, like, *The X-Files*, which I should not have been allowed to watch but my parents did not care.

Real TV inevitably meant either serious movies where nothing happened or sports, especially golf. Sometimes Real

TV meant nothing at all! They'd just flip through the channels and complain that there was nothing on. When an adult wanted to watch something, your ass did not have time to find a save spot or beat the level and get the password to come back later. It took me so many tries to beat *Super Mario Bros. 2* because the moment I hit a groove, some fucking adult would ask for Real TV.

That year, the birthday dinner at Chili's was unremarkable. We had food, they asked how school was, I probably talked about my progress on coloring inside the lines of worksheets or something, etc. I'm sure I was absolutely boring to them—especially compared to my sister, who had a bright, artistic personality as a kid. But I loved them and they loved me, and since love is only showable through material goods, they lifted a wrapped box out of a bag and put it on the table. This was a surprise, but I was cautious. I'd been burned before. I fully expected to open the box and find a polo shirt that would attach itself to every moist amoebalike fold in my body.

Under the wrapping paper was a blank cardboard box. No brand. No logo. This was already new to me. I was far more used to the two-part, top-and-bottom boxes that are the horror of every child opening presents. The box that makes you lift the lid and slowly move aside tissue paper to discover the new pair of church slacks that are going to make you look so sharp, just so handsome! Yes, my Jewish grandparents bought me church slacks. I think because they were technically also wedding, funeral, and—most importantly—golf clothes. They knew they'd get me into that sport yet!

I ripped away at the cardboard and inside, in its gorgeous cyberpunk-looking box, was the Game Boy. Lord, I screamed.

Yell-screamed. My grandpa whispered to keep my voice down. I was so loud that the waiter came over because he probably assumed that I'd swallowed shards of glass. It was guttural. It was primal. It was Game Boy.

As I rotated the box in my hands, I thought of all the possibilities. It came with *Tetris*, which I'd only heard about but had never got the opportunity to try. Apparently it was a puzzle game from Russia that people couldn't stop playing. It all looked like random shapes to me, but I was sure it was going to be okay. And I knew I could probably spend my remaining birthday cash on *Super Mario Land*, the very same game in the Nintendo comics. Portable Mario. Done. This was the entryway into a new world.

Lori and Shelly were naturally happy that I was happy. I'm sure it confused them in the past why I hadn't been thrilled with golf clothes. I loved games. They loved golf. Golf was a game. Clearly everyone should love golf. But none of that was important at the moment. They had finally understood that I didn't need golf, I needed the Game Boy.

"Can I open it up?"

"Absolutely not."

Fair. We were in a restaurant. I'd do it later. Having the box itself in my hands was enough to fill my mind with dreams of not being bored. I read the parts of the label I could and asked my grandma to read me the parts I didn't understand. As my eyes watered being in the presence of God's light, my grandfather smiled.

"Do you want another gift?"

I froze. Was this a trick? Clearly, the previous incident had left a mark on me, and I didn't want to fail here. I think I was afraid this was some sort of game show situation in which I could have the Game Boy *or* the mystery box, but not both. I wasn't going to take my chances on a gamble of this magnitude.

"No. This is okay."

Now my grandfather froze because I'd thrown that fucking curveball right back at him. I didn't know he was offering a *real* present! I thought he was testing me to see if I was an ungrateful piece of shit!

"You don't want another gift? Why wouldn't you want another gift?"

I considered this.

"I like the Game Boy."

"I'm glad, but do you want another gift?"

I stuck to my guns here.

"No."

Why did I say this? I don't know. When you get in trouble enough as a child, you really learn to try to avoid getting yelled at as much as possible. I'd seen my grandparents lose their shit when I spilled a two-liter bottle of Pepsi on their carpet. If that could set someone off, who knew what taking the wrong gift could do? Please remember I was a weird child.

My grandfather became frustrated and said, "Lori, just give him the fucking thing."

My grandma pulled another box from her purse, a small square one in plastic shrink-wrap. The first words I saw on the packaging were *Game Boy*. Oh my God. I'm such a dummy. They got me *Super Mario Land*! Yes! Of course they did! That makes sense!

As my grandma pulled out the rest of the box, I finally got a glimpse of the title. It wasn't *Super Mario Land*.

It was, ladies and gentlemen, *Golf*.

Golf for Game Boy.

Yet I was psyched! True, I thought golf was boring, but this was video game golf. Whether or not it was the game I wanted, it was still a game for the brand-new system I had just received. Plus, I didn't need to go outside or walk, which was about 80 percent of why I hated golf. So I thought, fuck it, let's play some golf. Or at least the childhood version of that thought.

I played the crap out of it. And boy did I suck. I ran into a bit of a chicken-and-egg problem: *Golf* for Game Boy kind of expected you to already know the rules of golf. It didn't really do a great job explaining where you should hit the ball, why, or what things meant. There was a manual, but I was too young to get what anything meant. Hell, you could've read it to me and I still wouldn't have understood it.

I didn't play *Golf* on a loop to make my grandparents happy. They never asked about it again. I don't even know if they remembered they bought it. My guess is that this had been their compromise: they got to be heroes by getting me the greatest toy of all time, *but* the catch was that it had to still have some golf in it. And God bless 'em for that decision.

Decades later, as happens in this shameful reality, my grandparents became sick and passed away, starting with my grandpa. He had smoked for the first fifty years of his life,[3] and even though he had quit, it still caught up with him. When I got the call that he might be dying, I was working at Nintendo. The

---

3   Well, probably not the first two or three of those years.

fact they'd brought a huge part of gaming into my life wasn't lost on me. I might not have had this career without that moment of strange, unusual deviation from their standard gifts.

Knowing the end was near, I flew back to Florida with that copy of Game Boy *Golf* in my pocket. Not as a tribute but as a reminder. The game I might have played the least on Game Boy was perhaps the game that meant the most to me. I never processed that until then. My grandfather, a proud, stubborn man, had met me halfway, and I still had (and have) playable proof of it to this day.

We were with my grandfather when he passed. We swapped holding his hand as his breathing became shallow. We watched his eyes slowly close and his mouth settle, and that was the end of Sheldon Drucker. If the afterlife is real, nobody is more relieved than him that he passed before the advent of *Young Sheldon*.

I'd later learn that my grandfather's golf life was far more interesting than I thought. In the 1950s and 1960s, my grandparents were a big Las Vegas couple. That was their vacation spot. They'd leave my dad and his siblings in Des Moines, Iowa, and go play poker and blackjack and slots at the various casinos. I also have a theory that they were into swinging, but that's mostly because they seemed very interested in dressing up and partying in different states. But I'll give you one guess what else they loved playing in Vegas. That's right: golf! In fact, my grandfather fell into a fun golf group of other Las Vegas guys. They became close, spending time together whenever they were in town at the same time. These people were cool! They dressed even nicer than Shelly did. They always seemed to have a lot of money and offered to pay for lunch every time. As far as my grandparents knew, they were just *legitimate* businessmen.

Turns out, my grandfather was the only person in that golf group who was not in the Mafia. They just really loved hanging out with him but didn't want him to know. My angry, loud grandfather was a hip, cool golf bro in his youth. He only figured out his friends were in the mob when one of them invited him to his house and there were multiple guards with guns. My grandfather and grandmother then commenced with what I'm assuming was the most careful, slow, and dangerous ghosting of all time. Maybe I'd have liked golf more if I knew all of this.

To nobody's surprise, Lori Drucker had happily granted one of my grandfather's final wishes: to be buried in his favorite golf clothes.

Throughout that day, I had my hand in my pocket holding that Game Boy *Golf* cartridge. It's silly, I know. But somehow that moment meant everything to me. Nobody knew I had it. I'm not sure they'd even understand why. Grandparents giving grandchildren gifts is the most boring who-gives-a-shit thing in the world.

I'm still bad at Game Boy *Golf*. I much prefer the casual versions of the sport like *Mario Golf* that recommend clubs and hold my little bitty hand the whole way. But every so often, I still take this original cartridge and play it. The Game Boy they got me died long ago. Between drops and water damage and pure negligence, it ended its life being donated to Goodwill with a note that it didn't work. But *Golf* for the Game Boy still works just as good as it did over three decades ago.

VIDEO GAME MANUALS
BY DECADE

1970s: Welcome to *Brick Ball*! In this exciting clone of an arcade game for your personal home computer system, you are an astronaut delivering the last medicine to a space station. To do this, you'll need to move a paddle and break bricks at the top of the screen! Be sure to insert the dinner plate–sized game disc with the label down or your computer may burst into flames. Good luck!

1980s: Listen up, soldier! It's Colonel Games here, and you've just purchased a certified *Colonel Games* product! Our seal of quality means quality! Now, listen up a second time, maggot! You are Robot Rabbit, and your mission is to move from left to right on the screen without getting hit by any of the ghosts created by Dr. Carrot! Here are five pages of blank space to take notes!

1990s: Whooooooa! Are you ready for the most thrilling

excitement ever? Sure, you are... *Not!* Grab four bodacious controllers, four radical friends, and be prepared for some off-the-chain shredding! Note: game only works with Double Super Pack Expansion attached to the Upper Core add-on of the Mark 3 version of the console. Your parents can help you set it up! Tubular!

2000s: Hello. Welcome to this game. In the following two pages, we will list the controls with absolutely no context. R2 is to Gotcha. X is to Spider Roll. A is to Spring. The rest of this manual will be legal disclaimers printed in size 2 font.

2010s: Insert disc to begin downloading patches overnight. Please go to the website listed on this card for a loose description of the game. We will be taking the website down in three days.

2020s: Here is a 36-digit download code. The rest of this $100 box is empty, just like you.

ACCESSORIES TO PAIN

The Power Glove was only good for one thing.

Before the Nintendo Wii, we all kind of assumed that motion controls were the future. Then they came out and they were…adequate. We loved wildly swinging our arms to bowl and play tennis until we realized that this was mostly only fun for bowling or tennis. To be fair, modern virtual reality devices like the Meta Quest have since improved upon motion controls. Mountain climbing feels like mountain climbing. Boxing feels like boxing. And, unfortunately, accidentally punching a wall while doing any of this feels like punching a wall.

Coincidentally, the prospect of virtual reality helped propel the dream of motion controls. Whereas now virtual reality is a fun way to make your roommates wonder if you're dead while you're watching a movie, back in the '80s and '90s, we thought VR was going to change the very fabric of humanity. For some reason, from about 1980 to 2001, pop culture was entirely convinced that we would eventually be able to enter a computer and—sometimes if we were really lucky—

even kiss somebody in it! So many movies and shows were based on this concept: *Tron*, *The Lawnmower Man*, *eXistenZ*.[4] I'd say approximately half of the children's fiction of the day involved getting sucked into the information superhighway. There was even a *Power Rangers*–style show called *VR Troopers*, which pivoted on the idea that some lame teens were actually superheroes in cyberspace! The show, for obvious reasons, did not put up *Power Rangers* numbers. I watched every episode. I could not tell you anything about any of them.

The Nintendo Wii was incredible for its time, but playing it was, even then, far from seamless. While the system could detect movement, it wasn't always great at detecting *where* that movement was going. And even when later controllers got better sensors, you still had to put the controller down on the table every two seconds so it could calibrate. And that was when motion controls were *ready* for prime time. Before that, so many gaming peripherals tried and got shot down like me asking out a crush while dressed as Mario.

Some early motion-control peripherals were absolutely bonkers. The U-Force was a controller released by Broderbund, the company behind *Carmen Sandiego*. They also made Print Shop Deluxe, which allowed teachers to create perfect-attendance certificates without having to put in any effort. The U-Force looks like a thick, open laptop with sensors where the screen and keyboard should be. Theoretically, you'd wave your hands over these sensors, which would register as movements on your Nintendo Entertainment System. The box says "Works with virtually all Nintendo games," with

---

4 You do not know how hard it was to get my computer to accept this spelling and stylization of that title.

that *virtually* doing some Atlas-level heavy lifting. What the box doesn't tell you is there's a parenthetical "terribly" between "works" and "with."

Another peripheral that should never have existed is the Sega Activator for the Genesis/Mega Drive. This was basically a plastic octagon on the floor that you were supposed to move your hands and legs over to replicate fighting moves in games like *Mortal Kombat*, *Street Fighter*, or—I dunno—*Eternal Champions*. I remember when I bought it with birthday money, I thought I was going to both learn martial arts *and* finally get in shape. Which, honestly, is kind of a sad wish for a child to make. So many cries for help! Whatever! As with the U-Force, it didn't work that well. What was a simple button press turned into repeatedly thrusting your leg over the sensor, hoping it registered your movement at just the right angle. It looked less like fighting and more like you were just really, really bad at the hokey pokey.

And then there was the Nintendo Power Glove.

The Power Glove came with one heavy advantage: it had the Nintendo name on it. We trusted Nintendo! They had their own seal of quality on boxes that was supposed to mean something that nobody ever really understood! The glove was a bulky, plastic gauntlet with gray fingers and a keypad on the wrist to enter so-called codes that would allow it to work with different games. The whole vibe was cool as hell. The Power Glove even appeared in *The Wizard*, the same film that promoted *Super Mario Bros. 3*. That's product placement, baby!

Ads for the Power Glove made it look like you could simply plug the device into your Nintendo Entertainment System, enter a code on your wrist, and then you'd be able to actually *box* your opponents in *Punch-Out!!* Also, *Punch-Out!!* is supposed to be written with two exclamation points, which is making my autocorrect want to die. The point being, the Power Glove was supposed to replicate the actual feeling of whatever it was you were doing in the game. In a driving game like *Rad Racer*, you could—if the ads were to be believed—control the car by moving your hand like it's on a steering wheel. For platforming games like *Mario*, you were supposed to be able to bounce your wrist to jump and wiggle your fingers to spit fireballs. It seemed like the next step in gaming evolution to me, a child who was six or seven when I finally got one. Then again, you could've shaken keys in front of my simple face and I would've thought it was the next step in gaming evolution.

Here's how the Nintendo Power Glove was supposed to work when you finally got it out of the box: you placed plastic sensors around your television, plugged the wire into the Nintendo Entertainment System, turned on the console, typed in a brief code, and entered a new dimension of gaming.

Here's how the Nintendo Power Glove actually worked: it didn't. It was a peripheral that hated you. It was an accessory that only wanted to cause you sorrow and pain.

Setting up the Power Glove itself sucked. The directions made no sense, and that meant I had to ask for help from my parents, who (importantly) knew how to read all the words. The plastic sensors that were supposed to rest on the television wouldn't stay the hell in place. Either they'd fall right off the TV or end up angled just a few degrees off, making the glove essentially useless. Everything had to be exactly right or the gloves were just pricey brass knuckles. And you know how I mentioned earlier that you needed to input a little code to configure the Power Glove for different games? That itself *also* sucked. Enter the code wrong, it would not work. Enter the code right, and it still usually would not work. It was a fun surprise to turn on the TV and find out how it wouldn't work this time!

The point being, using the Power Glove wasn't the one-to-one experience we were sold on. The platonic ideal of the device would've make us feel like Wolfgang Amadeus Mozart. The real version was a kind of arrhythmic jerking-off motion that moved your character sometimes if you were lucky.

As for me, I got the Power Glove for Christmas. Why? The television told me that I wanted it, all my friends said they wanted it, and I was a child with few leadership qualities. Ads have always been designed to sell you things, but between commercials and magazines and Fred Savage movies, it was hard for a kid my age to avoid the hype machine. Even the box was incredible with a picture of the Power Glove shooting lasers at a TV in the distance. I grew up surrounded by ads, but this was a full-on blitz. And if a company is willing to spend *that* much money on commercials, then certainly it must be a good product! No errors in that thinking!

I remember setting up the Power Glove for the first time. I needed my dad's help, which itself required a lot of cajoling and anxiety over getting yelled at. As I've mentioned, the first frustration set in when the sensors wouldn't stay straight on the TV. The thick cords on the device seemed to pull it just a *little* out of place, no matter where you put it. When they weren't twisting around, they were outright flopping onto the floor. We hadn't even turned on the Nintendo yet, and my father was already breaking a sweat and looking at me like I myself had designed the toy to torture him.

With the sensors finally secured with tape, we tried it out. When I was six, my dad was at least three or four reading levels above me: he was able to follow the instructions. But it barely worked. No matter how closely we followed the glove's manual or how hard I shot my fist out, I was not delivering punches in *Punch-Out!!* We tried programming another code into the buttons for *Super Mario.* Along with the buttons for programming the glove, there was also a basic NES controller built into the wrist. You could always tell as a kid when you were on the verge of giving up when you started using the controller part. And even that was uncomfortable and awkward. Worse, you could only also access those buttons with one hand because you were literally wearing the controller. But somehow it was still more effective than an electric glove that was designed for that specific purpose.

Anyway, my dad took a turn, and he quickly broke down and just started using the game pad. He was now furious. The tape got loose and the sensors dropped off the television again. He ripped off the glove and used two hands to program in a code and then, putting it back, still found it did not work. I learned a lot of new swear words that day. But in my defense, I kept telling him it wasn't a big deal, I could play with other stuff, etc. Even at that age, I would rather a toy not work than have my father curse his entire existence and every choice that had led him to this moment.

My dad removed the glove and stormed off, muttering under his breath that he might write a letter to Mattel. Oh, that's another thing about the Power Glove. It was *licensed* by

Nintendo, but it was made by Mattel. So while it appeared to be one of Nintendo's internally developed wonders, it was actually just a really shitty piece of junk made by some random people who are probably dead by now.

Yet I still tried to make it work. I spent hours over the next few weeks taking down and setting up the same terrible sensors that kept slipping off the TV. I tried to parse the codes on my own, hoping that I could enter them correctly even if my dad couldn't. The worst part? It *almost* worked. For a few brief moments, while I was racing little remote-controlled cars in *RC Pro-Am*, it felt good! This was what they were talking about! Then the sensors slipped off the TV, and it didn't work again. With a sigh and probably a cry, I put the Power Glove down. Christmas was over! Except for all the food and other gifts I didn't deserve.

Except the Power Glove *did* work, just not as expected. My sister, only a few years older than me, was extremely curious about it. Her age had just hit double digits, so she was wiser to the ways of the world. I handed the toy to her. She turned it over and looked at it, trying it on and flexing her fingers. She spoke as if she wasn't even paying attention.

"Dad said this doesn't work."

Yep. True. I confirmed that.

"What is it even supposed to do?"

My sister liked playing video games with me, but she wasn't as enthralled. She didn't read every gaming magazine cover to cover, she didn't make a Super Nintendo out of cardboard when our parents didn't have enough money for that gorgeous new system. She was busy being a human being doing human being things. I told her what the glove was for. You could actually move your hands to control the game the way you would in real life!

However, I made one mistake. I used *Punch-Out!!* as my example. I told my sister that when you punch with the Power Glove, it's like punching something in real life. That's definitely the way I phrased it, which was a bad idea.

My sister donned the glove. Then she punched me straight in the stomach with it.

"Hey," she said. "It works!"

YOUR SAD ELECTRIC SON

Let me tell you about my relationship with my dad.

You know that song "Cat's in the Cradle" by Harry Chapin? It's basically a guy saying that he can't play with his son and he's sorry for disappointing him. You're supposed to shake your wise head in sadness at the singer and feel for a child who just wants to play catch or something. The last part of the song is the dad saying he finally has time to play with his now-adult son and his son being like, "Nah, you had your chance, buddy." It's more poetic than that, but it definitely has Nah-you-had-your-chance-buddy energy.

Anyway, my relationship with my dad was a lot like that song. Specifically that last part. In fact, you could say that, throughout my childhood, we had a *reverse* "Cat's in the Cradle" situation. Rather than the song being about a boy who wants to play catch with his dad, our version of the song would be a dad depressed that his son never wanted to play ball. To be fair, my dad never criticized me for not playing sports. He just really wanted me to be interested in the same things he was interested in, and I really wanted to be left alone.

I didn't even hate sports, but what I did hate was being forced to *watch* sports. By the time I was in elementary school my favorite two activities were reading and video games, both of which I preferred to do inside with the comfort of air-conditioning and orange juice, away from the vampire-killing power of the sun. Sporting events, by their very nature, were usually outside. Stadiums in Florida were hot, crowded, and, most importantly, boring to me, a sensitive little dork. Watching sports—especially when I was compelled under the fist of an angry dad—felt and still feels like watching someone else have a better time than me.

The problem is that, as a kid, I was *required* to go to football and baseball games. I didn't have a choice. "Get in the fucking car or I'll give you something to cry about" may have been my father's catchphrase for a couple years. He desperately wanted his kids to love watching sports, and he would work overtime to make me and my sister hate watching sports in the process. My brother took to it, though, and eventually played for one of our county's first high school ice hockey teams. Dude could stop rockets.

As for me, I began pushing back at my dad when I was around seven or eight years old. Whining and crying all the time made my dad worried about my masculinity. Which I get. My dad grew up as a baby boomer in Iowa: he is the target demographic for believing that Big Sports = Big Man. Sports were something he could talk to guy friends and male strangers about. It was a common language that he shared with the other men in his life, including my grandfather. And whether I liked sports or not, when my dad, my relatives, and his friends watched a game, at least they were yelling at the players and not me.

I don't think my dad was outright worried that my not being masculine was going to ruin my life. He wasn't angry I didn't want to play Little League. I just think he was bummed. While my brother would fill the hole of the athletic child later, I was the oldest son. I was supposed to share the same bonds with him that he shared with my grandfather. So my not enjoying sports probably felt like a huge letdown. He might have also been a little embarrassed and confused. I was a heavyset, melodramatic child with hair that looked like a rat's nest. He didn't have a budding man to show off to his friends. So he kept pushing. Maybe if he tried hard enough, he could just break through to the other side. If I had to sit through enough baseball, maybe I'd want to talk about baseball.

And wouldn't you know it, Dad's embarrassment and confusion over this often translated into anger. Throughout my childhood, my parents struggled with various problems that parents struggle with. Getting sick, constantly changing jobs, having money issues, having even more money issues, and then having additional money issues. Depending on the mood of the day, our house could be a powder keg. I might have been a champion whiner, but it was still a fraught process that could set him off. Thankfully, this anger was never something along the lines of "My son is a [slur of your choice]." My dad wasn't and isn't a bigot. Don't worry: we'd just be told we were dumb, ungrateful, lazy, and basically any other insult that a child really takes to heart.

However, my dad is someone who very much cares how

people perceive him, so hopefully he's given up on reading the book by this chapter. He didn't want to lose his cool in front of his friends, so he'd get mad in private when my sister or I would protest going to a game. My sister was luckier in that she was the most dreaded thing possible: a girl. My dad would've loved her to be into sports, but her not having any interest was within the natural order of things.

When we'd make fun of the game *at* the game, my pops would give us a stern look that meant a long, loud car ride home with the possibility of him simultaneously trying to drive and swing his arm at us in the back seat. But very, very rarely did he lose his cool in public. Even as a child, I realized I could use this to my advantage. I might not have been as big or strong as him. But I could do one thing very well. I could be a complete asshole. It's a family specialty.

In the early 1990s, stadiums didn't have the same level of security as we have now. Sure, security guards might poke through bags at the (former) Joe Robbie Stadium, but they weren't patting kids down and calling the bomb squad if they had a Nintendo Switch. Also, Nintendo Switches didn't exist yet. What security guards really wanted to block was outside food and booze. They didn't consider a child might sneak in a Game Boy or a copy of *Men Are from Mars, Women Are from Venus* that I stole from a friend's parents. Which is what I did.

When I brought games or a book like *The Island of Dr. Moreau* to the stadium, it served two purposes. One, it embarrassed my father, which helped me feel a bit better about wasting my Sunday. Two, I was trying to keep from being bored out of my mind. The only advantage to being outside was that I could see the Game Boy screen pretty well and

Super Mario Land wasn't going to finish itself. I'd whip it out, begin playing, and eventually my dad would look around and theatrically whisper, "Would you put that away?!" Then he'd glance around to see if any other men had witnessed this outrageous offense.[5]

Even the times I wasn't actively trying to embarrass my father, I accidentally did. There was one Miami Dolphins game where, at some break or another, an ad for the fast-food joint Checkers played. At the end of the ad, there was a little 8-bit chiptune musical flourish. It sounded so familiar. Where was that from? I knew I'd heard that song before. What was it? What was it?

And then I had it! I had the solution!

"Dad! That's the theme from *Burger Time!*"

"Oh. No, it's an ad for Checkers, Mike."

"No, no, no. *Burger Time* is a video game!"

"Okay."

"And the music they were just playing for the burger place…was *Burger Time!*"

I've literally watched a relative die in a hospital, but to this day, that *Burger Time* interaction was the fastest I've ever seen the light leave a man's eyes. It was like every door my dad had hoped was still open suddenly slammed shut. My most recent victory before that had been asking him why the quarterbacks were always so handsome. That time I wasn't even fucking with him. It was just a question. But it was successful in that it did help me avoid a few home games for a month or two. And I never got an answer! Why *are* the quarterbacks so hand-

---

5 I hope they did, and I hope they judged the crap out of us.

some? I wasn't a fan, but even I could tell you that Dan Marino had that "It" factor, baby! What a star!

Either way, he never gave up on me. I was a difficult kid to connect with, especially if you were a dude from the Midwest who was brought up to believe that being a man came with a certain order of operations. You were supposed to love sports and you were supposed to live your life silently suffering. To this day, one of my great confusions is why some dudes so badly need to have their masculinity confirmed back to them like it's a permission slip from a teacher. I still don't get it. Just be yourself, buddy.

Fortunately, my dad wasn't trying to change me or fix me. It was more like he thought that if I kept having to watch sports, a piece of the evolutionary puzzle would slide into place and I'd be like, "I get it now! Manhood! What a concept!"

But there are two more embarrassing moments that truly broke him, both at Florida Marlins games.

One happened in 1997. I was at Game 7 of the World Series with the Florida Marlins against what was then called the Cleveland Indians. That's a pretty important game, folks! With every pitch and every swing, the entire crowd held their breath. I'm certain that this was one of the most powerful moments in a lot of those people's lives, something they'll look back on and remember forever.

Meanwhile, I wasn't even masking my boredom. Unfortunately, we were at this game with one of my dad's former work friends. This guy wasn't my favorite. I don't want to paint all my dad's friends with a broad brush, but just imagine combining Brick Tamland and Champ Kind in *Anchorman* and that's basically 99 percent of them. Just big old confident dummies. If you painted a tunnel on a wall, most of my dad's friends would march straight into it. Then they'd keep running into the wall, assuming that the plaster must be at fault here. I spent my childhood around these goofy fucks having to smell cheap beer on their breath as they talked about why Ross Perot had it in the bag.

Some of my dad's friends were even assholes to *him*! They were part of that generation where they'd do incredibly mean shit to each other and be like, "Ahhh! I'm just razzing ya!" I didn't like when my dad was mean to us, but I definitely didn't like when those hapless dipshits were mean to him either. So if you do feel like I might be talking about you, ahhh I'm just razzing ya!

The friend in question—let's call him "Bobby"—was the king of the douchebags. He somehow both looked like John Waters and a Bond villain at the same time while not being as cool as either. Whenever I saw him, he'd be condescending toward me about everything from sports ("Do you know what a home run is?") to romance ("You don't like that lady over there? Are you gay?"). Sitting near him was pure annoyance. I didn't always get along with my dad, but this dude sucked.

Here's the crazy thing: when the Marlins won, I got lost in the moment and screamed and cheered with the rest of them. Considering there had been an ongoing quest to make me like sports, one may have thought, "Hey, he's cheering—let's leave him alone. Right?" Just give me some credit for even participating! Instead, Bobby said, "I bet this is better than that *Pac-Man* shit you waste your time with!" Motherfucker was trying me and he was almost twenty years out of date on his references. Immediately, all excitement drained from me as my thirteen-year-old soul returned to its bitter form. I said, "Eh. *Final Fantasy VII* was better." He didn't even ask me what that was. He just frowned.

And then Bobby told my dad! He tattled that I said *Final Fantasy VII* was better than the Marlins winning the World Series! If you're making me choose between Billy the Marlin and Sephiroth, Billy will lose, folks.

My father, of course, was humiliated. On the car ride home, I was scolded for being so glib to my dad's friends, especially Bobby, who was a very precious man who must be protected against the slings and arrows of a middle schooler. That might also have been the exact moment my dad gave up on me and sports. We never really talked about it, but he slowly stopped making me go. If the biggest baseball game of the year wasn't converting me into a fan, maybe it was time to move on. And hopefully he realized that it actually cost him good money to force a child to be bored outside.

But the most embarrassing thing that I did to my father was purely by accident years earlier when I was about nine, in 1993 or so, since time works that way. What happened wasn't as important as watching the World Series, but this earlier moment probably should've signaled to my dad to cut his losses on the father–son sports relationship. Which is ironic, because it was also the greatest athletic moment of my life to this very day. Even better, it was something my dad had always wanted but never achieved himself: catching a foul ball. And why, yes, it was done in the most embarrassing way possible!

We were at a no-stakes, regular-season Florida Marlins game against the Chicago Cubs. That is to say, our family's current home team versus my parents' original home team. I had snuck a book into the game to distract myself, *War of the Worlds* by H. G. Wells. Every so often, I'd look up, see a ball get hit, and begin reading again.

Suddenly, there was a loud crack of the bat. The crowd cheered, and the people behind us started jumping and shouting. Even without looking, I could *feel* the stadium shake as everyone stood up and crowded around some spot above me. As for me, I passive-aggressively sighed and hunched over my book. You know when you're trying to read on an airplane but apparently every other person on the flight sounds like they're going to the same cocaine-fueled bachelor party? It was like that. I barely clocked what was happening, and then seconds later, a small object fell between my bent-over-back and the chair itself.

A baseball.

Nobody had noticed where the ball went but me, the boy holding it behind his back while darting his eyes around. I may not have been there by choice, but even I recognized that catching a baseball was kind of cool. I also had seen enough baseball games to know that adults will rip a baseball right out of the hand of a child, so I kept it hidden. This caused a lot of confusion and complaining in our area of the crowd. People were searching around the ground and under seats for the ball. But to paraphrase Brandy and Monica, the ball is mine.

Quietly, I bent back down in my chair and reached around for the ball. It was real. I had caught a baseball. And even better? I had caught a baseball because I was specifically *not* paying attention to catching a baseball. There's some sort of philosophical lesson in there that I still haven't learned. But, confirming I had the foul ball, I quietly handed the ball to my dad and said, "I think I caught it."

Again, it's fascinating to see the light leaving a grown man's eyes. My dad at that point was at the end of his thirties, and he had told us multiple times how he'd always dreamed of catching a ball someday. Home run, foul, it didn't matter. Ever since he was a little boy in Iowa, he thought it would be the coolest thing on Earth to catch a ball at a baseball game. But he never did once. Instead, his child who immediately went right back to reading did!

My dad wasn't mad at me. He was somehow both confused and proud and a little disappointed that I caught the ball. I had lived one of his all-American dreams by putting in literally negative effort. The universe had shown him something Lovecraftian: that the person least excited to be at the sports game was the one who just had the best moment at the sports game. It was like seeing his brain turn off and reset.

On the drive home, my dad was a little bit manic. He was proud! It was so great! We had to get a little plaque for it! Man, how he wished he had caught the ball! Ha ha! Pretty lucky that Mike had that book with him, right? I wanted to pat his shoulder and say, "Hey. It's okay, man." I almost felt bad, like I'd stolen something precious from him. He was happy a Drucker had caught a foul ball. He was baffled by which Drucker. I mean, he was fine. But I did feel bad.

When we got home, my dad asked for the ball. I gave it to him. He's always loved collecting sports memorabilia, and his son's first (and definitely only) foul ball would have fit perfectly in his collection. "Would have" because none of us ever saw that ball again. He didn't get rid of it. It's probably somewhere in my parents' house, stuck between boxes of newspapers from when Pope John Paul II visited Miami. Either way, he never ended up displaying that ball.

I'm still not a massive fan of watching sports. I can definitely *play* a sports game. I can even sweat profusely and breathe heavily while playing a real one outside with any temporary friends. But I don't think I'll ever be able to break into the stats and the histories and the storylines and the excitement and the camaraderie, which is a shame. And to my dad's credit, he did make an effort to help me understand why he enjoyed it. Although, I will be honest, he still won't tell me why quarterbacks are the handsome ones.

KING GRAHAM AND THE QUEEN OF COMPUTER GAMES

The stories in games used to be more important to me than the actual *games* themselves. For me, in a lot of role-playing and adventure games, the story *was* the adventure. Oh, I know that sentence is cringey. I just don't care.

In the '80s and early '90s, most adventure and role-playing games were PC exclusive. Occasionally you'd get great ports like LucasArts's adventure game *Maniac Mansion*, which made its way to the NES. But early adventure games suffered from obtuse user interfaces where you'd sometimes need to type out exactly what you wanted your character to do while hoping they'd do it. In the very earliest of adventure games, like *Zork*, that's all there was: text. Which ironically still holds up today because reading never goes out of style! God, I hope anyone has read this far.[6]

As for me, I didn't really get into story-heavy games until

---

6   Except for my dad.

we got our first CD-ROM drive. Only one or two years after being told that we absolutely, positively needed to get a *personal computer*, we were now being told that we definitely, indubitably needed to buy a CD-ROM drive. They were the wave of the future! Displays in stores ran copies of *Myst*, an adventure game with vaguely confused live actors playing parts to the best of their ability. While *Myst* was never my cup of tea, including because it's a game and not tea, even I was grabbed by the magic of vast, computer-generated vistas in eye-popping colors.

The propaganda was twofold. Computer stores and gaming magazines promised that CD-ROMs would change everything, and we actually got to use them fairly often at school. Because, just like us, schools were getting a hard sell on those plastic discs. And they were amazing! *Encarta*, the once-iconic encyclopedia software, featured *videos* of historical events! They had *audio* of famous speeches! Meanwhile, we got access to other CD-ROM programs that would read us children's books! It didn't just benefit us: teachers around the world had a new way to distract students while they nursed a hangover.

There are moments in technology that feel incremental, and there are moments that feel like something big has just shown up and wants to fuck your wife and sleep in your bed. CD-ROMs were promised to bring live video and voice-over by real actors. These games would have bigger, more intricate landscapes with images that could only fit on a technological marvel that held a whole—you're going to need to sit down—700 megabytes of data. Seven hundred megabytes! The microSD card in my Steam Deck is a full terabyte, which is about 1,428 times more space. I'm now *relieved* when I have to download something as small as 700 megabytes.

Our first CD-ROM drive was, in hindsight, a piece of shit. It was attached to the computer by a series of cables that definitely aren't made anymore, and the drive itself ran as slow as possible, if at all. Half the time it would make a whirring sound and then just stop, which always made me afraid I'd get blamed. My parents talked about every new device, including video game consoles, in exactly two ways: "Hey, everyone! Gather around! We've got this stunning, new device that's going to give us joy forever!" and then, seconds later, "If you touch this with even a small finger, I will rip your soul bones out through your chest."

When CD-ROMs were still new and developers were trying to figure out how to use a whole 700 megabytes of storage, everything seemed impressive. I distinctly remember one game called *Quantum Gate*, which is a name that a twelve-year-old boy would think is very, very cool. It's a science fiction adventure game with full-motion video. Characters moved and talked! Games would never be the same! Unfortunately, the story behind *Quantum Gate*—you're on an alien planet trying to eliminate bad guys who turn out not to be bad guys—is pretty lame, even by kid standards. A problem with early CD-ROM games was that a lot of developers spent so much time taping actors and animating visual effects that they forgot to write something actually interesting that was also fun to play.

Still, this was groundbreaking technology. Real voices. Real music. I cannot explain to you just how much *The 7th Guest* scared the shit out of me as a kid. You play a mysterious visitor to an abandoned haunted house. Your job is to solve a series of increasingly difficult puzzles that each reveals a little more of the story as it goes. Ultimately, it becomes clear that the ghosts in the house are meant to catch a little boy for a dark ritual to fulfill their greatest desires, as one does. And, in a twist of fate, *you* are the ghost of that boy, trying to prevent the cycle from continuing. *The 7th Guest* might not be Shirley Jackson, but its gothic story, devious puzzles, haunting rooms, and creepy music really did make it feel like it was breaking ground. In all honesty, most of the cool effects were just animating movement between scenes until another static screen appeared that you had to click around. But that was like half of the PC games in the '90s.

On the bright side, CD-ROMs were cheaper to make and thus often cheaper to buy than cartridge-based games like those on the NES. There were already bargain bins at computer stores filled with weird random collections of discs that usually had no cohesive theme. My favorite things as a child were these odd plastic vertical value packs. They'd cost next to nothing and were a fun little dice roll to see if you got anything good. The CD-ROM value pack almost always had a couple essential elements: a questionable health application, a useless business program, an educational program aimed at a narrow category, and a disc with hundreds of shareware games. Or, as humanity still knows them, *demos*.

I made some amazing discoveries on these shareware discs. It's where I first played *Doom*. *Doom* had already been available via floppy disks. But I didn't know that! And when you're a child and see the word *Doom* on a large list of games, you click it *immediately*. I'd seen a few first-person shooter games like *Wolfenstein 3D*, but this was one of the first games to really make me feel afraid. I was scared of the monsters and the sound design and the claustrophobic corridors. The game still rocks to this day.

There was another game I discovered from these shareware packs, one that has all but fallen down humanity's memory hole: *Hugo's House of Horrors*, the adventure game where Hugo—and this is going to blow your mind—enters a house of horrors! No? Not blowing your mind? Because literally that's about it. You walk around a creepy house, trying to interact with various objects as you get closer and closer to shutting off the program. I think it was supposed to have a quirky *Abbott and Costello Meet Frankenstein* vibe. The important thing is you absolutely do not remember that game.[7]

Overall, the CD-ROM bargain bin packs tended to produce far more duds than hits. *Space Invaders* clones that weren't as good as *Space Invaders*. *Pac-Man* knockoffs. Countless side-scrolling games that wanted to steal Mario's lunch. The closest we got was *Duke Nukem*, an '80s cliché bad dude with sunglasses. His side-scrolling game was adequate, but he'd later become famous for *Duke Nukem 3D*, a game like *Doom* but with a lot more gross-out humor and boobs. We children loved it!

But the one CD-ROM game from the vertical value pack that changed my life was *King's Quest V.*

I had spent years struggling to get literally anyone in my neighborhood to play Dungeons & Dragons. I almost got a game going in elementary school, but my D20 got confis-

---

7   If you do, please become my friend immediately. I don't have many.

cated because my teacher thought it was intended for gambling. But I wanted that experience! I knew this was who I truly was. I wanted to be an adventurer in a magical land! Or an adventurer in a normal land! Or an adventurer anywhere that wasn't Florida! And I wanted to be the one who controlled my own journey. This was not an early, healthy form of self-actualization. This was me learning an important but tragic lesson that would inform the rest of my life: if human interaction fails, the solution to all your problems is behind a screen of one kind or another.

And no, I didn't know there were already-existing Dungeons & Dragons video games. And definitely not ones I would've understood. I'm sure D&D games like *Pools of Radiance* were incredible when they first came out, but I had zero access and zero ways to find them. I thought *King's Quest V* might be my only chance to confront mythical monsters... or at least some other stand-ins for my parents.

But what I got was so much more.

During the '80s and some of the '90s, *King's Quest* was the top-selling computer game franchise. And there were a lot of great computer games bouncing around! Both *Ultima* and *Wizardry* still influence role-playing games today. We're talking the birth years of *Civilization* and *SimCity*. The market for PC games wasn't as big as the market for consoles, but we had fun, folks. While *King's Quest* may not have been putting up *Mario* numbers, it was still at the top of the ladder.

Part of what drew me to *King's Quest V*, and later the rest of the series, was its lightness. In a lot of fantasy-themed games, everything is so motherfucking dire. Your village has been sacked and your family murdered. A villain is burning the countryside. Only you can go into a dark, dangerous dungeon to punch skeletons and find keys to treasure chests. Instead, playing *King's Quest* felt like watching a Disney cartoon. Hell, it felt like *walking into* a Disney cartoon.

In most *King's Quest* games, you control a member of the royal family of a fictional country called Daventry. It's basically Fairy Tale Land with little cute references to various Mother Goose stories. As with most adventure games, you're essentially trying to solve puzzle after puzzle to make your way through the plot. The first *King's Quest* involved finding three treasures that would allow Graham to become king of Daventry. The second was Graham finding a wife. The Daventry royal family expanded as the games expanded. We even get a long-lost prince in there!

But in *King's Quest V*, you're King Graham, a silver fox with a nose for adventure. An evil wizard has magically stolen your castle. An owl, himself magical, takes pity on King Graham and flies him to a strange, different fantasy-themed setting to take down the wizard in question. As a child full of anxious wonder, this was the fantasy adventure I'd been hoping for.

But *King's Quest V* was just beginning to stretch its multimedia legs. There weren't any fancy CGI sequences to show us the wonders of ten-frames-per-second pre–*Toy Story* computer animation. We'd get those in *King's Quest VI* (along with a truly mortifying end-credits song). Meanwhile, *King's Quest VII* would bring us beautiful hand-animated sequences (along with a truly mortifying opening-credits song).

Despite my burning need to get into role-playing games, *King's Quest* is nothing like Dungeons & Dragons, outside of the fact that some games have dungeon-y areas and dragon-ish characters. In fact, playing the two couldn't be more different. Dungeons & Dragons is a game in which you create a unique character with stats that allow you to do anything you want and change the story to your whims. *King's Quest* is a linear adventure game in which, if you don't do everything exactly fucking right, you will die over and over, again and again and again, until you dole out money for an overpriced strategy guide. Thank God walk-throughs of games are free these days.

I love *King's Quest* so much. Every few years, I play through the entire series. True, they're all nightmares that run on unfair rules and absolutely absurd logic. A few of the puzzles were easy—you just needed to check the manual for the solution to prove you legally owned the game. But some of the games would *mess you up* with pure nonsense. There's one puzzle in the first *King's Quest* where you have to say Rumpelstiltskin's name backward. I'm sorry, I mean you have to *guess* that you're supposed to say Rumpelstiltskin's name backward.

To creator Roberta Williams's and her team's infinite credit, the *King's Quest* series was part of an early wave of games that proved the medium could have actual, interesting stories. Maybe it wasn't as deep as *Ultima*, but at least there's more to do than in *Dragon's Lair*, an arcade game where you had to instantly match on-screen prompts with button presses. There was no interactivity past that. It's just a beautiful Don Bluth cartoon that you never finished because you died every ten seconds.

That said, *King's Quest* games are hard as fuck. And I was a little weirdo who handled adversity with the strength of wet toilet paper. *King's Quest V* literally has a sequence in which you're trying to steer a boat with zero idea of where to go. I can't emphasize how lost I was trying this on my own. As far as I can tell, this water maze was made to simply add hours of trial and error to the game.

That's where the strategy guide came in. And not just any strategy guide, reader! Peter Spear's *King's Quest Companion*. It included every game in the series both as a walk-through and as factionalized novellas that still contained all the answers. The strategy guide showed you how to beat those impossible puzzles, traps, and mazes, and if you couldn't even afford the games themselves, at least you could still get the complete story. I was under ten years old at this point, so, yeah, I 100 percent made my mom read to me from the book. Even better, Sierra rereleased the entire series on CD-ROM, including earlier games that were only available on massive floppy disks. Finally, I could experience the full adventures of King Graham, Queen Valanice, Prince Alexander, and Princess Rosella. I still know a fictional royal family's lineage by heart but really don't know the names of all my cousins. To be fair, I have a lot of cousins.

Like *Mario* before it, *King's Quest* captured my soul. I'd draw fan art of King Graham and Prince Alexander and read everything I could on the making of the games, which wasn't a particularly difficult task considering there was no internet and only a few hobbyist magazines that even covered the industry. I learned about the game's creator, Roberta Williams, and her Disney influences. I learned about *King's Quest*'s sister series *Space Quest*, which, unfortunately, was not a Roberta Williams joint. I'd later appreciate other great adventure game designers like Tim Schafer, Ron Gilbert, and Jane Jensen, but for a large portion of my childhood, Roberta Williams was *the* pinnacle of interactive stories.

When I was in the seventh grade, we had to do a small presentation on a woman we admire outside of our families. Other kids did reports on musicians, actors, politicians, athletes. I, as you can expect from reading this chapter, chose Roberta Williams. Between magazine profiles and interviews about her games, I was able to *sort of* trace her career, starting with the first graphical adventure game, *Mystery House*, up through the live-action horror game, *Phantasmagoria*.

There was one problem. My teacher did not believe Roberta Williams was a real person. At all. She gave me an F. If you think it's fucking bleak being someone who's too into video games now, you have no idea what it was like trying to be academic about them in middle school in the '90s. I could not let this stand. It was unjust! King Graham wouldn't have let this happen in *his* kingdom! As a rebuttal, I brought the *King's Quest Companion* as well as a copy of *InterAction*, a promotional booklet that was half magazine and half catalog for Sierra On-Line games, including a picture of Roberta Williams with her name under it. She was real!

The teacher reversed my grade to an A. Although, I don't think she was happy about it. On the last page, she added a short paragraph in pen explaining that she had intended this assignment to be for bigger figures. She'd let it go this time, with the caveat that, in the future, I needed to choose someone "more prominent." But Roberta Williams, the Queen of Games, could not have been more prominent in my life. That said, if I met Roberta Williams now, I'd shed tears of happiness and tell her that her games helped make me the person I am today. Which, considering the person I am today, could actually be a negative. I'd probably mostly just keep repeating "You're Roberta Williams" and "Thank you" over and over again until she left the room and blocked me on all social media.

Perhaps because I had hubris before I even knew what that was, I ended up sending a *King's Quest* game pitch document to Sierra On-Line. This would've been around when I was ten or eleven, after the release of *King's Quest VII*, but before the release of *King's Quest: Mask of Eternity*. I was going to break into the video game industry the same way everyone does: by sending a letter to a major corporation as a child nobody's heard of before.

Now, I once talked to a developer who complained that most people who say they have a video game idea actually have a *story* idea that might work in a video game. A zombie apocalypse is a great setting, but it isn't a fucking game. You want to make a murder-mystery video game? Great! There's, like, two thousand ways to do that. Do you have a plan? Do you even know *how* the mystery is solved? No? We'll figure that out later? Great!

Anyway, the annoying dummy who was pitching a story rather than a game was ten-year-old me. I hadn't even seen game-development documents before and, like I said, I lived for a good tale. I couldn't sketch out puzzles because I was bad at puzzles. I certainly didn't know what a fucking storyboard was. All I could do was write a very thorough plot outline. The fact that the document was in four or five different typefaces and font sizes probably didn't help. But as a child, all you got to do is believe hard enough and wishes can come true!

In my imagination, a secretary of some sort would gently knock on the door of Roberta Williams's gilded wood office. Roberta would say, "Enter!" The secretary would give her an envelope with handwriting that looks like someone broke my fingers with a hammer. She'd initially toss it aside, but then, in a fit of deep curiosity, she would open it.

Inside the envelope, she'd find the pitch for her next game, *King's Quest VIII*! She'd read the story of Prince Alexander saving King Graham from a *new* wizard named Leahcim, which is definitely not my own name spelled backward. Every one of the six pages would fill her with the joy of creation. She'd break down, wailing and laughing in equal measure. Her secretary would ask Roberta Williams if she was okay. Roberta would say, "I am. But I've been touched by this young boy's triple-spaced, typo-filled story. Games are stories, and that's all that matters!"

Tragically, Roberta Williams never wrote me back[8] and moved forward with *King's Quest: Mask of Eternity*. Unfortunately, from what I've read, it seems like she was slowly pushed out of her own project by business dummies who thought the way to increase sales of *King's Quest* was to change every single aspect of it. Instead of an adventure game featuring the royal family of Daventry exploring colorful landscapes, it was a (very bad) action role-playing game in which some random dude explored dark, boring areas. But hey, at least it swapped out the hand-drawn cartoon art of *King's Quest VII* with bland, rudimentary 3D graphics!

Mask of Eternity was a critical and commercial flop, but

---

8 That document 100 percent never came close to hitting her desk.

that didn't change what the rest of the series meant to me. It filled my vacuous little mind with wonder, and inspired me to write what was, essentially, my first fan fiction. And God bless Roberta Williams. During a time when I had fuck all to look up to and when—to paraphrase the Muppet Babies—"my world looked kind of weird and I wished I wasn't there," her games helped. I'd always loved stories, but she showed me I could live them.[9]

---

9   If Roberta Williams is reading this, do I have a pitch doc for you!

MY FATHER, THE STREET FIGHTER

A couple years back, when I was in my midthirties, my dad and I had an argument. I honestly don't remember what it was about, but probably something involving me calling every piece of art in their house *creepy*. I swear to God, there's a painting of twelve children whose eyes follow you as you move. Anyway, at some point in this argument I must've brought up something from the past because my dad said something that a lot of people hear from their parents: "You only remember the bad things. You never remember the nice things we did!"

It's a phrase that usually comes with a slice of guilt. Your— or rather, my—parents feel bad about something in the past. But they don't want you to dwell on it or ever mention it! They wish you'd call them out for the cool shit they did! And so I did just that. I told him that I, in fact, had an extremely important memory from my childhood in which he was my hero. Let me share it with you.

So! Capcom's *Street Fighter 2: The World Warrior* was the

coolest game I'd ever played. Of course, when I was eight, you could have put a picture of dogshit on a Nintendo cartridge and I'd probably have thought it was art, but *Street Fighter 2* was different. It's hard to overstate just how brilliant it looked and played when it hit arcades in 1991 and, later, the Super Nintendo in 1992.[10] Sure, there had been plenty of games where you could fight people. Obviously, there was a *Street Fighter 1*, but even in that game, you only had the option of two characters (Ken and Ryu) and the fighting felt slow and laggy. You'd trade simple punches and kicks until someone fell down.

But *Street Fighter 2*! Even in the game's original version— i.e., *The World Warrior*—you had the choice of eight different fighters from eight different parts of the globe with eight different fighting styles. Well, seven, really, because Ken and Ryu were the same person the same way I used to think Billy Joel and Elton John were the same. It turns out one is a piano man, the other is a rocket man.

The game was also *beautiful*. I was so used to characters being tiny sprites. Even when Mario ate a super mushroom, he still looked relatively small on-screen. The battlers in *Street Fighter 2* were massive. They dominated the space and had more colors in a game than I knew were possible in reality. Each fighter had their own personalities and backstories and endings you'd see if you beat the game. People identified themselves based on which character they liked the most (Blanka and, later, Chun-Li for me). The kooky karate arcade game subgenre turned into an entire industry. Soon, other

---

10   And then later, when they felt like it, on Genesis.

companies would pop up and imitate *Street Fighter 2*'s success, to the point of actual lawsuits.

I was eight, and *Street Fighter 2* was the most grown-up game I'd played up to that point. The sound and graphics made you feel it in your bones when a character fell or crashed into a box. This was adult, albeit bloodless, gaming! We were still a year away from *Mortal Kombat*'s head-ripping fun. As far as I was concerned, this was maximum violence and carnage, and I lived for it.

There had been games like it, and there had been games in adjacent genres, but with those giant sprites and magnificent animated backgrounds and blasting, high-intensity music, *Street Fighter 2: The World Warrior* was truly a trip around the globe. It was also a somewhat racist, cliché-filled trip around the globe, but that's not the point. I was learning about different countries through the wonders of punching.

When I heard *Street Fighter 2* was coming to the Super Nintendo, I did what kids have done since time immemorial: I begged for it for Christmas. Pleaded for it. Prayed for it. Needed it so bad that I'd *die* if I didn't get it. It would've actually been pretty funny if my parents called me on that bluff. But if I was going to get any gift at all, it needed to be *Street Fighter 2* for the Super Nintendo. This was—and still is!—one of the most innovative games of all time. The only problem was, it also came with an exciting, new innovative price: $70.

Yep! We complain about games costing too much now, but companies have been pulling that shit for years! Explaining why I wanted a $70 karate game was difficult. That's a lot of money for a game for a kid who already ate more Taco Bell than he was worth. I tried telling my parents that you could throw fireballs and do flying uppercuts and electrocute your enemies but, believe it or not, that didn't move the needle with adults. My dad is into cars, so I thought I could interest him with the sumo wrestler character, E. Honda. This made sense to me. Instead, my dad thought I was insulting him by comparing him to a, you know, sumo wrestler.

Still, they got the game for me. When I opened that gift, I almost had to leave the room. This was it. Life was complete. My parents may have spent most of the year screaming at us and telling us we smiled wrong in photos, but they sometimes landed that plane on Christmas morning. A solid family foundation if there ever was one.

Street Fighter 2 did not leave my Super Nintendo for weeks. I made my sister play it with me despite her wholehearted lack of interest in fighting games. While she and I had grown up playing video games together, she was entering her teenage years by the time the game came out. She was a popular student with a lot of friends and admirers. Despite her new teen ways, she could still throw down in a game when she had to. Before I got good, she absolutely decimated me with my dad's favorite sumo wrestler. My sister had figured out something before I did: certain characters would do special moves if you just tapped the button very fast.

The game dominated my life. At school, my friends and I discussed strategy and rumors. One kid heard that there was a secret cheat code to let you play as the villainous boss, M. Bison. Of course, Capcom would soon become known for releasing an endless string of versions of *Street Fighter* that expanded the cast and adjusted the gameplay. But back in the

Maplewood Elementary School cafeteria, we were hungry for any *Street Fighter* content we could get. One kid brought an official *Street Fighter 2* card game that was promptly confiscated.

To eight-year-old me, *Street Fighter 2* represented the power of the new generation of consoles. More colors, more sounds, more action, more buzzwords! I could freaking electrocute people as Blanka! I could stretch my arms as Dhalsim! I could brush my stunning hair as Guile!

Life was perfect, and nothing could ever go wrong again.

Despite only being a teenager, my sister had always seemed decades older than my brother and me. But in her life, things were actually starting to become interesting. She got a boyfriend. She became passionate about painting. She smoked, which was something cartoon camels used to tell kids was cool. But as the oldest sibling and the only one tall enough to reach the phone without a chair, she was still in charge of babysitting us. She was fourteen, knew she was a mature adult, and had total control of the house most nights, which meant she was about to completely blow things up.

One Saturday when my parents were both working late, my sister had a supposed get-together at our house. We Druckers are an antisocial bunch by nature, so this terrified my brother and me. Teens? Like, as in *teenagers*? In our house? No, thank you! I didn't look up to the guys my sister dated so much as treated them like T. rexes: if I was completely still, maybe they wouldn't see me. Making friends with them wasn't an option either. They just didn't last long enough. One boyfriend bought me a nice little picture frame for my first communion, and then my sister broke up with him a week later for what I hope were unrelated reasons.

My sister didn't plan this get-together as a party. Again, the Druckers are antisocial. The word *party* brings terror to our hearts. Really, she just wanted to stretch her wings and have a good time with more than one person. So she invited some friends. And then her friends invited their friends. Those friends of friends invited their friends. You've seen this movie before. What was supposed to be a handful of people became a three-bedroom ranch house packed with strangers. They were poking around cabinets, opening doors, making the place their own. My sister either became worried or didn't want us underfoot, because she told us to go to and stay in our rooms.

The problem was that my parents' house was not a good party house. My parents had no alcohol. They weren't in recovery, they just never drank at all. All their anger came from an honest place.

So the anonymous teenagers scouring our house for booze were disappointed. I know this because the phrase "No beer? What the fuck?" was shouted by at least one dude who probably couldn't even drive yet. Their options were milk in the fridge or older milk in the back of the fridge.

But these thirsty gents (and they were mostly guys) weren't going to let a little thing like a lack of alcohol stop them. Instead, they skipped to phase three of the plan and ripped our house apart. A glass shattered. A couple plates broke. Some of my parents' bad wall art was mercifully put to death. Even while I was in my bedroom, I could hear things getting out of hand with my sister growing angrier. We were being robbed or, rather, over the course of just an hour or two some dudes casually walked out with our stuff.

By "our stuff," I mean a VCR, a few VHS tapes, some knickknacks, and most of my video games.

Including *Street Fighter 2*.

Somehow that was the one that hit me the hardest. Losing the sci-fi racing fun of *F-Zero* hurt, but I'd already beat it. Never seeing *Pilotwings* again was a bummer, but that flying game gave me motion sickness. For a while, I was only able to play it in short bursts. No huge loss. But seeing that *Street Fighter 2* had been taken? Oh, man. I was crushed.

At first, I lied to myself. Maybe we hadn't been robbed. Maybe things were just strewn about the house. I got on my little hands and knees and looked under the furniture, as if some teenage dude had accidentally kicked the game cartridge into a corner. No such luck. I tore through closets and cabinets. No game. I asked my sister if she'd seen it. She hadn't and tearfully told me she had bigger things to worry about. We were both feeling it that night.

I understood *Street Fighter 2* wasn't the most important item lost in the pillaging. My parents didn't really give a shit about a few missing video games when their trust in my sister was broken; these friends of friends of friends had done actual damage to the house, and they were upset, to say the least. Hell, this wasn't even like a movie where the party happens while the main character's parents are on a big vacation; they were just working late at their jobs!

I tried to avoid talking to my parents at all. They were screaming at my sister, and each other, and I felt like if I said one goddamn word, blame would somehow fall on me, too. I could imagine my mom pointing a finger and shouting, "Why would you leave your games in the living room, where the games are located?"

While noting the damage with the police, my parents finally realized that a lot of the video games, those plastic gray miracles that kept their son from talking to them about feelings, were gone.

When my mom asked me if I knew where the games were, I lost it. "Th-th-they...they took everything!" This was actually a little dramatic. They hadn't taken everything. They had grabbed what games they could and ran. For her part, my sister was still just relieved that nothing bad had happened to us. She's a good sister!

Once I calmed down, I was able to tell them what was stolen, which my parents were able to then tell the police officer (for all the help he was). As you might expect, we got the old "We'll let you know if anything pops up" and never heard from them again. What were they going to do? Find every suspicious teen boy in a thirty-mile radius and ask if they had *Street Fighter 2* for the Super Nintendo?

That's when something flipped a switch in my dad. Not because I was inconsolable. I was born inconsolable. I think my dad cracked because the world had once again been torn from his control. My parents struggled enough trying to make ends meet, let alone deal with a situation that was completely avoidable. This wasn't the straw that broke the camel's back, but it was the straw that made the camel realize, "Shit, I'm carrying a lot of straw." My dad grunted and grabbed his keys.

He asked me what game I wanted back the most.

The answer was clear. *"Street Fighter 2."*

"Fine. Get in the car."

We proceeded to drive to every toy store and department store still open in the city. This must have been eight or nine o'clock at night. We'd go in and ask if they had *Street Fighter 2* in stock. If they didn't, we left. If they did, my dad would ask to speak to a manager out of earshot from me. I had no idea what this process was about or represented. My dad really liked talking to other men about their jobs, so I wasn't sure if this was some sort of adult thing I didn't understand.

After each conversation with the store manager, if they were around, we'd leave and my dad wouldn't say a word as we headed to another store. It made zero sense to me. These hushed conversations weren't confused and angry like when my parents sent a plate back at Cracker Barrel. They just seemed quiet, fast, and, looking back, a little sad.

Up to that point, I didn't know why I was being dragged around the city, but I knew it was a situation that had the potential to get me yelled at, so I shut the hell up. My dad had clearly brought me for a reason, but I still didn't know if and when the shouting would start. Like I said, he and I had a weird relationship, and most of our interactions were me trying to avoid getting yelled at and him trying to get me to like him by yelling at me.

After what seemed like hours of driving, we finally got ahold of a manager at a Service Merchandise, sort of like a Walmart or Best Buy from the early '90s. All their stores closed for good shortly thereafter, so maybe this was what killed the business. My dad and the manager talked out of earshot, and the manager nodded and put his hand on my dad's shoulder. He grabbed a copy of *Street Fighter 2* from behind the counter and rang it up.

It was significantly less than $70.

My dad had somehow convinced the manager to give him a discount. I think about that now as an adult, and I understand that's why he didn't want me to know what he was talking about with those managers. He told them what had happened to his family and, "man-to-man," asked for a little help during a hard time. My dad had humiliated himself in front of strangers so he could afford to buy back at least one of the games that had been stolen. Even then I recognized this. I might not have known what he was saying, but I understood he was doing something extremely kind. Plus, I'm sure bringing me to the store with him prevented it from seeming like he was trying to scam them.

When we got in the car, he threw the bag on my lap. "Don't tell your mom about this," he said. "She'll be mad I spent the money, and I can't take it today." I said I wouldn't tell anyone, which was easy because that was something I usually only had to promise after bad things happened, and I was more than eager to not think about bad things. Enough bad things had happened that day, man.

I still have that copy of *Street Fighter 2*. And that night with my dad was probably one of the most wholesome memories I have of our relationship from my childhood. That game represented money I knew my parents didn't have during a time when they really, really needed that money. They sacrificed so much for us and then sacrificed even more when things went awry. They may not have always been happy with their situation in life, they may not have always been happy with us as their weird children, but they cared. My dad cared.

Cut back to a few years ago, when my dad and I were arguing. After he said I never remembered anything nice, I told him this very story. I told it to him with tears in my eyes. I told it to him with love in my heart.

My dad then looked me in the eye and said, "I don't remember doing any of that!"

MORTAL MONDAY

Between October 1992 and September 1993, *Mortal Kombat* became an international controversy. Parents rushed to protest the dangers of this incendiary game, news networks breathlessly reported on the violence, and politicians gave speeches denouncing it as a threat to our humanity. A game where you ripped heads off? What next? A game where you killed people on the street while the police chased you for committing grand theft auto? I wouldn't even know what to name such a game!

Those poor souls had no idea what was coming for them. Yes, before *Mortal Kombat*, there *were* gory games. But most of those were cartoonish like *Splatterhouse*, where a Jason Voorhees–type character bashes monsters in explosions of blood and guts while walking through a mansion of horror. It's a good time. But nobody I knew as a kid owned a copy. I also can't remember seeing many ads for the game, likely itself due to its extreme, over-the-top violence for the era. So, yes, gore in games existed. But before *Mortal Kombat*, it often felt shady, like those games should be kept behind a beaded curtain for grown-ups only.

Mortal Kombat, with all its guts and gore and brains and blood, was decidedly not for the children. Except, you know, it 100 percent *absolutely* was marketed toward children. And it marked my first taste of violence for "mature" audiences only.[11]

The original ad campaign was simple yet very effective: people shouted *"Mortal Kombat"* really loud. This wasn't an entirely new formula for a video game ad. *Super Mario 3* also had an ad in which people shouted "Mario" a lot until you got it stuck in your head. Something about this period convinced ad executives that if enough children screamed in unison, other children would buy their product.

And while it would soon become the most infamous name in games, I didn't have access to a *Mortal Kombat* machine. And I definitely wouldn't learn about slightly rarer, hip NeoGeo arcade fighting games like *Samurai Showdown* and *The King of Fighters* until middle school. Meanwhile, most games coming out then were specifically *designed* for young audiences. The same year that *Mortal Kombat 2* hit arcades, *Super Mario Kart* and *Sonic the Hedgehog 2* landed on their respective home consoles.

All I had to go off for *Mortal Kombat* was the screaming ad campaign and previews in game magazines, which were often the same thing back then. In one issue, game writers would describe a luxury vacation they got for free to play the latest, hottest game. And then in the next issue, they'd give

---

11   It was also my first taste of misspelling words for effect. The developers loved having most (but weirdly not all?) words that begin with *C* start with *K* instead. Probably to fuck with kids' ability to spell. I remember once a relative bought me a knockoff T-shirt that said *Mortal Combat*, and it was a whole thing.

it a half-decent review. This is unfair: plenty of hyped games got bad reviews. But you did get the sense those free vacations didn't hurt.

Anyway, the magazine previews said this game was unfathomably violent, a bloodier version of *Street Fighter* (a few called it the "*Street Fighter* Killer," which would actually be a pretty good nickname for a real murderer). It was going to be released on a Monday, which the ad campaign called "Mortal Monday." I hope whoever thought of Mortal Monday gets those same free vacations as the game reviewers for the rest of their life. It was a great tagline that was easily remembered. At home, I sang the words "Just Another Mortal Monday" on a loop until my sister hit me.

The original *Mortal Kombat* isn't that flashy. It had only seven fighters, two of which—Sub-Zero and Scorpion—looked identical, kind of like *Street Fighter* (although, in an improvement, they had completely different moves). The game's stages were few in number and generally pretty bland outside of the Pit, where you could knock someone off a bridge onto spikes. The music was okay. The fighting felt heavy, like *Street Fighter* in molasses. But it looked awesome, and that's all that matters in life. They used real actors in *Mortal Kombat*. Behind-the-scenes photos showed 1990s Chicago's finest martial artists ridiculously bending and posing in costume. Unlike the horrid, sure-to-not-hold-up-forever pixel art in *Street Fighter 2*, *Mortal Kombat* was real, dude!

Even more real was the promise of violence. Older kids who had already seen *Mortal Kombat* in faraway arcades knew. Magazines like *Electronic Gaming Monthly* wrote in detail how gross the game's secret moves could get...and then would give you all the button combinations you needed to pull off those moves! But the real kickers were the Fatalities. That's what got the game on the news and taught an entire generation the definition of a word mostly associated with traffic accidents. *Mortal Kombat* wasn't just about fighting, it was about *murder*.

At the end of the match, after either player had won their second round, an ominous voice said "Finish him" as the words flashed across the screen. Depending on the character, you could rip off someone's head or tear out their heart. Or show a skull under your mask and light your opponent on fire. Or blow a kiss that *also* lit your opponent on fire. There weren't *many* options in the game, but every fatal act of violence—hell, even all the blood that fell through the air during a match— made *Street Fighter 2* look childish by comparison.[12] It was shocking and gritty and *real* the way that all annoying kids confuse something being edgy with being realistic.

I wasn't a superviolent child,[13] but the game was filled with a fearful delight I would later associate with horror movies and sex with other human people. Or rather, it would fill me with a fearful delight once I actually got my hands on a copy. That, folks, was harder than Sub-Zero's head-rip Fatality.

We also knew that *Mortal Kombat* would be released on four consoles: Super Nintendo, Sega Genesis, Game Boy, and Game Gear. Super Nintendo: the powerhouse console made by a famous company for children. The Sega Genesis:[14] a rival

---

12 Which is hilarious and stupid considering I was a child back then.

13 My siblings and I will likely disagree on the level of fighting and who instigated said fights.

14 Also known as the Mega Drive in Europe and Japan. I can't choose and don't want to choose which name is cooler.

console made by a company famous for edgy games and making fun of the first company I alluded to. The Game Boy: a weak handheld system with a black-and-white screen that was nearly impossible to see. The Game Gear: a slightly less-weak handheld system with a color screen that was, somehow, also nearly impossible to see. A PC version came out later that same year, and was apparently a great port of the game, albeit on DOS, which usually meant you had to jump through a dozen hoops and probably rewrite system files like Autoexec.bat to get it to run correctly.

Choosing which version to buy was a process. Each had their ups and downs. The Super Nintendo edition of *Mortal Kombat* might have looked and sounded the best, but because of Nintendo's more family-friendly image, they changed the color of the blood to look like sweat and altered half of the Fatalities to be a slightly nicer type of murder (i.e., Sub-Zero didn't rip off your head, he just turned you into ice and shattered you). The Sega Genesis version, however, was considered the gold standard (classic Sub-Zero head rip). Contrary to popular memory, it also didn't have blood from the outset—until you entered a very publicly available code to turn that sweet red liquid of life back on.

Sales for the Sega Genesis version blew the others out of the water. That was the one to get. While I was and still am a Nintendo fan, Sega knew that audiences were getting older. I wasn't eight years old anymore! I was nine! That's practically two digits already! To me, Sega was more mature. This despite Sega having one commercial in which a teenager has to beat himself in the head to enjoy the less cool Nintendo. Meanwhile, Nintendo was so protective of its family-friendly appeal that it forgot the one activity that really brings families together is everyone tearing each other apart.

When you played *Mortal Kombat* on Genesis—especially with the system's special six-button controller[15]—you found an experience of pure bloody chaos. It is absolutely wild that this was the biggest game in my—again—*elementary school*. America didn't have a consistent games rating system yet. And these games were being released on multiple platforms with one giant ad campaign. *Mortal Kombat* wasn't being hidden behind the store counter like an open bottle of vodka on Black Friday; it was the main event of the season. It was for us!

As I played the game at my friends' houses, my imagination took over, and I thought about saving our world through martial arts. According to *Mortal Kombat*, if our dimension loses enough tournaments, the monsters of Outworld could invade and kill us all. I know it doesn't make complete sense that an interdimensional war would rely on a fighting tournament, but a lot of things in life don't make complete sense. Either way, I imagined I was the character Liu Kang and, through button presses and hope, I would bring about humanity's salvation.

After breaking glass jars of coins and dumping out every birthday card that might have still had five bucks in it, I finally had enough money for *Mortal Kombat*...on the Game Boy. Great! It seemed like *maybe* it could still be good? The logo on the cover of the boxes was the same: a stylized dragon on a dark red background. And, again, I was cognizant enough to be grateful that I got any version of this game at all. I flipped through the game manual and read a story that has now been

---

15 Using the Genesis's original three-button controller for fighting games suuuuuuuuucked.

retconned a thousand times. Over the years, *Mortal Kombat* has changed its backstory so much that newer games' plots literally involve rebooting previous timelines.

Even back in 1993, we knew the versions of *Mortal Kombat* were different. The portable systems were far less powerful than their home console counterparts. I understood the Game Boy port would be missing the movie-star heartthrob fighter Johnny Cage. Meanwhile, the Game Gear version was missing the Australian criminal Kano, *but* it had color and a secret code to unlock blood like on the Genesis. As the ads said, *"Sega Does What Nintendon't."*

But despite missing a few bits and bobs, I fully expected the Game Boy *Mortal Kombat* to give me a taste of that festival of flesh. Perhaps not the full feast, maybe a sampler platter of flesh. Ultimately, the Game Boy version was more like someone at a free sample table in Costco asking, "Hey, you want to try a little violence?" Besides missing a character, it's also missing some of the stages, special moves, music, and the basic fun of the fucking game itself. It was *Mortal Kombat* the same way lipstick on my hand is a girlfriend I can kiss. Yes, technically, it is happening, but I need to stretch my imagination to make it work. I can fully attest it is a video game. Past that, nothing. Let's forget what I said about the hand thing.

It wasn't until years later that I finally got a chance to play the original arcade version. The arcade *Mortal Kombat* had a heaviness to the gameplay. Characters were slow, and hits sounded and felt powerful. And while the Super Nintendo and Genesis versions played a little faster and lighter, the Game Boy edition changed the game's speed from "slow" to "glacial." Characters don't walk across the screen, they tiptoe like

Scooby-Doo entering a haunted house. They don't punch so much as press their hand into an opponent over eons.

Getting special moves to work in the Game Boy version was more painful than the moves themselves. Even if you had a list of the button combinations, the dead-slug, frame-by-frame crawling speed of the game made it almost impossible to pull off a Fatality. I've tried many times since then. I tried again before writing this essay. I know the Fatalities exist because the computer opponent can still do them when you lose. But actually making them happen? You gotta have magic fingers, baby! And if you think the Super Nintendo Fatalities are a little watered-down, wait until you see them with three frames of animation in black-and-white on a pea-green display!

But I didn't care. I was nine, and I owned *Mortal Kombat*, the most controversial game of 1993. Ads with kids running through the streets screaming were effective. Magazine previews showing all the blood and guts were effective. Adults on the news panicking about the game completely ruining us were the most effective. Owning *Mortal Kombat* was cool. And being cool was not something that came naturally to me. Do you know how cool it felt to be cool? Let me tell you, it feels pretty cool!

Of course, I couldn't play Game Boy *Mortal Kombat* with friends. Nobody owned the game besides me, and the cables you could use to link up two systems were relatively rare before Pikachu turned us all into animal wranglers trading beasts on the black market. But I could examine the depths of every magazine and every crappy official comic book to read the lore, to figure out why characters like Sub-Zero and

Scorpion weren't friends. They looked like friends! Ryu and Ken from *Street Fighter* are friends! But it turns out Sub-Zero might have killed Scorpion's entire family, and I've since learned that some people actually like their families.

What's crazy is that it's not the Game Boy's fault. Back in the day, reviews scoffed at the idea that the Game Boy would even try to have the majesty of this fighting game grace its pixelated shores. "This tiny machine, she cannot handle these fighters!" Except it fucking could! I know this because the port of *Mortal Kombat II* for Game Boy is amazing. It only came out a year later, 1994, and somehow its characters are larger, move smoother, and—really importantly!—actually respond to the controls you're hitting. I played it again while writing this: it still holds up![16]

Mortal Kombat remains special to me. As I write this, the twelfth game in the franchise was just released, called *Mortal Kombat 1* because the series has internally rebooted itself twice now, and nothing makes sense. But, Lord, is *Mortal Kombat* still great. People my age who lived through Mortal Monday have a deep, deep love in our hearts, and playing the new *Mortal Kombat* gives me the same sense of joy that I got from playing the original *Mortal Kombat*.

I loved these games so much that I even ended up having the slightest cameo in the eleventh entry in the series. My friend, a screenwriter named Ben Mekler, had a podcast about *Mortal Kombat*. The dude loves it even more than I do.

---

16   Unfortunately, *Mortal Kombat 3* on the Game Boy went right on back to sucking. Also, I'm not mixing up the numbering style. The second MK is stylized as *Mortal Kombat II*. The third is stylized *Mortal Kombat 3*. It's madness but I don't make the rules!

Each episode breaks down a different character and their backstory and what makes them so cool, etc. For our part, we talked about Scorpion, Sub-Zero's enemy-cum-friend-cum-enemy-cum-stop-saying-cum. We turned into little kids saying Scorpion's catchphrase "GET OVER HERE" and describing Fatalities and joking about the characters. The *Mortal Kombat* series' developer, NetherRealm Studios, was listening. When they released *The Terminator* as a playable character for *Mortal Kombat 11* through downloadable content, one of the Fatalities included a shot from inside the Terminator's robot head. To the side, quickly scrolling, is a list of the names of victims it's already killed. Including me. My name. I was murdered. I'm dead in the *Mortal Kombat* universe. And since the *Mortal Kombat* universe uses alternate timelines and different dimensions, that is *canon.*

I've spent my whole life trying to impress an imaginary version of myself as a child. If I went back in time and visited myself, I'd tell him a couple things. One: "Please don't call the police, I'm just you from the future." Two: "No, really, don't call the police. I can prove to you who I am. Just ask me anything." Three: "One day, your name will flash on the screen as one of the Terminator's confirmed kills in a *Mortal Kombat* game." Little me would hang up on 9-1-1, put down that telephone, and smile into the warm face of God.

That's why we shouted *"Mortal Kombat."*

THE FALL OF BIGFOOT'S ARCADE

I don't know exactly when Bigfoot's Arcade opened. It definitely felt older than the '90s move toward more kid-friendly places. While I had visited Chuck E. Cheese, that little strip mall wonderland was designed to be bright and friendly: a place to throw birthday parties and hang out with classmates whose parents guilted them into going. And, not for nothing, it was easier to see your children when windows allow sunlight into the facility. Bigfoot's Arcade, meanwhile, was a dark, labyrinthian gauntlet of arcade machines, pinball, and Skee-Ball.

I also wish I could tell you where Bigfoot's Arcade was or even *used* to be.[17] It moved locations at least once, and I was too young to have any sense of where things were on the planet. Nearly every sun-bleached nightmare strip mall in

---

17 It doesn't help that, going by old listings and a loose game token, the name may have also been written as "Bigfoot Arcade," "Big Foot's Arcade," or possibly all three.

South Florida looked the same. All shopping plazas in Florida usually consisted of three or four elements: restaurants that were eternally "Under New Management," a gun store that loved using multiple fonts on signs, a crystal shop that never had any customers and definitely was the front for a heroin business, and then a wild card spot. If you see a combination massage parlor and dentist's office, you've got your wild card. If you walk into a store that only sells baseball cards and suddenly realize it's in an abandoned Pizza Hut, big wild card energy. Regardless of what was slotted into that wild card spot, it would close within a year.

My parents, ever dedicated to finding new ways to keep me from bothering them, ran across this arcade in our area. Outside of Chuck E. Cheese, I'd heard legends of other arcades. Growing up, every kid in South Florida dreamed of a place called Grand Prix Race-o-Rama. That's where rich kids had birthday parties. It was a bit of a drive and it was expensive, but it had to have been worth it for go-kart racing, mini golf, and playing the newest arcade games like *Hydro Thunder*, where you raced boats in 3D. Also, I just realized how old I am in that I wrote the phrase "newest arcade games like *Hydro Thunder*."

Bigfoot's Arcade emerged—at least into my consciousness—ironically as the concept of the neighborhood arcade was dying. Consoles had begun to catch up to the quality of arcade games. Near-perfect home versions of older games like *Space Invaders* and *Pac-Man* had existed for years. And by the time the Super Nintendo and Genesis landed (and, to be nice, the TurboGrafx 16), console ports of arcade games were close enough to be basically the same. The arcade edition might have still *looked* better, but it was far more fun playing *NBA Jam* at home than constantly inserting tokens to play all four quarters of a basketball game. Do you remember that? If you wanted to play a full game of basketball, you needed to keep feeding it money. Wild.

Bigfoot's Arcade existed when arcades were becoming less cool. In the '70s and '80s, adults with pearls to clutch determined that arcades were causing their teenagers to cut class and smoke Mary Jane. Arcade owners pivoted toward a more family-friendly atmosphere with new, money-guzzling games that could earn you prizes.[18] Out went many of the more obscure arcade games—like *Bubbles*, where you have to clean a sink and that's it—and in went more games of chance to win tickets that could be exchanged for cheap toys.

Not all the cultural changes arcades went through were *that* terrible. My hometown and a few cities around it were already cracking down on smoking indoors, which was nice. It's also probably why my grandparents avoided the place like the plague.

Bigfoot's Arcade was often empty, often weird, and often desperate, and it became my go-to arcade. In the same way you might find yourself gravitating to the same bar over and over again because the bartender sometimes flirts with you even though you both know it's a polite way to keep your business. Same deal, without the flirting part, thank God.

Despite moving between locations, the arcade generally had the same layout each time. When you opened its doors, you were greeted with flashy, new ticket games. Then you

---

18 So many plastic spider rings and paper finger traps that were immediately thrown out.

came across a glass display case that clearly used to be for a deli. Inside were your usual ticket prizes: sticky hands, hard candy, green toy soldiers, and then of course something like a Hot Wheels playset for some insane price like a hundred thousand tickets.

Once you left that front room, you got to the real arcade. It was dark and always smelled like popcorn—weird, because I don't remember them selling popcorn. If they had, my parents did themselves a financial solid and kept me from ever finding that out.

The back of the arcade was where the actually fun machines were, dark and pristine. No adults smoked near them. No kids left pizza grease on the buttons. The machines worked. For better or worse, the owners actually took care of their machines. Classics like *Frogger*, *Robotron: 2084*, and *Space Invaders* were in one massive row. Newer games—like *Killer Instinct* and *Primal Rage*—were prominently displayed in the center. Pinball and Skee-Ball had a space on an opposite wall where they could shove all the machines that were a dozen feet long. There were also a handful of old shooting games in which you held a model gun and fired at little physical targets.[19]

Regardless, Bigfoot's Arcade was my world to explore. Yes, I needed that $5 ($20 if it was my birthday) from my parents to get a fix. But I was able to just try games, see what I liked, and even glimpse the future. State-of-the-art, gorgeous 3D fighting games like *Virtua Fighter* and *Tekken* always landed in arcades first. I got to see the world of games change in real

---

19 I'm assuming this worked the same way the light pulses worked for Nintendo's analogue *Duck Hunt* game. To be honest, I assume a lot of things.

time. Each visit to Bigfoot's was its own video game convention. The new and the old combined to show me the reality I wanted to exist in.

Even my father and my brother found peace here. While they let the least chill member of their family (i.e., me) explore to his cholesterol-clogged heart's content, my dad and brother discovered a quasi-forgotten game called *Lucky & Wild*. It's a combination driving game and shooter in which one person drives the car and—wait for it—the other person shoots.

Despite my family's love of the place, the business was clearly not sustainable. Bigfoot's Arcade was too large and too empty, even when we went on Saturdays. I remember there being a piece of paper hanging off the door announcing the business was moving to some random shopping center that was even more inconvenient. I was too young to ever meet the owners of the business—especially because I was very briefly under the impression the place belonged to Bigfoot—but looking back, I can tell just how much they wanted to keep the lights on.

The last time I remember being there was on some preteen birthday. I'm going to guess it was my eleventh?[20] The only problem was, I was also heavily sick. So before I tell you the rest of this story, yes, I should not have gone out sick. I understand that now as an adult. But I was a goddamn child, and I was going to get some goddamn gaming in for my birthday.

When we got there, I was in weak shape. I could barely play anything. Fortunately, it was a weeknight, and the place was even more empty than usual. When I was healthy, an empty arcade felt like my kingdom. Sick as a dog, the glam-

---

20   Time is an illusion that imprisons us.

our of the place faded quickly. Worse, I myself was fading quickly: I think I fell asleep while sitting on the racing game *Hard Drivin'*. This all seems very dramatic, and I don't mean it to be. I wasn't dying. I wasn't being carried around by my best friends and longtime colleagues so I could say goodbye to *Bubble Bobble*. But even then, that birthday was bittersweet.

Worse than being sick, I could tell Bigfoot's Arcade was short for this world. Without the rose-colored glasses of the games, I noticed the carpets were fraying. The prizes on the shelves never seemed to move. There were different employees every time, looking just as mind-numbingly bored as the ones before. One or two older arcade games no longer worked, while more than a few game screens suffered from burn-in, with images of old logos eternally etched into the glass.

The isolation I had enjoyed before grew ominous. There wasn't really anybody there. I spent years dreaming about getting locked in there overnight, but what would I have done? Played *Pac-Man* again? Missed more baskets in *Pop-A-Shot*? With what money? Something about being sick and just a little bit older sucked out the magic and turned it into just another short-term business in a Florida strip mall. To quote Bigfoot himself: "Me not enjoy it."

Eventually, as my family grew bored and noticed me dying on machines, we decided to leave. And that was the last time I ever saw Bigfoot's Arcade. Again, I'm not exactly sure when it closed. Our visits had already become increasingly infrequent. It had also got harder to sell our parents on taking us. "Don't you already have that?"

"Yes, but it's not the arcade version."

"Why do you need the arcade version?"

"It looks better." There was no world in which they had the time, energy, or money to think that difference mattered.

Next time I convinced them to go, the arcade was gone. No note on the window. No signs that there had been an electronic entertainment complex. Just a little notice that the space was up for rental if you had a business that would work well between a pawnshop and a karate dojo. But this time, they hadn't relocated. I think they'd just simply…stopped existing. Less like a death and more like a friend who suddenly moved away and you never heard from them again.

I miss Bigfoot's Arcade. It marked the sweet spot in arcade history, after they'd stopped being smoky hideouts for frighteningly cool kids but before they'd reached the Dave & Buster's world of expensive booze and cheap carnival games. Its closure marked the point at which I became responsible for my own fandom and my own discoveries. Bigfoot's Arcade may not have existed forever—or, honestly, probably very long at all—but I was lucky to feel like at least one arcade belonged to me.

BOOKSTORE BOY

When I was a kid, there were three types of ads that aired during Saturday morning cartoons. The first were commercials for cereal, part of a "well-balanced breakfast." Which, of course, was nowhere in the vicinity of healthy. Nothing that you eat by the handful in the middle of the night can possibly be part of a well-balanced breakfast. The second type of ad was, of course, for toys, board games, and video games. These were the types of ads where a kid would smash a *Power Rangers* figure through a fake brick wall, and then, at the end of the commercial, a voice would quickly tell you that the fake brick wall was definitely not part of the playset.

The final ad was the public service announcement. We loved our PSAs, folks. They were the height of herd protection! Sometimes they could be fun, like when Woodsy the Owl told you that the only way to give a ~~fuck~~ hoot is to not ~~polfuck~~ pollute. More often, it was celebrities looking dead straight into the camera and telling you that drugs, while clearly something a lot of attractive people wanted to do for fun, were very bad for you and not fun in the slightest. But the biggest PSA, the one we had to see and hear the most, the idea that was drilled into our minds for decades, was that without exception—if you were a child—every stranger on Earth wanted to kidnap and murder you. If you stepped outside your front door, you would die in one second. You gotta stay inside! Close the blinds!

"Stranger danger" was the big phrase. I'm certain whoever came up with that rhyme patted themselves on the back for years. Parents were told to watch their children like hawks and be ready to fight any adult they didn't know personally. Perhaps encouraging us to only be wary of strangers might have been a mistake that steered a lot of kids away from clocking the charismatic monsters in our everyday lives. We were all on the lookout for a guy in a fedora and a trench coat when the real problem was the fun math teacher who wanted us to know that at twenty-four he could still party.

Obviously, strangers were an actual problem. They're still a real problem. But in the '90s, everyone was so obsessed with stranger danger, it must have been impossible to imagine leaving your young child alone for hours in a public place where unknown adults shopped.

Unless you were my parents.

From the ages of eight until maybe thirteen, my parents would drop me off at bookstores like the Coral Springs, Florida, Barnes & Noble and just leave.

Not leave to shop in or around the store. They would leave the geographical area of the shopping center and tell me to make a collect call if there were any problems. There was rarely a time frame for when they'd come back. This wasn't a punishment or some way to force me to enjoy reading. In fact,

I loved reading! When I was the bookstore boy, I thought my parents were just really supportive of my education. Now that I'm grown, I realize they either had a shift at work or needed some time away from their son, who was a lot.

Their strategy relied on one (honestly true) assumption: I would take all the time in the world to pore over video game magazines and strategy guides. All video game news, reviews, and previews I got came from magazines. True, the internet existed, but just barely: it was something you heard about on TV but seemed to only be for scientists and hobbyists who understood the arcane cultures of early message boards. We wouldn't even get the brand-new America Online until I was ten. And even then, it was mostly people yelling at each other over pointless head canon lore like when Cecil in *Final Fantasy IV* lost his virginity.[21]

My parents knew that if they dropped me off in a bookstore, I'd stick to the magazines, game guides, and *sometimes* the computer programming books when I was feeling frisky. I was still convinced as a little kid that my path to fame and fortune would be through learning C++ or something. The truth was that I was incredibly awful at programming. This wasn't helped by the fact that when I later took programming classes in high school, our teacher really didn't feel like teaching us. We just ended up using the school computers for games.

Fortunately for my parents, I wasn't the type of kid to wander off. They weren't concerned that I was going to split from the bookstore and head to the hardware store to check out the latest in hammers. My main interests were books and video

---

21 You may use the space below this footnote to add your own theories.

games. So I'd sit in bookstores near our home, bookstores near my relatives, bookstores near my parents' jobs, and I'd read every printed word possible about video games. *Electronic Gaming Monthly. PC Gamer. Nintendo Power.* The various magazines that tried to be *Nintendo Power* for other consoles but eventually died out one after the other.[22] I became an expert in which publications had truly great information and which didn't. I learned the names of the editors of the magazines so I could recognize whose reviews I could trust. I figured out that video game magazines on April Fools' Day included cruel jokes to confuse young children into trying to unlock *Street Fighter* characters that never existed.

(Stop doing April Fools' pranks. Stop getting my hopes up. I'm a goddamn adult now, and I still fall for it. If I'm not going to get better at critical thinking, the least you could do is get better at having less fun.)

In the early days of bookstore-boy bumming, my whole thing was just cheat codes and walk-throughs. I wanted to see the end of *Mega Man 3* without having my spirit crushed by Magnet Man every time I looked at his angry robot face that had a giant stupid magnet on the front. I needed to know how to do Scorpion's Fatality. How else was a child to show dominance over their friends in an absolutely healthy way? Years ago, when I was going through boxes in my parents' house as an adult, I found some of these notebooks I kept filled with button combinations and passwords and cheats and solutions. Without them, I would never have beaten most of these games. And I still sucked half the time. I didn't even finish

---

22 And then Nintendo Power died, too. RIP. I will mourn you until I join you.

the first *Castlevania* on the NES until I was in high school, when I discovered I could cheese it on an emulator by saving and reloading at every step in the game. Lord almighty, that game convinced me I would be terrible at killing Dracula. So there went another career option.

After I learned all I could about the games I already owned, I moved on to what was coming. There was so much else out there. As my family slowly adopted computer technology, I learned about the vast storage space of CD-ROMs and the stunning, groundbreaking titles like *Myst* and *The 7th Guest* that I've already mentioned would bring D-level video acting to monitors.

As my reading grew, my tastes grew. When I saw my favorite video game designer, Roberta Williams, was creating a *serious horror game* called *Phantasmagoria*, I knew it was time for me to become a *serious horror fan*. Despite barely cracking two digits in age, I became fascinated by the sexuality and gore of *Phantasmagoria*.

Phantasmagoria was a bit of a hybrid: a traditional adventure game like my beloved *King's Quest*, but with full-motion video actors like in *Quantum Gate* or *Plumbers Don't Wear Ties*. The latter promised that it was a romantic comedy thriller that played just like a movie![23]

Video game marketing teams often liked to use terms like

---

23 This was not a good game. It's essentially thirty minutes of two creeps hitting on a woman applying for a job. It's poorly acted, weirdly written, and the gameplay choices are both rare and somewhat inconsequential. Three decades later, I ended up writing a mocking-yet-somehow-official novelization of it for *Limited Run Games*. If you can't get that book, don't worry. Just hit your head against the wall a few times, and you'll feel what I was going for.

"cinematic" because they had zero confidence in the ability of games to actually be good on their own without needing comparisons to another media as a compliment. "Movies are good, right? That's a real art form! Let's go with that." There was this feeling that video games were for children, but *interactive movies* were for discerning adults. Hence the sex and violence.

Still, *Phantasmagoria* looked fascinating. It appeared gory and sublime in equal measure. While the game didn't turn out great per se, I can say with genuine sincerity that the strategy guide was a blast to read. I probably got more shivers reading the summary of the villain's murders than I did eventually watching the ham-fisted scenes in the game. It was a good idea that just doesn't quite come together. I've replayed it multiple times since.

Strategy guides became my new obsession. Magazines could only scratch the surface. They were pretty good if you wanted to learn about how to skip levels in *Super Mario 3* with a whistle. But some strategy guides told you even more! They even gave you behind-the-scenes material about the game's development. I wasn't just reading about how to beat *Phantasmagoria*, I was looking at images of the actual death scenes and descriptions of how they played out! I had so many nightmares about it and loved every second.[24]

Sometimes the Barnes & Noble staff would get curious. A couple people at a local store began to think of me as a regular and gave a little wave when I waddled by to get to the magazine section. They rarely talked to me, likely because

---

24 I implore everyone to not let their kids read that strategy guide.

they themselves had been warned that they could be accused of being a stranger bringing the danger. When someone did talk to me, it was less about me spending nothing while reading hundreds of dollars' worth of merchandise every week and more about the fact that, you know, just wondering, and no big deal, but a little boy has quietly spent five hours flipping through the back pages of a computer magazine that featured oblique descriptions of all the dirty games you could buy through the mail. Things used to be much weirder: the back pages of computer magazines often had cheesy ads for interactive porn, mostly in the form of puzzles and card games that slowly revealed a very pixelated naked lady. It's probably good I didn't understand most of it. I can't imagine the damage it would've done to someone like me if my sexual awakening was kicked off with a Microsoft DOS strip poker game. I'd probably be the exact person most people think I already am.

Eventually, hours into my stay at the store, my parents would come back to get me. Sometimes it was because I called them and said I was hungry and the sun was now gone, other times it was because they suddenly remembered they had three children and not two. I'd tell them about all the things I didn't think they'd get mad about. Often, I'd ramble for an entire car ride about how great the PlayStation was going to be and there was this game coming called *Final Fantasy VII* and they didn't even know that it would change everything! They'd smile and nod and not ask questions. I think they were simply relieved I was interested in something that kept me out of trouble and didn't need their direct participation.

It is wild that my parents left me alone in bookstores for hours. Full work shifts. I was there so much I probably could've got a job minding the shelves and sneaking off reading about the upcoming Game Boy Color (it couldn't do many colors, and it didn't have a light, but it was a Game Boy in color and sometimes we had to thank the video game gods for the little blessings we could get). I think my parents told themselves that I was street-smart enough and that I could handle myself. I also knew they needed to work a lot of hours to keep food on the table, and anything I read in the store was pretty much free. They figured nobody was going to make a target of a sour-faced overweight boy who kept whispering "Sushi X loves *Street Fighter*."[25]

Being left to rot in literary paradise also made me an important font of information at school. If anyone wanted to know what was coming up in the gaming world, they talked to me. I could tell you about Capcom making a mature, edgy Mega Man called X, or the upcoming Ultra 64 and how its graphics could rival *Jurassic Park*. I could tell you about E3, a gaming convention so magical that only the purest of souls and the greatest of minds were allowed to attend.[26]

Ultimately, being left alone in a bookstore was perhaps the most consistent pleasure I had as a child outside of games in the house. Birthday parties were fun. Parks were good. But every new page was a pixel-perfect picture of something I wanted to play. Every review felt like a clairvoyant voice telling me what to try and what to avoid. It was peaceful. There

---

25 Sushi X was a fictional video game reviewer for *Electronic Gaming Monthly* who the real writers used to cartoonishly gush over fighting games. Like I said, things were strange back then. We took what we could get.

26 Most of this information ended up being wrong, by the way. Especially the part about E3.

was no yelling. Nobody could kick me off the TV or tell me that Nintendo was a waste of time. It was just me, the books, and the games.

SECTION 2:

DANCE DANCE TEEN ROMANCE

A TWO-HOUR LINE FOR
THREE DIMENSIONS

The line to play the new demo of *Super Mario 64* stretched out of the Toys "R" Us and down the sidewalk. The South Florida sun laughed at us as waves of heat rose off the concrete. All of us wanted a taste of the future. Or, at the very least, what was being marketed to us as the future. Regardless, there was something important on display here, something vastly vital to the continuing existence of the human race: *Super Mario* in 3D.

Super Mario 64—and the Nintendo 64—had been built up for months, if not years, as the newest innovation in games: three dimensions! The hype machine intentionally ignored that there had already been 3D games for years. It wasn't even the first 3D game by Nintendo: *Star Fox* came out in 1993 and plenty of games used the Super FX chips to render games with extremely low frame rates. And, hell, the Sony

PlayStation and Sega What Were They Thinking (Saturn)[27] both hit the market with advanced 3D graphics a year before Nintendo did. None of this mattered. It only counted to us as 3D when *Mario*'s creator, Shigeru fucking Miyamoto, said so himself. Sony and Sega were upstarts waiting for the true king to take the throne. All of this was utter nonsense, but I was twelve and taking orders from advertising propaganda.

Every drip of information thrilled me. I saw screenshots from an early *Legend of Zelda* demo in which a 3D Link fought a silver knight as the camera dramatically cut around them. If *this* was what games were going to become (to paraphrase a great man who'd later work at Nintendo), all of our bodies were ready. The PR machine even implied that the system— at that point code-named Ultra 64—could produce graphics on par with movies, which was nowhere in the realm of true, but we were feral with excitement nonetheless.

As each detail leaked, we only got more pumped. Features like the console having four controller ports, and thus allowing four players as opposed to just two, made our dreams of big multiplayer parties a reality.[28,29] The fact that neither of the *two* launch games, *Super Mario 64* or *Pilotwings 64*, used those extra ports didn't bother us.

Then the day came when I found out the local Toys "R" Us would be getting a demo of *Mario 64*. The news spread

---

27   If you don't know, the Sega Saturn was surprise-released in America early, both confusing fans and infuriating retailers.

28   Unfortunately, *parties* turned out to be the difficult part for me, not the number of controller ports.

29   True, multiplayer parties were already a thing, but most children did not have the resources to set up a local area network of computers.

through my neighborhood like wildfire. We talked about it like a celebrity was coming to visit a small town, and we all had to prepare. If we had the ability, I'm sure we would have asked the mayor to put a banner up and hire a small brass band playing lovely tunes to welcome the Nintendo 64 demo.

Upon arriving in the demo line, we were told there would be a strict time limit. After a few minutes, you had to hand it over. These instructions were given to us by employees like we were waiting for bread during the Great Depression.

I don't blame the employees for being stressed. It couldn't have been easy watching hungry-eyed people trying to get their hands on one specific thing in the store—a thing, I should add, they could not yet buy. Teenage employees not much older than myself were trying to keep a child-sized riot from breaking out. It was kids managing slightly smaller kids. Let's be honest: we were in the way of *them* getting to enjoy *Super Mario 64*. *We* were the schmucks.

My parents dropped me off, thinking it wouldn't take long. They told me to call them from the nearby Barnes & Noble when I was done. Was this Barnes & Noble across a busy four-lane thoroughfare? Why, yes, it was! I can't stress enough the amount of times I should have been killed or murdered as a child.

It was a long wait. For some reason, I didn't think to bring a book or a Game Boy (why would I? This wasn't a sporting event!). The anxious anticipation was made even worse by the beatific smiles on the faces of people who had tried the game before us. Watching the aftermath of people's experiences with the Nintendo 64 had the weight of a religious experience without requiring a tragic Netflix documentary.

Then the line stopped. An employee came out to tell us that the demo machine was having problems. Maybe the television wasn't working right or some kid with sticky fingers accidentally glued down a button on the controller. Who knows. The guy who told us looked like he had pulled the short straw. The line was furious. Dads said the catchphrase that every father has to say at least once in his life: "I can't believe this!"

Rumors spread through the still-growing line. The demo kiosk "having trouble" eventually became "it's broken." The line grew restless. Then it moved a little. Good news: they'd fixed the problem. We were going to get to play the game. A wave of relief flooded the people who'd spent hours waiting. Dads were ready to go back to believing this.

The sun began to set. Another wave of horror hit as people realized that the store might close before everyone got a chance to play. It was essentially the opposite of the old "If you're in line to vote, stay in line to vote!"

Some kids said they just wanted to see the game. They didn't need to play it. Could they just go inside and watch someone else play it? We were begging for scraps. We were weak and sucking down every ounce of marketing that had been thrown our way. If we couldn't touch the clawlike, three-pronged controller, at least we could confirm with our eyes that it actually existed, that it was real.

Some folks began pushing. Others broke off and did what we thought people were trying to do earlier: lie about going in to shop and then trying to sneak in toward the Nintendo 64 kiosk. If we could kiss the feet of the demo and ask our souls to be cleansed, we would have. But they wouldn't let us get that close. Those that got in the cheap way watched from a distance, behind a thin toy rope that was now being used as actual rope. Dads started not believing this again.

But finally, gloriously, I got inside. I was maybe ten or fifteen people away from the kiosk. I could see the game being played. The energy was only more nerve-racking, people checking watches to make sure that whoever was in front of them didn't take up precious minutes one could spend moving a fictional character around a fictional field in a fictional world. But the expression on people's faces! The experiment in a new dimension had worked. And it was almost my turn.

Then a little bastard tried to cut in line, and people flew into a rage. That Toys "R" Us turned into a dry run for January 6th.[30] Even as the mob overcame employees, the only thing we wanted was a chance with Super Mario. The hero of the hour. The only man who ever understood us. Or probably just me. He was a husky man in denim overalls just trying his best. I understood that well.

Kids and adults alike crowded the machine. Someone handed the controller off to another person who was not next in line. People erupted. Civilization was falling apart. We were seconds away from slap fights. The vibe had gone from excited to anxious to angry. The closest description I can give it is a Black Friday sale mixed with *Lord of the Flies*.

Someone who I assumed was a manager finally pulled the plug. He was older than the employees waving their arms and

---

30 Considering it happened in Florida, there probably was some overlap between participants.

shouting, and this did not look like his first rodeo.[31] The manager announced at the top of his lungs that there would be no game until everyone got orderly. We could either leave or line the hell up like human beings with dignity and self-respect.

After hours of waiting, I got my turn. My palms shook as I held the controller. The game came on, and I was immediately taken to another, happier world. *Mario 64* was everything I thought it would be. Any doubt in my mind was erased when I put my thumb on that stick. I didn't know that, in comparison to today's games, the camera controls were like pushing shit through molasses. This was the '90s, baby! Nobody had figured out how to make a good 3D camera yet.

The game was and is brilliant. I ran across Bob-omb Battlefield, the first real level of the game. The music alone was an upgrade: big, bouncy, beautiful. The gameplay flowed like water. Jumping, moving, diving, it all felt natural. That's the magic trick of *Mario 64*: it might not have *all* aged great (especially that camera), but when it came out, it was the most intuitive 3D game ever made.

I experienced all of this in just two minutes. The manager of the store was literally holding a stopwatch. The moment my two minutes were up, the manager put a hand on my shoulder and said, "That's all for now." That's how drug dealers talk to you in movies after giving you a hit.

The Nintendo 64 came out in America on September 29, 1996. My family got one on the first day of its release through a mixture of long-term begging and luck from my mom's em-

---

31 I saw him again when I waited in line for the *Star Wars: Episode I – The Phantom Menace* toys. Of everything embarrassing I've shared, that might be the worst. I owned a lot of Jar Jar Binks toys.

ployee discount. While there were two games available, I'd learned my lesson from *Duck Hunt*: I had to go with *Mario*. Although, I want to reiterate that *Pilotwings 64* is *lovely*.

Until the early 2000s, I'd have said *Mario 64* was my favorite game of all time. Easily. And it's still on the list somewhere between the fun family game *The Sims* and the sad horror tragedy *Silent Hill 2*. Playing *Mario 64* now is like playing a first draft of a better game. Nintendo would continue to experiment. *Super Mario Sunshine* added a weird water cannon. *Super Mario Galaxy* allowed you to walk around tiny planets. *Super Mario Odyssey* let you possess a T. rex and then stomp around. Each iteration added to the last, which—I guess—is the way this is supposed to be.

That all said, *Mario 64* holds up. Even today, there's an awe-inspiring magic to walking into Princess Peach's castle and hearing that soft (artificial) string music. The camera deeply sucks, but the movement and platforming and puzzles all work well to this day, 10/10. It was a triumph, and I'm glad I wasted an entire day getting sunburned to play it.

AERITH GAINSBOROUGH AND MS. RED

Nobody on this planet deserves to go to middle school. There should just be a three-year-long hibernation where you're kept in an ice-cold box and fed through a tube connected to your mouth. A little machine softly rubs your throat so you swallow. Sometimes it reads you a story. Sometimes you miss that machine.

I was lucky that my experience at Parkway Middle School wasn't universally awful. My biggest bullies were the people waiting for me at home, so it wasn't like I was going to get it worse from some kids who didn't even know my biggest weaknesses. What were they going to do, insult me? I'd been called "ugly" and "stupid" my whole life: the only difference was that it wasn't happening at Disney World or on Christmas morning.

According to an assumption I'm making with no valuable expertise, the main driver of middle school's problems is puberty. Puberty didn't hit me hard like it does in a movie. My voice didn't crack. I simply expanded vertically and horizontally. I had more hair and slightly more crushes than I'd had before. You can't become *more* awkward when you're already at *maximum* awkward.

I wish I had some story directly connected to my body's changes. Something about summer camp in the woods, which actually sounds like my version of Hell. Or getting a weird boner on the bus, which actually sounds like my version of Purgatory. As with other issues in my life, the main problem was that I always felt bad. It's not like I went from Little League star to the kid who gets picked last; I merely went from "not good" to "even less so." My body constantly felt weird, and I've never known how to talk to other people. The free flow of new hormones didn't change that.

But puberty did line up exactly with my entry into the world of *Final Fantasy*. A friend had shown me *Final Fantasy III*.[32] And not only did he show me *Final Fantasy III*, he showed me that opera scene where the characters participate in a poignant chiptune song with pixelated lyrics written on-screen. This is around the same time and place in the game where you fight a giant, sarcastic octopus, but that somehow did not reduce the deep pathos.

As much as I loved *Super Mario 64*, it didn't really have a story per se that I could chew on. It had been a while since the last real *King's Quest* game had come out, and I needed something adventurous in my life. To be fair, there *were* a lot of games with great stories during this period of time. Tim Schafer and other folks at LucasArts were churning out clas-

---

32 i.e., *Final Fantasy VI* in Japan.

sic after classic. But I didn't quite *get* them yet. They'd click later, but for a moment I was a complete philistine.

But here was an RPG with the same focus on narrative as those games! *Final Fantasy* was all about the story! I remember an older student saying that we (my friends and I) weren't ready for what happens in *Final Fantasy II*,[33][34] a game that had a famous line where one character called another a "Spoony Bard." That student was probably only a year older than us and didn't know shit. We ignored him. My friend group was a loose band of students who mostly just talked about video games whenever we were in the same class. An eighth-grader telling us that we weren't ready for the game made us want to play it even more.

The downside was that *Final Fantasy* games were hard to come by. Half of the early games weren't officially localized from Japanese into other languages until years later. And because the games were seen as esoteric experiences for a small subset of fans, stores didn't really carry a lot of copies of the ones that did come out. In fact, none of the stores in all of South Florida seemed to have new copies of *Final Fantasy II* or *Final Fantasy III*. I know because I called. So I put my name on the waiting list for any used copies that might come in. It was the same situation with *Chrono Trigger*. I know that's not a *Final Fantasy* game, but people spoke about it like it was a phantom dream that only existed if you saw it out of the cor-

---

33   i.e., *Final Fantasy IV* in Japan.

34   Okay, so in the '90s, because Japanese game companies didn't always localize every game in a series, they thought they'd somehow make things less confusing by renumbering them for other territories. Fortunately, this has since been fixed in subsequent rereleases.

ner of your eye. I still protect my SNES copy of *Chrono Trigger* with my life. Mostly because I don't value my life, but still.

Of course, the game we were all excited about was *Final Fantasy VII*, which, thank God, was actually called *Final Fantasy VII* in every region. For my entire life, I'd been a Sega-curious Nintendo fanboy, but *Final Fantasy VII* made me want a PlayStation more than anything I could hope for, including the safety of my family.

The ads for *Final Fantasy VII* promised cutting-edge graphics. Not just cutting-edge, *cinematic*! (As I mentioned earlier, it's been almost thirty years since the release of *Final Fantasy VII*, and the industry still loves advertising new titles as movie-like experiences.) This was a bit of a cheat: the ads almost exclusively featured prerendered computer-generated scenes. These weren't what we'd be seeing or playing most of the game; they were sweet little full-motion video treats that were the main reason the game spanned three CDs. That's right, folks! Three. Whole. Compact. Discs. In an era in which *one* CD-ROM felt like it could hold all the information on Earth, *three* felt truly decadent.

In fact, part of the reason the creators of the *Final Fantasy* franchise, Square (later Square Enix), ditched Nintendo was so they could use all that CD space. Nintendo had stuck with cartridges for important reasons like money, faster loading times, money, durability, and money.

Final Fantasy VII was also supposed to make the franchise more gritty and mature. *Final Fantasy* was growing up and joining the ranks of other *very serious* games like *Resident Evil*.

It was even rated T for Teens, and I was 13![35] Gone were the cartoonish characters and colorful kingdoms. Instead, the game took place in a giant city that's filled with steaming pipes and magic power plants. Also, you're an ecoterrorist who carries around a giant sword. Whoa! This was clearly the developmental boost all of us needed. Playing this game counted as having a role model.

When it came out, *Final Fantasy VII* completely lived up to our expectations. We didn't care that the next-generation graphics in all those ads were noninteractive, prerendered cutscenes. We loved those cutscenes! They were like prizes for playing the game correctly. Sure, the in-game character models looked like origami people with Legos for hands, but the moment those video sequences kicked in, the characters looked real. Well, maybe not *real*. More like if Pixar made an anime, which is honestly much cooler anyway.

I got the game the same day I got a PlayStation. This was my sole reason for buying the console. Before *Final Fantasy VII*, I had mocked—*mocked!*—PlayStation games like *Crash Bandicoot* for being mere Nintendo rip-offs. Now I knew that if I could get this system connected to the living room TV, I'd never have another negative emotion ever again. At least, I would've felt that way if I had known I needed to buy a memory card to save the game. I don't know what I was thinking; I even owned memory cards for the Nintendo 64. In my haste to get the greatest game ever made (I assumed), I left out the item that would let me actually play the entire story. Nor did I have the budget for one! I could not save this

---

35 Time for serious grown-up material! Maybe characters would even kiss!

game and, more importantly, resume it later. For weeks, I'd make it hours into the game before someone in my family turned it off or accidentally kicked the console. "Accidentally" existing within giant quotes.

It didn't matter. I could play the beginning of that game for an eternity. The opening sequence starts slow with stars and green flickers of light and then a long, awe-inspiring zoom out from the industrial city of Midgar leading straight to our hero, Cloud Strife, and crew jumping off the train. All role-playing games seem to exist in only two forms: amazing immediately, or thirty hours of setting the table. In *Final Fantasy VII*, the fun begins right off the bat, thank God.

The game became like a religion to my friends and me in the seventh grade. These were the early days of dial-up internet, so resources were scattered. A deep-dive search for music from the games came up with horrible MIDIs and other types of sound files that I'm relatively sure don't even exist anymore. Today, you can stream every *Final Fantasy* soundtrack in full, high-quality audio. The companies are actually proud they exist! Back then, we were just praying that our download of the final battle theme, "One Winged Angel," didn't give us a virus. This was also when computer viruses would just ruin your computer rather than hold an entire hospital hostage. We used to be afraid of things that were so simple.

It shouldn't matter that *Final Fantasy VII* came out while I was at this specific point in my life. Except for one issue: my seventh-grade English teacher, Ms. Red, looked exactly like Aerith Gainsborough.[36] And this ruined me and a few

---

36 "Aeris" in the original translation, before anyone gets mad at this book. At least she didn't go from "Toadstool" to "Peach."

of my friends who shared her class. There were maybe three or four of us. One student who might've been handsome if he didn't have a long, dirty ponytail. Another student who played baseball but secretly just wanted to do nerdy stuff. And me, the main character of reality.

Ms. Red looking like Aerith alone wouldn't have been enough to break us. We knew her before we had played the game. But Aerith is one of the romantic leads of *Final Fantasy VII*, and her tragic death at the hands of Sephiroth was the exact type of story twist custom-designed to make a middle schooler feel deep. Plus, we already all had crushes on Ms. Red. Really, I feel like anyone who might have been attracted to a human woman was in love with Ms. R.

Like *Final Fantasy VII*, Ms. Red was catnip for us dorks. She looked angelic but was bookish enough to make us feel less stupid for liking her. She was kind to everyone, and she didn't talk down to us like other teachers. Moreover, she encouraged everyone to do creative writing projects. She even read her own poems in class. At any other age in my life, I would have hated this. But, man, Ms. R hit that button at the exact right time. I still remember her quietly reading a poem about a little girl who was too sick to leave her bed so she imagined a magical world around her. At the end of the poem, we found out that—yep, you've already guessed it—that little girl was her! We gasped!

Looking back, I'm also pretty sure Ms. Red knew we were smitten with her. She was a sweet lady, not an oblivious one. The same few weirdos raised our hands for every question and definitely asked to stay late for advice. For her part, she navigated this quite politely and kept us at a very long, professional arm's length so we wouldn't singe her when we self-immolated from passion. This wasn't cute. We were delusional.

But when I say she looked exactly like Aerith, I mean it. Same green eyes. Same long light brown hair. Same slight build. She wasn't magical and didn't have a staff to beat the shit out of monsters, but we were more than willing to let that slide. All of us had projected a fictional character onto a living woman.

Fortunately, Ms. Red wasn't aware of *Final Fantasy VII* or our belief that she resembled one of the main characters. That is, she was unaware for, like, five minutes, until we *made* her aware. Brother, we went and *told* her! We even tried to explain *Final Fantasy VII* after class one day. And she listened! She asked questions about the story! We showed her the game's official art of Aerith and asked her if she saw a resemblance to someone. She didn't and asked who. We explained the picture resembled her. She said, "Oh, okay. I see it now." This was the complete wrong move on her part! Oh my God, if she had just treated us all with disdain, we might have avoided this whole business. The more she stayed interested, the more we fell in love.

Each of us had our own strategy. The student with the ponytail was a very good artist in the way that any middle school student will draw anime characters that just look a little off. He drew a side-by-side comparison of Ms. R and Aerith to show it was more than just *a bit* of a resemblance. She was kind of impressed! The baseball nerd had the genuinely brilliant idea to ask if they could do a book report on the game. She said *no*! Totally okay! For some reason, we really wanted her to stay interested in this game. That was step one. There was no step two planned.

What did we expect? We were twelve- and thirteen-year-olds. There was likely no point in our many detailed explanations of the ending of the game that joy was going to fill her eyes and make her say, "Oh, I'm beautiful! You have convinced me! Now I will go on a date with all of you!" That's the problem with learning about romance from video games and novels: you do kind of believe that could happen. Video games are a lot like teen movies from the '80s: oh, they're fun! But do not ever take their romantic advice.

For example, as a young adult, role-playing games taught me that the most romantic thing you can possibly do in any situation is to say nothing. In games like *Final Fantasy VII*, stoic men like Cloud respond to dramatic moments and pleas of romance with a text box reading "…". In other games like *Chrono Trigger*, the protagonist doesn't talk at all. If you're an idiot (and I was), you begin to think that's how you're supposed to attract people. This seems cool until you put it into practice in the real world, where people just think you're a giant asshole.[37]

Since we *were* taking romantic advice from a hastily translated role-playing game for the PlayStation 1, we were going to keep on talking about it with Ms. Red until she was on board or the year ended. One of my ideas was to play "Aerith's Theme" for her, with its soft flourishes and big, tragic crescendos. I got the audio by holding a Talkboy Tape Recorder up to our TV—and no, I'm not bragging. I don't remember

---

37 It turns out you need to be attractive to be stoic.

how she reacted to hearing the music, which probably means I didn't *want* to remember how she reacted.

Ms. Red put up with us, likely because it was easier to show light interest in a few kids' passion than it was to say, "Hey, guys, don't do this to women. It's weird and, at some point, downright creepy. I'm begging you to stop before it becomes a pattern." Instead, she patiently learned the story of *Final Fantasy VII* again and again and again. She saw character art—from both famed *Final Fantasy* artists Tetsuya Nomura and Yoshitaka Amano, no less!—maybe a thousand times.[38]

Obviously, we couldn't be in Ms. Red's class forever. We soon hit the end of the school year and the end of Ms. Red. Literally. She told us that she was engaged to be married, and she was not planning to keep her name.

Fortunately, by this time, our infatuation had calcified into a less desperate, more distant worship. We moved on with our neediness. Like Cloud Strife after the death of Aerith, we had to continue our quest to save ourselves and the world. Except nobody died, and we were just moving on to a slightly harder English class with a teacher who had the bitter energy of the food critic in *Ratatouille*.

Years later, I reconnected with Ms. Red on social media. This was in the early days of Facebook, when you'd just add literally any person you'd ever met in your life. Still, I was surprised she friended me, and I sent a message saying hello and that I had appreciated her class. I did not mention video games, hoping she'd forgotten how embarrassing we'd acted.

---

38   Side note: this was not our only route to making Ms. Red love us. For her birthday, we put together a gift box filled with snacks and poems based on her name. It made more sense to us then than it does to me now.

The following week, we had a nice phone conversation. She had been doing well (hopefully true). I had been doing well (definitely a lie). She mentioned talking to Ponytail Kid a little while ago. He seemed to be doing "all right."

Eventually, after she politely listened to my ongoing college plans, we said our goodbyes. It had been nice talking. We should do it again sometime. Good luck with everything. And then, as we were hanging up, she said, "By the way, are you still obsessed with that weird game?" I laughed and said, "No, of course not." And then I replayed *Final Fantasy VII* to feel something again.

GOOD GAME, NO REMATCH

I've mentioned that I'm not a big fan of watching sports. Usually the interpretation of this is that I hate sports altogether. But I don't hate sports. Sports are *games*, and I like playing games. The first time someone told me (way too late in my life) that football was a turn-based strategy game, I was very close to being sold on the idea. Then I thought a little about it and realized that's not entirely true, but I did appreciate the attempt of a friend trying to connect our worlds. That guy and my dad would *love* each other.

Despite years of trying to get me to enjoy sports, my parents were intensely weirded-out when I asked for *NBA Jam* for the Super Nintendo. I'd shown literally zero interest in anything ball-related before this, and my dad barely played any games outside of the occasional *Tetris*. Until my brother was older, video games and sports mixed together like peanut butter and battery acid.

"But you hate sports!"

"No, I don't."

"Yes, you do! You never wanted to go to a Heat game."

"But here I get to play as the Heat! I can get set on fire and dunk!"

"Oh."

And that's where the conversation stopped. One, because telling your parents that a game sets your character on fire is alarming to them. Two, because my dad—God bless him—has a habit of rebooting whenever one of us says something that his brain isn't ready to process. The idea that I didn't want to see LIVE basketball but did want to play FAKE basketball probably felt like I was mocking him.

Not that *NBA Jam* was my first sports video game. Besides Game Boy *Golf* from my grandparents, my earliest childhood crush, a seven-year-old with the inexplicably adult name of Darlene, gave me *Ice Hockey* for the NES when she moved away from our neighborhood.[39] I was the younger man at six and willing to pretend I enjoyed sports if it got Darlene's approval. It's also a pretty great game. It may be part of Nintendo's earlier line of sports games that everyone seems to ignore, but the fights, Zamboni interludes, and extremely short playtime have kept it as a game that my brother and I play to this day.

The one thing that *Ice Hockey*, *NBA Jam*, and the granddaddy of even-people-who-are-bad-at-sports-will-like-this games, *Tecmo Bowl*, have in common is that they heavily simplify the rules. As much as movies portray athletes as brainless jocks, I can't imagine having to remember where I have to stand at all times or know what I did wrong when I get whistled at by a man dressed as the Hamburglar. I understand the

___

39 I tried to prevent her family from moving by knocking down their For Sale sign every time I came to her house. It did not work.

utility of rules in real life. I know that taking fouling out of basketball would turn it into a blood sport. I just don't know *what* a foul exactly is. And with *NBA Jam*, I never needed to learn! The lazy will inherit the Earth.

With games like *NBA Jam*, rules barely matter. Forget about whether or not the rule book says a golden retriever can play basketball; I could make a cartoon pixel Bill Clinton dunk over Scottie Pippen. (There was a code in *NBA Jam* to get Bill Clinton on your team. And Al Gore for the sexy freaks.) So I like sports video games, but I'm really not good at the realistic ones like *Madden* or *NBA 2K*. Never have been. I can read a football play, but I can't bring myself to give enough of a shit about it to really figure out the exact strategy I'd need to defeat my brother, Dan.

Dan was actually incredible at sports games. He still is. Of the sorrows of his life, Electronic Arts discontinuing their college football video game series was high up on the list. Of the greatest joys of his life, Electronic Arts bringing back their college football game series over ten years later was at the *top* of the list. There are likely far greater tragedies or victories, but none of them involve video games, and therefore none of them are important to me.

To this day, my brother always wants to play sports games with me. He loves them. He loves me. He also probably loves the fact that I'm so terrible at them. A game with my brother usually involves a first quarter in which I do moderately well and then three quarters in which I realize he was just fucking with me before going in for the kill.

Except for one time.

Almost.

While I'm four years older than my brother, my friends still enjoyed playing sports games with Dan since he was competent in them, where I was not. The *NFL Blitz* series may have ended because it celebrated players hitting each other as hard as possible *right* as athletes started taking concussions more seriously, but it was also fun as hell and boiled the rules of football down to nearly nothing. That game was my bread and butter. Dan was still better. To be honest, Dan is better than me at a lot of things.

One guy who especially loved competing with my brother was Carlo. Carlo was another student in my high school and a weird dude in the best way. He was tall. He was handsome. He had a tattoo of the Pokémon Butterfree. Except it wasn't real. He simply bought a lot of the same temporary tattoo of Butterfree and applied it to his arm every few days. When talking shit after delivering kill after kill in *Unreal Tournament*, he'd roll up his sleeve and say, "Butterfree did that!" I was from a family of unlovable losers; he was maybe the first person I'd met that was made of pure confidence and charisma. But he was also a good dude.

Carlo and I were in high school, but the bus we rode to school each day also carried middle school students. One time on said bus, we noticed a middle school kid getting bullied by some other boys. It was the same shit I myself had heard for years, too: ugly for being overweight, dumb for being quiet. That said, we weren't going to get our own asses suspended for starting shit with the little fucks harassing this kid. We simply absorbed that bullied kid into our fold and named him King.

We didn't expect anything from King. Every time he walked on the bus, we'd shout "The King is here" and bring him back to where the high school students sat, away from the jerkoffs. We weren't exactly protecting him, we just wanted him to not feel bad for existing. He was still shy, but his experience riding the bus was far less hellish. We made his ass laugh and there was nothing the front of the bus could do to stop it.

Carlo loved video games just as much as I did. That makes sense considering we took most of the same engineering and programming classes. And since one programming teacher appeared to believe his own attendance was optional, we were able to spend hours playing *Quake 3* and *Unreal Tournament* and every emulated console under the sun. The computers were relatively new, but they weren't locked down by the school's IT department. Whatever we wanted, we could install and play as long as our teacher was sick or just didn't care that day. For some reason, we also really got into the strategy game *Star Trek: Birth of the Federation.*

The real fun was that we role-played these games as the leaders of different factions. Since all the nerdy students (including Carlo and me) were in the same computer lab, we were able to shout accusations at one another in character. The selfish, greedy Ferengi, the faction I liked to play as, couldn't swear on TV, but they sure as fuck could swear when they were getting a shit deal from one of the other dumbass factions that don't know anything about the Rules of Acquisition. I loved them so much. I loved bribing other players. Our games became their own little *Star Trek* stories of space politics, exploration, and turning off the computer extremely quickly if a school administrator came to check on us.

Where Carlo and I did diverge was sports games. Carlo loved them. He was naturally athletic. Playing basketball in real life was as easy for him as it was on Super Nintendo, whereas for me, playing basketball on Super Nintendo alone was a challenge. Was I going to push the shoot button or the pass button? I'll tell you this: whatever I wanted to do was the opposite of what I actually did. In real life, the only way I could make a basket was if I wanted the ball to land anywhere *but* the hoop.

And because Carlo hung out at my house sometimes (one of the few friends of mine that regularly visited), he and my brother connected on sports games. I could keep up with my brother in *NBA Jam* or *NFL Blitz*, but when it came to the serious sports games—the ones that came out every year promising even more verisimilitude than ever before—I was terrible. Later in life, when I worked at *The Tonight Show*, there was nothing that filled my heart with more joy than being asked to play a video game with famous people, and then more sorrow when I discovered that game would be *FIFA*.

I'd spent years trying to beat or even get close to matching my brother in a sports game that didn't star Mario or start its life in an arcade. Again, I could decipher the little drawings of plays in *Madden*, but I just didn't really know what to do after they went into motion. No matter who I'd throw the ball to, it would be the wrong person. There was no preprogrammed dialogue for the automated announcers to describe just how much I sucked.

Except for that one time.

Another friend in our gaming group was a guy named Francis. We loved Francis. My man could deliver the goods. He pirated Dreamcast games, and that was a big boost for any broke kid in high school. No, I don't condone pirating now.

Yes, I know that the fact that Dreamcast games were so incredibly easy to pirate was a large reason the system quickly failed. Remember that this was about twenty-five years ago and you'd be lying if you said you wouldn't take *Cannon Spike* for free. I was a child who wanted to play *JoJo's Bizarre Adventure*, despite having no idea what that was or why it was so bizarre. All I knew: free.

Like me, Francis wasn't particularly great at sports games. He enjoyed sports in general more than me, and he knew how the games worked better than I did, but he was still bad at them. He was a great source of bootleg games and VHS tapes of *Dragon Ball* episodes that hadn't aired in America yet but not a wonderful digital quarterback. He was prone to locking up at big moments in any game. My man could be dominating *Unreal Tournament*, getting that announcer smoker voice to shout "Monster Kill" as he racked up headshot after headshot…and he'd still blow it at the end when the pressure was on. To put it another way, as a team we were absolutely helpless. If you left us in a forest alone with two newborn babies, the babies would survive and we would not.

That's why Carlo and Dan so enjoyed playing against Francis and me on the same team. We were easy pickings. Online play wasn't nearly as common as it is now, and there weren't many other challengers in the neighborhood. All my brother and Carlo had to play against were the chumps. And if they were going to play the chumps, they sure as hell were also going to dominate them.

The game we played was *NFL 2K* on the Dreamcast. Oh, man, that game felt like you were watching football live on TV. It looks like complete shit now, but at the time the players looked real. Magazines actually marveled that you could see individual holes in the football jerseys. Unlike the players in *Madden* with their blocky beach bum bodies, these athletes didn't entirely consist of sharp, polygonal edges. It was a revelation to us as kids, which means that it's also hilariously bad in the present.

My brother trained day and night on *NFL 2K*, as did Carlo. Any game involving me and them ended with them having a double-digit lead, at least. I'm certain there were times Francis and I played so much fucking worse than that. But the higher the score, the happier they felt. I didn't really care about losing that much because it was a foregone conclusion. If anything, my main goal was to score at least *once* so it wasn't a total sweep.

In this specific *NFL 2K* game, Dan and Carlo chose the Miami Dolphins, as usual. We lived in South Florida, and the reigning champions wanted to be on home turf. Francis and I picked the Dallas Cowboys because I was relatively sure it was a good team. In *The Little Giants*, the Cowboys were the unstoppable team of rich, physically fit children. And weren't the Cowboys in the Super Bowl a bunch in the '90s? Good enough for me! I didn't pay attention.

Initially things seemed to be going the way they always did. In the first quarter of the game, Carlo and Dan drove the score up to 15, adding insult to injury by going for two points after their second touchdown. They didn't hold back from shit-talking. They were respectful enough to not spike the controller when they scored, but they were disrespectful enough to dance in the middle of my living room and call us losers. Which was, to be fair, an accurate assessment.

The second quarter Francis and I began to pick things up.

We realized that our best bet for scoring was to prevent *them* from scoring and just kick a field goal whenever the opportunity presented itself. A button-mashing defense was easier to pull off than a well-planned offense. We were slowly but surely putting numbers on the board. Not that it worried them. We were still down by at least 9 at the end of the half. The shit-talking continued. Successful kicks were treated like the sad, meager attempts to save face that they were.

And then the second half started. I won't act like there was a big moment that pumped us up. I wish I'd given a dramatic halftime speech that ended with me screaming, "Do you want to live forever?!" But ultimately we didn't even need one.[40] Dan and Carlo got cocky. The opportunity to showboat was too hard to ignore. Usually when they got arrogant, they had the ability to back it up. You know how a lawyer should only ask questions they already know the answer to? Well, people should only talk shit when they know they're absolutely going to win. Dan and Carlo were only up by a touchdown and change, but they were choosing superlong Hail Mary passing plays to fuck with us.

They chose poorly. We caught interception after interception. Twice in a row, they threw the ball, and twice in a row, we were shocked that our players picked it off instead. It's not like we were doing anything special. We didn't suddenly get good. They got bad. The first turnover they shrugged off. What did it matter? Carlo and my brother had the quality of a villain watching James Bond try to escape: it didn't matter if he got one rope loose, he was still doomed.

And, like a Bond villain, they were wrong. After the in-

---

40 And I most certainly do not want to live forever.

terceptions, we kicked two field goals. The plan still worked well enough. Move down the field as far as possible. Kick the ball the second we were close. Get the ball again. Yet something had thrown them off. While our chipping-away-at-the-lead strategy shouldn't have been successful, it began to freak them out a little. They scored again, but by now they were barely in the lead. The trash-talking quieted. Before, they were mockingly announcing which plays they'd run next. Now they were quietly conferring. *Conferring!* They started to go with more conservative running plays.

In other words, they were spinning out. We weren't beating them so much as they were beating themselves while we just kept our eyes forward and tried to score when the moment presented itself. They threw another interception—this time one so incredibly ridiculous that I was able to run the ball for a touchdown. Francis and I had never surpassed the other team's score, but we were getting close. The mood in the room turned serious. Everyone spoke less.

As the fourth quarter started, we were down by two. Our teams had closed the gap. Carlo and Dan scored a touchdown. Their celebration was palpable. Francis and I were back to facing two people who actually knew what the fuck they were doing. Carlo laughed and said, "Did you think it would be that easy?"

And then we got a touchdown. This should not have happened. Dan and Carlo were back on their game. They should've been able to quickly stop us, but there was our man running into the end zone and keeping us neck and neck. They were the best video game football players we knew. The absolute best of a very, very small sample size. But we now had a chance to win.

With less than a minute to play, Dan and Carlo had the ball. All they had to do was run out the clock. Run the ball. Get tackled. Let the time expire. Easy. They also knew that if they could drive the ball to the opposite side of the field, we'd run out of time before we could score. They were counting on this so much that they started right back up with the assholery and were complete dicks to us. I think they needed it. They had just spent half of a football game worried that two massive losers were about to beat them. Maybe they thought it would psych us out in those final moments.

With a few seconds left, they fumbled the ball. We *got possession*, a term I had to look up to make sure I was using it correctly. Down by two, thirty yards away from the end zone, we had one option and one option only: kicking the ball. We were so close. Francis and I looked at each other and probably felt the same thrill: we might actually win this thing. In the movie *The Little Giants*, Rick Moranis's character gives a dramatic speech to the kids about how, even when the odds are against you, if you win one time in a hundred, that's still *one time*. This could be our one time.

Everyone held their breath. Francis kicked the ball, and it went in a straight, superb arc toward the goal. When it got through those bars, we'd have three extra points, and we'd win the game. There was no prize. No reward. No trophy. But we'd fucking win for the first time, and they'd fucking lose, and that's all that mattered to any of us.

The ball sailed. Time froze.

And Carlo kicked the console. Motherfucker kicked the

Dreamcast across the room, unplugging it and shutting it off in the process. I could tell it wasn't with malice in his heart. He didn't damage my Dreamcast, and he didn't intend to. Thank God, because if he had, it would've been a brutal breakup, and I don't know who'd have got custody of my brother or King. But either way, the game was instantly over. Literally one second before the ref would've shouted "It's good!" all of us stared at the blank TV screen.

"Did you just kick my Dreamcast?"

"Still undefeated," Carlo said and high-fived my brother.

We pressed the point. We were about to win the game, and he had turned it off. That didn't count as them winning, that counted as them quitting midgame. Their rebuttal: It was a video game with no stakes, and why were we whining when that ball was definitely going to miss anyway? This was a dirty lie, and they knew it, but it was enough to keep us from complaining even more. And there were other games we could play. We asked for another round. Maybe our luck would change.

Except there wouldn't be another round. We were told it was a good game, but there would be no rematch today. Plus, the Dreamcast still worked, and Francis had a burned copy of *Power Stone*, a 3D fighting game where you basically run around a room and beat each other up with stuff, every child's dream.[41]

So we didn't win the game. In a real football match, if a bird had flown in the way of a field goal, I assume it would've

---

41 They only made two entries in the series because humanity didn't deserve more.

had the same technical result. A sense that nature had taken over and returned things to their default state.

But it still marked the greatest video game sports moment of my life.[42] It was the closest I'd felt to being the underdog in the Super Bowl. We might not have won, but we were *going* to win.

When they bury me and write my obituary, it'll likely be short. But if there's one thing I hope they leave in there just for the sake of it being known for all eternity, it's that Mike Drucker nearly beat Dan and Carlo in *NFL 2K*.

---

42 There are not many.

WHAT YOUR FAVORITE CLASSIC ARCADE GAME SAYS ABOUT YOU

Pac-Man: You have a lot of time to kill at a laundromat.

Galaga: You have a lot of time to kill at a *fancy* laundromat.

Samurai Showdown: You have a lot of time to kill at a Pizza Hut.

Frogger: Big *Seinfeld* fan.

Gauntlet: You want to play Dungeons & Dragons but hate math.

Space Invaders: You prefer to just sit back and let death come for you.

Missile Command: You *really* prefer to just sit back and let death come for you.

Marvel vs. Capcom 2: YOU WANNA TAKE FOLKS FOR A RIDE! DOO DOO DOO DOO, DOO DOO DOO DOO! YOU WANNA TAKE FOLKS FOR A RIDE!

NBA Jam: As excited as you are when it happens in the game, you wouldn't know what to do if someone was actually on fire.

Crazy Taxi: You'd commit manslaughter if it meant getting $50 and a nice Uber review.

The Simpsons: You still think about the moment in the game when you get shocked by electricity and it shows Marge with rabbit ears under her hair. You wonder how the world would've been different if that were canon.

Paper Boy: A small voice in your head begs you to hit pedestrians with your bike.

Street Fighter 2: You're already a little mad I didn't specify which *Street Fighter 2*.

Pong: You've just woken up from a forty-five-year-long coma.

Breakout: You've just woken up from a forty-five-year-long coma and have no friends.

I'LL NEVER HAVE A REAL
FAKE FAMILY

I've disappointed my family in more ways than I can count. I'm not into outdoor activities. I didn't become a doctor or a lawyer. I don't visit my parents and siblings very often. Also, it was impossible to get me to smile correctly in a photograph from ages nine to forty. None of these are my fault, except perhaps at this point the lack of smiling. But the one thing that I feel a little bad about is that I'll never give my parents grandchildren. I say *a little bad* because I don't necessarily owe anyone the creation of a life so they can have a fun weekend once a summer.

The silliest reason I'll never have kids—beyond the fact that I'm not sure I need to pass on the abject sadness genes that fill my blood—is *The Sims*, the life simulation game where you build a house and get a job and start a family. This game felt created for me and me alone. As a child, I'd gone through a weird phase in which I designed houses in cheap CD-ROM computer programs made for architects that allowed you to lay out a house in 2D and then do a very rudimentary, very slow walk-through in 3D. It *always* impressed me. I loved building massive, empty homes and just walking around them as if I was moving in.[43]

I was also a lonely budding teenager when *The Sims* first landed in 2000. I don't think the gaming world expected how big it would be. Sure, we were excited! We already loved Maxis's other games. Everyone created towns in *SimCity* and then blew them up with natural disasters. But *The Sims* delivered on the promise of actually running (and ruining!) individual people's lives. With the ability to literally make up people who would be friends with an improved, fictional version of myself, I could live like someone with self-respect! Do other people even think or talk this way? I bet they don't! I don't know! I believe in other people more than myself.

With *The Sims*, life would no longer have to feel like I was watching it from the outside. Sixteen-year-old Mike Drucker was going to be somebody, baby! Specifically, he was going to be older than sixteen, because if I wanted to date other fake computer people in the neighborhood, I had to make my character an adult. I was out there seducing both Mortimer *and* Bella Goth. I might have just moved into the neighborhood, but I was going to blow up everyone's lives and create some broken families. This wasn't the plan, but it wasn't *not* the plan. Digital Mike lived for drama.

I just never really managed to get the family part right. No matter how many iterations of characters I made, no matter how many relationships those characters got into, no matter how much money I made at a fake job, I could not keep my

---

43 God, I clearly needed personal space as a child.

baby from being taken by in-game Child Services. This has ironically haunted me ever since I was a child myself. I have spent decades trying. (Well, honestly, I tried a couple times and went, "That's okay.")

Let me repeat that: I have never raised a child to adulthood on *The Sims*. Which is wild, because it is not supposed to be that hard. The game wants you to actually do this activity as part of the *fun*. When I ask other fans of the game, they're often surprised how bad I am at it. Nice home? Steady job? Too bad. Still required leaving the house to go to work and earn a living. And the baby can wait safely in its crib alone for hours, right? Of course not! I'm a moron! The authorities still came and took my baby away. Apparently the cops will do this in real life, too, so be on the lookout.

There were times my Sim did stay home with the baby. It didn't work. Maybe I just wasn't picking up on the cues. I knew I could just make a larger family from the get-go and they could watch the baby while my favorite characters went off to work wild jobs like being a professional athlete, but that felt like cheating. It takes a village to raise a child, but that doesn't mean I wanted to build an entire digital village for the sake of keeping Child Protective Services at bay.

Do I feel like I'd have this exact problem if I became a parent? No. I don't think I'd abandon a child in a crib for an entire day to train to become a professional athlete, because that career path has never been quite accessible to me. And I'd remember to feed the baby better than my guy in the game did. But the fact that my best defense of myself is "I'd probably remember to give it food" is itself a red flag. Even calling the baby "it" gives you a pretty big hint that I still just can't handle the responsibility.

I think when the fourth or fifth baby got taken in *The Sims*, I got the hint. The game was not a big fan of my parenting techniques. I would not be receiving any prizes for my work in the field of child-rearing. And honestly, fine! I got to have characters make out and design bathrooms that were both too large and had a terrible layout.

And who knows? Maybe one day I will start a family, but I don't think it's happening. Do I want children? Not really. To be honest, I'm not even sure I wanted children *before The Sims*. My dad once asked why none of his children had kids of their own, and my sister said, "What do the three of us have in common?" It was a generous way to explain that my parents were pretty open with us as kids about how much harder and worse we'd made their lives. I cannot think of a single moment from my childhood where I thought, "I can't wait to share this with *my* son someday!" But I do have plenty of moments from my childhood where I thought, "Hey, Mom is really good at throwing shoes!"

Also, kids are expensive. I get why my parents were mad at us all the time! I really do! I'll die surrounded by strangers with cold faces, but at least I can afford to buy a new Xbox game anytime I want. That's a pretty good deal that I certainly won't regret in a dark future.

But saying *The Sims* put me off parenting is not a total exaggeration. It definitely didn't help sell me in the other direction. I don't care if it makes no sense. It doesn't affect anyone else, and it's my senseless choice to make. Sometimes people get mad at you when you say you don't have kids or you're not having kids. They say it's selfish. Which is funny, because I've never been in line at Disney World behind a giant family and thought, "Wow! I'm glad those parents are so generous!" Some people seem to consider my decision to not have kids as an attack on *them* and their decision to become parents. Or that I'm a misanthrope who hates humanity at its core, and by not having children, I'm condemning my own bloodline to extinction. And, I'll be honest, that last part is pretty nice! But I don't think I'm better than you because I don't have kids. I think I'm better than you because I own two Nintendo Virtual Boys, one of which actually works. You having children only proves you've had sex. Me having two Virtual Boys actually makes it impressive that anyone has ever touched my body at all.

A lot of my friends and coworkers have children, and from what I've seen of them, they sure seem to be human beings with wants and needs of their own. When I see a friend's kid, I just want to make a weird face, get them to giggle, and then find my way to the exit before I'm asked to hold it.

That's the other thing: I will not hold your baby. Look, congratulations to you. I'm happy it's happened. I will still not hold your fucking infant. I'm not the one. I once ruined Halloween by dropping a jack-o'-lantern on the carpet of my dorm. If I dropped a baby, that's all anyone would know about me for the rest of my life. I'm not saying "no" because I want you to feel bad or don't appreciate your unique achievement. I'm saying "no" because I don't want you to have to shop for a tiny coffin.

I'm happy people are happy with their kids. If you are reading this and you have started or want to start a family, *good*.

Unless you're my parents, in which case, you really whiffed on that one. Don't worry; my parents have filled in the grandchildren gap by getting a dog that hates us and sending my sister's cats birthday cards with gift certificates for pet stores.

I know I'm being a bit glib about something people do and should take extremely seriously. And maybe if I happened to stumble into a new relationship where the person already had kids or had a burning passion to make some new ones, I'd change my mind. Much like pickleball, parenthood is something I'm sure I'd enjoy but really don't want to go through the process of finding out. The reality is I just don't believe I'd be a good parent and would rather the job go to those who want it. As much as people say, "I bet you'd be a good dad," the word *bet* still implies a pretty massive gamble. I appreciate the compliment, but I'm not going to see if the house wins.

Still, I always think about the other fear. The one created by *The Sims*. There would be nothing more horrifying to me than having children and then hearing a knock on the door. When I open that door, there stand the authorities. As they take my baby out of the room, cradling its red-faced sad little body, one of the authorities looks me in the eye and shakes their head. I'll sit on my floor in my empty house and cry, "*The Sims* warned you. Why didn't you listen? Why couldn't you listen to *The Sims*?"

THE GREAT *STARCRAFT* CONSPIRACY

StarCraft almost got me expelled from school.

I was a little over fifteen when Columbine happened. It's hard to remember the feeling now that mass shootings have inexplicably become part of the fabric of our country, but when Columbine happened, schools across America basically stopped everything to reassess. One of the high schools in my county had almost a week of assemblies discussing how students felt about the incident. It was a massive tragedy that nowadays would take up maybe two, three hours tops on the news because life is a nightmare. It's not a good sign for a culture when someone says, "It happened again," and we're all pretty sure we know what "it" is.

As with many schools across the country, my school was put under a strict no-tolerance policy without defining what that meant. No toy guns—got it. But then you saw kids on the news getting hauled out of class because they drew a picture of a sci-fi ray gun, and even back then we were like, "I

dunno about that." Rather than rooting out problems like un-
treated mental illness, ignored behavioral issues, and easy access to firearms, officials were throwing spaghetti at the wall
to find *something* to blame. School administrators were desperate for a policy fix that would require no money or extra
work. A few folks at my school concluded that their best bet
was to shit on the students.

With that zero-tolerance policy enacted, some school staff
acted like they *knew* if they caught the next shooter, they'd
be set for life. I'm not trying to be mean, but there was a type
of adult at my school who was absolutely certain that in the
face of a school shooting, they would've been able to stop any
tragedy from happening through sheer pluck and machismo.
That included one of my school's security guards. (I forgot his
name because he was a dick. Let's call him "Mr. L.")

This specific dick was certain that our school must have
someone planning something terrible. What that plan was, he
seemed not to know. He demanded teachers send him any sad
poems, pass on any drawings that looked a bit off. He'd stop
people in the hall with weird hair or baggy JNCO jeans or
whatever he thought was a sign of trouble. This dude wasn't
just acting out of fear, he was acting out of a strong desire to
be the school's hero. None of this was done carefully or remotely sympathetically. He had a huge grin on his face when
he thought he got you. Even though, ultimately, he got nobody and would stomp off.

Unfortunately, I was kind of gothy and hung out with people who were *really* gothy. One of my closest friends, Phil,
looked like a model right out of *Vampire: The Masquerade*.
The dude dressed like he was taking Satan out on a date to

a Michelin-star restaurant. We were a bunch of nerds who wore black and played games like *StarCraft*, *Quake 3*, and *Unreal Tournament* in the computer lab. And Columbine, for better or worse, flattened out everything goth into the Trench Coat Mafia.

To this particular security guard, every goth wearing dorky black clothes was a supervillain rather than a kid who liked Tim Burton and could've just used a few more hugs. He immediately started centering his suspicions around my little friend group. To be fair, a bunch of teens who mostly wore long trench coats in the South Florida heat was its own form of weirdness, but that had nothing to do with danger. Also, *The Matrix* had come out just a month before Columbine; that movie is all big coats and tight black outfits. Goth kids dressing like a pagan version of the *Men in Black* was not a new concept even then, and it definitely wasn't popularized by two evil fuckheads.

But Mr. L didn't know any of this! I can't imagine the man's seen a movie or any art that might cause him to empathize with someone. He began monitoring us, which we found out from teachers who felt uncomfortable when he asked them to feed him info. When you're fifteen and a teacher says, "Be careful what you say. You're being watched," you feel absolutely terrified. And a little cool because that's the shit they say in spy movies. But mostly terrified.

Soon, the security guard was finding the supposed proof he needed. His biggest discovery was our love of the strategy game *StarCraft*, which had only come out the year before and was immensely popular. According to his research (asking a teacher), *StarCraft* was a game in which different races tried to kill each other. The thing was, those were humans and *alien* races. As in different species with entirely different body structures. It's basically humans vs. space insects vs. star elves, but Mr. L jumped straight to *Helter Skelter.* Sure, *we* were the strange ones.

That security guard heard the word *race*, and he was off to the...races. He took each of us individually into small rooms and demanded we talk about our feelings on *StarCraft.* What "race" did we all play? How did we feel about the other "races"? Did we want to start a "race war"? He was an acrobat *stretching* to try to link a real-time strategy game with a desire for mass murder. No matter how much we all tried to individually explain to him what the game was, he thought he cleverly saw through our charade. It didn't matter that our school was mostly Black or that my group of friends was as diverse as the cover of a pamphlet for a college. Race war!

In a way, this was a fitting way to cap off the 1990s scare over video game violence. Oh, don't get me wrong! People are still *very* worried about video game violence. Every time a *Grand Theft Auto* game comes out, some weirdo on the news says, "You kill hookers to get the high score!" Which is madness. *Grand Theft Auto* games don't even have a high score. In the 1990s, people such as infamous anti-fun lawyer Jack Thompson tried to work the refs in the government and get violent games banned. *Doom* and *Mortal Kombat* almost seem quaint now, but there were full-on congressional hearings about games. *Night Trap* was a crappy, hilariously bad CD-ROM horror game that had grainy clips of women in barely revealing clothes. Nobody on Earth played it, but adults on the news couldn't shut up about it.

The fear that violent games poison the minds of children isn't any different than the fear that rap music, rock music, television, movies, vaudeville, ballroom dancing, and novels would poison the minds of children. But it was a fear that had been in the air for a while, especially as technology improved graphics and games began to look more realistic. It makes sense that when Columbine happened, a lot of talking heads pointed to video games as a likely contributing factor to the violence. There wasn't any real proof of this, of course, but it just seemed logical based on the public panic.

Back at my school, there were near interrogations conducted over a couple weeks. One friend tried to *show* the guard what *StarCraft* was so he could wrap his mind around it. Nope. Was not having it! It didn't matter what the game *looked like*. It only mattered that games like *Quake* and *Street Fighter* were convincing innocent children to hurt each other. Our protests to the contrary only made him more curious about what we were doing in class.

It wasn't that he wanted to protect the school. That we understood, even then. It was that we were being targeted for being dorks, a position we already weren't always in love with. A kid named Gary was found to have written a depressing poem about loneliness and worrying he'd die without anyone loving him. Emilio had drawn some *Final Fantasy VII* fan art of Cloud Strife and his giant sword, which was deemed "threatening." Bird McSparrow (some of these names may be fake) had once sworn at a teacher during an argument. These were all seen as actual hard "evidence" and were brought up in our little talks. I've seen enough true crime shows now that I understand he wanted to play us off each other.

But we were just some kids who brought Dreamcasts and *Dance Dance Revolution* pads to school. We weren't really angry at anybody: our school treated us pretty well, and other students played video games with us all the time. Being into anime and PlayStation was not really a negative in my school. It turns out that the one time our high school group was bullied was when an *adult* on staff had a problem with us.

Education!

We spent days being pulled out of class and talked to together, alone, and—at one point—even with parents. My father was furious. He didn't believe the security guard. He didn't think I had it in me to hurt other students. But he was mad that he was off work that day and did not expect to need to put on pants. It was as rough a day for him as it was for me.

For months, Mr. L kept trying to catch us out. He thought if he asked the same questions multiple times in multiple different settings, he'd get someone to spill. A few teachers believed him and began treating us like we were a threat. We learned this when Mr. L began inquiring about specific things we'd said in various classes. "What did you mean when you told Ms. Clay that *The Catcher in the Rye* bored you *to death*?" This motherfucking Dumbo thought he was Columbo.

Fortunately, most teachers did not believe him. Unfortunately, some teachers still decided to fuck with us over it, including one who accidentally stepped on my shoe and then jokingly knelt down to polish my sneakers while saying, "Please don't blow up the school." It was a *thing*. I know that's an insane joke to say to a student, but let me assure you that the story is absolutely true. Plus, that guy was also a *very* good English teacher who introduced us to authors like Zora

Neale Hurston and Nella Larsen. And, while I know it's a very grim bit, it did make us nervously laugh in the moment.

Sadly, Mr L kind of won. He didn't get in trouble for harassing kids. There was no confrontation. No calling-out. Instead, some students in my goth group just began to skip school. These were smart people who were already disaffected by abuse and other issues at home. And while I was only fifteen, a few of the friends in my group were older and had the legal ability to just drop out. So some did. A few, including Phil, Emilio, and Bird, simply entered the military. I believe one or two of them eventually saw some combat in the Iraq War. My friends felt they weren't really welcome in the school, so they left.

And…I don't know what happened to them after that. Early on in the war, I'd check lists of casualties to find their names. After about a year of this, I couldn't bring myself to do it anymore. There weren't easy ways to find them either. Nobody I knew from then was on MySpace. Facebook was still a young, exclusive app that only let in a couple colleges at a time. I didn't even have the names or numbers of their families; we mostly just hung out at school. Hell, some of them still aren't on social media—or at least not easy for me to locate. I hope they're happy. I hope they're safe. I hope they read this and they think I'm being histrionic while remembering that I sucked at *Soulcalibur*.

As for my friend Phil, I only know a little of what happened after he left for the military. Phil and I were our own minigroup. He may have looked like the IT guy for a Rammstein concert, but, Lord, did I look up to that man. He was my rock. When I was rejected by a girl, I talked to him. When his mom and dad were divorcing, he talked to me. I believed wholly in Phil and would've walked into Hell for him to have that Michelin-star dinner with Satan. I definitely had some form of crush on him that I did not put together until later in life.

Phil joined the military and, from what I heard, became a sniper, which is ironic considering the reason he was pushed out of the school. I only have old second- and thirdhand accounts, but it sounds like he might have had some personal troubles after that. I hope that's not true, but if it is, I hope he's got what he needs. Last we ever communicated was about seven years ago, when he wrote me a cryptic email. Not cryptic like a puzzle that could be solved, but cryptic in that it was a small congratulations on a semiviral video game tweet after not talking to me at all since high school. I don't remember what the tweet was, but I do remember writing a long, rambling email asking how he was doing and explaining how I was doing. There was never a response, which is very mysterious and very like him.

If you're wondering why I don't just google Phil, it's because his real first name is very common in all English-speaking countries and his last name is also a very common noun in all English-speaking countries. The search results I get are only helpful if the truth was that he had aged quicker than me and was a dentist in New Zealand.

Of course, what I suffered in high school isn't anywhere near the suffering of people who've experienced the actual danger and terror that happen in school shootings. The two aren't even in the same fucking universe of fear. I'm lucky in that I was in high school at a time when school shootings weren't treated as if they were uncontrollable natural disasters like tornadoes and earthquakes.

But I'll never stop thinking that a security guard with an ego made some of my favorite people leave. They were nerds who had found a school that treated them all right, and they were punished for enjoying it. The games they played with other students suddenly also made them a supposed threat to other students. Protoss, Zerg, Terran, it didn't matter what race you played in *StarCraft*: evil was afoot. Also, now that I think about it, Mr. L never picked up on the fact we also played a lot of *Diablo*, which is so demonic and violent that it makes *StarCraft* look like *Paw Patrol*. That man should have his photo just slightly off-center in the Dumbfuck Hall of Fame.

This story doesn't end badly for me. I continued to be lucky. I continued to be okay. I did well in school, which provided me with some protection from teachers when Mr. L got overly judicious or wanted to randomly pull me out of class. Plus, those teachers had begun to become annoyed with what everyone knew was bullshit. Meanwhile, I entered high school engineering and language competitions and took home prizes. I liked school to begin with, but I sure as hell had to keep being the model student until Mr. L was satisfied he'd driven off enough kids.

Ultimately, I was the valedictorian of my high school. I gave a speech that actually got some applause breaks, but it felt hollow. What mattered was that some of my best friends weren't there to see it, even though they could've been. Phil and his common-noun last name weren't there. Gary wasn't there. Emilio wasn't there. Bird McSparrow wasn't there either. I'm still too self-satisfied with that name.

I wish I could have some meager sympathy for Mr. L and his righteous quest. Columbine, and later 9/11, would change society and break our brains in the process. Some people were looking for heroes, others wanted to become heroes, a few wanted to be *seen* as heroes without doing any real hero work. Mr. L was in that last category. He saw an opening to get his name in the paper, and more importantly, he saw us dressed as his newborn idea of *bad kids*. So he wasted our time, filled us with paranoia, and ultimately broke us apart. Not because we liked video games but because liking video games was seen as suspicious. I still enjoyed high school, but I can't imagine just how incredible my time would've been if those guys weren't forced to leave by the constant harassment. I lost some of my best friends and never saw most of them again.

I miss them all, I hate that security guard, and *StarCraft* is still about aliens.

DANCE DANCE TEEN ROMANCE

I had never seen a *Dance Dance Revolution* machine before. Back in the late '90s/early '00s, arcade rhythm games seemed like something only lucky people in Japan got to experience. These mysterious wonders allowed players to pretend to dance or play musical instruments: that is, they could pretend to be cool. We had all read about them, but we had no idea if or when any would ever grace our shores. Decades ago, about 99 percent of the amazing things you'd see in a gaming magazine would end with a sentence begging the developers to please release it in America.

So when I first came across the game in an Orlando arcade in 1999—I believe near Universal Studios—I knew what it was, but not really what it was going to mean to me. While there are now as many versions of *Dance Dance Revolution* as there are stars in the sky, each massive machine still looks like an intimidating rainbow. Even if you haven't played it, you've seen it in a movie: bright neon lights, loud music, and two giant directional pads on the ground with a little barrier behind them to ostensibly keep you from suing the arcade when you fall off like an idiot. Absolute perfection.

Coincidentally, the very first person I saw playing *DDR* fell off like an idiot. I don't think he knew what he was doing. At first, he and his companion treated the machine with the same mixture of wonder and fear that I had. He looked a bit like me: that is to say, his body was not prepared for what was coming next. Thinking himself something of an arcade connoisseur, he immediately put it on the hardest difficulty level. The ways of arcade rhythm games were still mysterious to many of us. Sure, we'd had music games like the *PaRappa the Rapper* on the PlayStation, but—and this might surprise you—there is a bit of a gulf between playing a game on a controller and flopping around your useless, god-cursed body.

If that man did not hurt himself on the outside, he definitely hurt himself on the inside. His performance wasn't very steady. He did his best to keep his feet stomping on the directional pad to the beat of the music, lining up his rhythm with the arrows on the screen, but those arrows move fast, especially on the difficulty he chose. His face flooded with sweat, and his smile turned to a frown. It looked less like he was playing a game and more like a bad guy in an old West saloon had said "Dance!" and started firing at his feet.

On the screen, two arrows pointing apart from each other rolled down the screen. He jumped with his legs spread. It then went up and down and then returned to side to side and then a corner. That was the almost cool portion of the performance. During a complicated jump move, the man tipped over onto a *Marvel vs. Capcom* cabinet. Nobody laughed at him because it wasn't the type of fall that seemed like he was okay. Luckily, he *was* okay. But, hoo boy, for a second it looked like a man had died playing a dancing game.

He got up and—I'll never forget this—said to his companion, "Let's get out of here," in the tone of someone who'd just lost a fight in a teen romance film. It's like he had challenged the *DDR* machine to a downhill ski race and lost. It wasn't the machine's fault the dude sucked. He didn't even suck! But his hubris had led him to choose the hardest setting, which was his downfall.

Since I was next in the slowly forming line for *Dance Dance Revolution*, I figured, why not? The revolution might not be televised, but it *would* be on a screen in a Florida strip mall arcade. I fed some grubby money into the machine, smacked the start button, and was on my way. I took time to scroll through the music, searching for the right thing to match my mood and my ability as an awkward teen with a large body. I wasn't afraid to suck at this game, but I didn't want to fly off it. That was the bar for success set by the previous player: do not fall off.

I ended up choosing what is still my favorite *Dance Dance Revolution* song: "Butterfly." It's a Japanese pop song about a young woman searching all across Japan, just to find, to find her samurai. It's kind of like "Holding Out for a Hero" but less urgent and a little happier and not featured in the 1989 John Candy classic *Who's Harry Crumb?*[44] It's a great starter song for *Dance Dance Revolution*: light and perky, with actually semicoherent lyrics. Konami's entire music series has (mostly)

---

44 You knew this book wasn't gonna get printed without a topical *Who's Harry Crumb?* reference.

great music, but it is (mostly) club music, and sometimes it's aggressive club music. "Butterfly," by comparison, eases you in with a moderate tempo.

The good news is, I was terrible right away. But at least I didn't flop my ass onto the ground of the arcade, which seemed like a win on its own. True, I started off on the easiest difficulty level. But that's because I'm a somewhat self-aware human being who doesn't think I'm the master of Video World. The other dude did not know what he was doing.

Worse, that guy falling had made people only more interested in the game. By the time I was on the third song, I had an audience. A confused audience that wasn't entirely sure what they were watching, but an audience nonetheless. I began to sweat. I don't know why I wanted to impress these strangers, but my entire living is now based on impressing strangers, so I get it.

When I finished, the crowd politely applauded. I gave the type of wave that could generously be described as "weak." You know the wave a celebrity gives to the press after meeting with prosecutors? That's about where I'd say we were at. I wasn't confident enough in myself to feel as if I'd deserved the praise. Nor self-aware enough to figure out if they were making fun of me.

In reality, this was likely just a group of people trying to shoo one of God's mistakes off the dance pad. They wanted their turns, and applauding me was the best way to keep *things* rolling. Clap, clap, clap, very nice, great work, *let's move it along!* But, baby, I still wanted more of it. I needed another hit of that validation.

After I finished dancing to my little songs, I went straight back into the line.

A few players ahead of me struggled with the game. Even on the easiest game mode, I was surprised to learn that I was more coordinated than a lot of people whose fashion sense went beyond Target's latest Looney Tunes collection and XXL shirts shot out of a cannon at a Florida Panthers game. Fortunately, none of the goofs playing ended up hurting themselves, and we were all a little too self-conscious to laugh at the people who did fall. It was a supportive environment, which, in video games, is really a coin flip.

To move things along, people in the increasingly impatient line began playing everything two-player. Two total strangers would dance together to the same song, smile, and then loop back around to wait for another chance. We all loved this new, musical thing. It was unlike anything we'd seen in an arcade before. It was a game that tricked you, if not the people watching you, into thinking that you were actually good at dancing. Any video game that makes you feel cool drives people insane. If we could replicate this everywhere, we'd have world peace for at least the length of Konami's version of "Butterfly."

By the time I hit the end of my spending money, I was the closest a beginner could come to thinking he's an expert. I had the basics down, and I could play most of the songs on normal difficulty without bleeding out of every hole in my body while crying out for the Lord's mercy. Which is something they warn you about on the screen before you play the game.

That day I became obsessed with *Dance Dance Revolution*, much to my parents' confusion. I was a kid who mostly played games involving slaying dragons, running countries, and stacking blocks in neat rows. I didn't even like most games *emulating* physical activities. And yet here I was, ready to bounce my ass around an electronic mat like I just got cast out of pity in a budget version of *The Nutcracker*.

I don't remember telling my parents about the game, but I imagine it went like this. I twirled into the kitchen and said, "Mother, Father, I've found my true calling. Dance." At which point we probably hugged and they realized I truly was the most special boy. More likely, I told them about the game while they stared into the distance, imagining the life they could've had if they'd spent their youth traveling rather than having children. Their firstborn son hated football and loved dancing. Oh, man. My poor parents never stood a chance. There would never be a normal entry about me in the family Christmas letter.

I was in high school by this point, meaning I had enough internet access to begin hunting down a home version of *DDR*. My local game stores didn't have it, but my friends had heard about it, and magazines reviewed it. I knew it was out there. By now, my mom had moved on to a different job; we didn't have an in at any stores. I'd left my name with GameStop, Toys "R" Us, and Best Buy to call me when one came in, and somehow I was able to track down a copy of the game. Which is great, because almost *none* of the stores I called had *any* idea what I was asking about, so I'm sure I sounded like I was describing a game I'd half seen in a melatonin nightmare.

While getting the game on PlayStation was easy, the actual dance pad controllers were a little more difficult to find. Since I was searching for this stuff around the time of my birthday, I was able to convince my parents to ship in a pad from Japan as my gift for the year. That's right—we had to import controllers that would later become so common that people would just give them away after receiving them from someone else who just gave them away.

Success. Finally, against all odds, I had *Dance Dance Revolution* for the original PlayStation and two *Dance Dance Revolution* pads. I believe they must have come as a pair, because there's no world in which I would ever assume I'd be playing with another human being. I'm a man who plays fighting games alone without considering the depths of sadness that represents. There are entire tournaments around games I deeply love that I will never watch or participate in because I'm playing *solo*! So, so low.

Thankfully, my parents were supportive of my new lifestyle choices. It confused them, certainly, but I think they saw their son hopping around a thin layer of wires and plastic and thought, "At least he's moving?" Hell, I bought into the idea, too. I really believed I'd cracked the code, and with video games I'd finally transform into the handsome, godlike man that existed nowhere in my genetic family history.

As embarrassed as I was waving to the audience my first time playing *DDR*, I realized that I was kind of naturally good at the game. When I showed my friends, they were amazed by what I was doing. Like, they didn't even make fun of what was *clearly* some foolishly bad dancing. What I didn't understand was that I was simply ahead of the curve. Once the game was discovered by people who actually understood how music and dancing work, I was just moderately okay at it. But until that point, I'd been the best dancer in a ballroom of one. I *taught* people how to play.

Like the hero I am, I brought my PlayStation and dance pads to school. I rode the bus with a completely full backpack and a duffel bag. It probably looked like I was shipping out to the fucking Marines rather than seeing if I could impress every student in the school in one dramatic performance, even a girl named Marci who I had a huge crush on. (She didn't like games, and we had nothing in common.) I hoped that I'd blow everyone away with my moves and rumors would start to fly about me: "Mike Drucker? The kid who doesn't own pants that go all the way down to his shoes? A dancer? Well, how about that!" I remain this naive to this day.

I even challenged a few other students to dance-offs. After all, I had *two* pads. No reason to not try your luck against the fastest feet in Dillard High School (outside of our football program, and the basketball program, and the track team, and the rest of the school itself).

Other students started to pick up their own equipment and bring it in. We'd have two TVs on wheelie-carts running the same game at the same time with four people competing to dance, which, to an outside observer, must have looked like the most inane bullshit they'd ever seen. We were young. We were dumb. And we were full of the spirit of dance. As our South Florida god Gloria Estefan tried to warn everyone, the rhythm did, in fact, get us.

Nor did it end there. We were at the birth of the insanely impractical peripheral era, and with the launch of the Dreamcast, I had another gaming obsession: *Samba de Amigo*. You've probably already figured out from the word *samba* that it's another music game. It's really as much of an artifact of the

'90s as possible. "Macarena" and "Livin' la Vida Loca" and the opening song from *Austin Powers* were all there to party.

As with most great works of art, *Samba de Amigo* stars a monkey in Mexico who loves playing the maracas. This monkey needs your help bringing joy to the world. And the only way to bring joy is music! Ta-da! Like a lot of rhythm games, this meant on-screen targets would scroll by and you would have to hit them to the beat of the song. *Dance Dance Revolution* had arrows that told you which foot to move, *Guitar Hero* had lanes of color that instructed you to play a certain note, and *Samba de Amigo* had three circles on each side of the screen: upper, middle, and lower. Depending on where the notes were on-screen, that's where you shook the maracas.

Thankfully, the music in *Samba de Amigo* is great! And it's a fine, if less exciting, game to play with a regular game pad. Like most rhythm games, playing with a controller is way easier but also far more boring. The plastic musical instruments that served as controllers for *Guitar Hero* may have been cheap shit that most of us lost sometime between leaving college and remembering that other things need to fit in a closet, but at least they were briefly cool cheap shit. The main problem with this cool cheap shit was that, technically, they worked with all games, but not well.[45]

Samba de Amigo had superspecial controllers that were shaped like maracas. These were wired to a little bar on the floor that both connected to the console and helped sense the movement of the controllers. You played the game by holding the maracas in the correct position on-screen and then

---

45 That's why you could barely get past Margott in *Elden Ring*, but some superhuman weirdo beat the game with the drums from *Donkey Konga*.

shaking them with the beat. On easier difficulty levels, this makes you look like a doofus slowly conducting plane traffic. On harder difficulty levels, you look like a tourist who got drunk in Mexico and just embarrassed your entire family.

In other words, the *Samba de Amigo* controllers were glorious. I know I've made them sound silly, but holy shit were they silly fun. You didn't need as much coordination as the *DDR* game pads, meaning I could trick more people into embarrassing themselves. This was still a couple years before *Guitar Hero*, where the one-to-one illusion of using a fake musical instrument to play the song on-screen was more convincing. Dancing to music was one thing, but playing it felt amazing, and *Samba de Amigo* was the best early precursor to party games like *Rock Band*.[46]

For a short time in junior and senior year, we had a decent little unofficial rhythm game club. We realized we could slip out of programming into the computer storage room and use the vast concrete floor space to dance. Considering that none of us had any physical skills or knowledge of dancing, this was likely a mistake. Concrete is a very hard material. Falling (and people did fall) left bruises.

Also, once a maracas controller flew out of someone's hand and slammed into another student's face, nearly breaking his nose. We wanted to create an electronic dance game society and ended up looking like we were in *Fight Club*. That's just the world, folks.

Since my high school was big on video games, none of this was ever *that* weird. We only had to hide it to avoid being

---

46 Hey, you guys remember *Rock Band*? Hoo boy, time just keeps marching on, doesn't it?

seen by teachers who'd say "What the fuck?" and then repeat "What the fuck?" and then threaten to take away my precious dance mats and maracas controllers. It *would* have been funny if it was Coach P who found us. She couldn't make our asses run circles around a track at school, but here we were, going full Richard Simmons in a dank back room filled with old computer monitors.

Sadly, as in any situation, I had to find a way to make it embarrassing. I pitched playing *Dance Dance Revolution* at our high school prom. Oh, my friend, I didn't even think I'd have to pitch it! I thought they'd know about it and decide that, yes, it would be absolutely reasonable for them to add a PlayStation to the school's biggest social event of the year. I really believed this was a great idea. I was certain that a group of seniors planning their end-of-the-year party wanted to see me and two other sad students jumping around a floor pad.

The second part of this assumption was that the prom committee would approach me when they realized they needed my help. In this fantasy that would not have occurred in an infinite number of universes, the prom committee would ask to speak with me after school. I'd think at first, "Oh, God, I'm being banned." And they'd be like, "No, we love you. And we love video games that turn dancing into jerking leg movements. Can you please bring your copy of the game to be a hero to us all?"

That they didn't laugh in my face is a credit to their maturity, empathy, and probably the fact I was in half of their classes. Their response was that it wasn't fair to let one student change the prom at the last minute, and how every student would want something, and it would be hard to wheel out

TVs and make room for a video game area. All of this was legit. I was devastated. Prom was going to be boring.

Sure, I had a date to the prom, who was a wonderful person to go with and who I'd been seeing for a while! That's all the details you need because this person does not deserve to look back with more horror than is already warranted. I don't remember much about how I asked her to go, which hopefully means that I didn't humiliate myself in front of yet another girl. I'd been known to write very long, dramatic poems to ask people out—and receive a very polite, earnest *no* as a response. Thankfully, I didn't attempt that strategy here. It also helps that I couldn't come up with any good rhymes for "vampire" in my romantic poems.

What about the prom itself? Well, it certainly happened! There was a prom. Teens danced. Guys stained their nice suits the moment they touched literally any liquid. I'd love to tell you that there was some dramatic incident, a villainous popular kid got their comeuppance, or a young woman discovered she could make fire with her mind. Something interesting. We didn't even have the old sprinkler system prank. It was a fucking prom in a hotel ballroom.

The only notable thing I can remember about my prom is they actually raffled off the role of prom king and queen. There was no vote. Our school wasn't the type to have the two most popular people awaiting coronation for months. They simply tossed everyone's names into one of those bingo barrels, turned it a few times, and pulled out a couple slips of paper. I forget who ended up with the jobs, but I do remember them barely knowing each other and having the most delightfully awkward dance as everyone watched. It was nice.

Also, they kicked out a student who brought a date that might have been in his fifties. I forgot about that part. That's also something that went down.

But I'll tell you what would've made that prom really pop: *Dance Dance Revolution*. I knew for a fact in the most logical part of my brain that playing a rhythm game at prom, especially our middle-energy, raffle-filled prom, would not result in people being impressed. Neither my date nor anyone else would have felt a strange, new explosion inside their bodies. If anything, they would've stared at me in abject lack of horniness. And it should come as no surprise that I didn't get laid after prom. I didn't expect to, so I wasn't disappointed. It's not like *DDR* would've helped, anyway.

But I like to imagine a prom in which the lights go down as I walk through a crowd parting like the Red Sea. People whisper to each other that I—the fucking mayor of normal-difficulty video game dancing—have arrived. The PlayStation is already on and loaded. The music is turned up. Anyone still dancing stops to observe the most profound moment of their lives.

As I select my first song and begin to twirl, I imagine the other students shaking in awe. They're touched that this man, this sour-smelling man, has found joy in the primal expression that is movement. They think back to the times in their lives they've come up short, the times they didn't try because they didn't believe they could succeed. I inspire them. One day, they might look back and wish they'd told me how much I changed their lives. But I'd know. I'd always know.

SECTION 3:

THE FORMER NINTENDO EMPLOYEE

TOM NOOK UNIVERSITY

I went to New York University for college, the only other college I applied to besides the University of Miami. At the end of high school, I was completely burnt out from the stress of keeping my grades up, the exhaustion from school clubs, and the loss of friends who dropped out. By my senior year, I was number one in my class, but I had quit the National Honor Society, math club, German club, robotics club, and the programming club. I was tired, man. I did well enough on standardized tests and AP exams, but I knew I wanted a change of pace when I went to college. I wanted to go to a school that didn't feel like it was a school.

While NYU is a college like you see on the big screen in movies, it does you the courtesy of not having a campus. The school has a lot of buildings around Washington Square Park, but they also have a lot of buildings all over the city, including dorms. I spent all four years in a dorm called Third North, which wasn't the worst and wasn't the best.[47]

A lot of people who come to NYU are not from New York and, like me, are desperately trying to escape home and/or learning how to drive. At forty, I still don't have a license. The weirdest part? I love racing games! I played *Gran Turismo* 7 in virtual reality for *days*. But much like with having children, I don't trust myself in a role that could lead to the instant death of another person. Plus, once you don't drive long enough, it starts to become kind of a funny bit to foist on unsuspecting friends who will absolutely hate you for it. But don't worry, because it's very much a relationship deal-breaker, too!

That's not a lesson, kids, that's a warning. Don't be like me. You can get out. Just because you love video games doesn't mean you have to end up this way. I can lie to myself about saving the environment as much as I want, but I would absolutely die first in a *Mad Max* situation.

The dorms in Third North were mostly suites, almost like their own little apartments. We had a small common room, a little bathroom, a tiny kitchen, and three bedrooms with a bunk bed in each. This was more or less an introduction to having strangers for roommates in New York City, an activity that I'd continue for years after college.

My roommates were all from different parts of the country. A wealthy guy from New York City whose parents wanted him to learn a lesson by having to live with regular people. A man from Texas who finally had his chance to live the

---

47 Fun fact: apparently Lady Gaga was in the same dorm as me at the same time, which is crazy when you think about how similar our lives turned out.

life he wasn't allowed to have in his small town. A guy who played the violin in the middle of the fucking night like he was Sherlock Holmes. A kid from Florida who brought every video game imaginable to a microscopic six-person dorm. We weren't at cross-purposes, but we didn't share a lot of interests or goals. For my part, I was at NYU because New York City seemed like a cool place to become a writer and also to escape Florida. This was a terrible idea, but I still managed to double major in journalism (a degree I've never used) and English literature (even less useful). We each had different interests, different majors, and very different backgrounds.

But what brought us together was *Animal Crossing*.

At first, the game that we'd gather for was *Smash Bros. Melee*, one of the greatest games ever made. When the original *Smash Bros.* came out on Nintendo 64, people were *wary*. I remember reading a magazine preview that kept bringing up the same question: "Do people *really* want to play a game with Nintendo characters punching each other in the face?" We soon learned that the answer was "Dear God, yes, very much, please." So by the time its sequel hit the GameCube, everyone was on board. Even roommates who weren't really into games could understand the idea of Mario and Luigi fighting. Plus, with four players able to go at it at once, it seemed perfect for us.

But *Smash Bros. Melee* quickly started to stress some of us out. It caused too much animosity in our dorm. And, folks, this was a dorm that was already packed with drama. It makes living with roommates later in life easier when your first go is pure chaos. Without going into detail, one roommate briefly dated another roommate, and the breakup was *insane*.

You know how retro game enthusiasts always say that a CRT (cathode-ray tube screen, not critical race theory) is the only way to play old games? Well, that's true! Classic games look far better on a CRT, which weighs roughly a thousand pounds and is made of metal, plastic, and hard corners. Follow-up question: Have you ever seen someone *throw* one at another person? Like I said, it was a wild breakup.

But then we got *Animal Crossing*. The original GameCube version came out during my freshman year of college.[48] The game allowed up to four people to decorate their own homes in a little cartoon village where they had to do favors for passive-aggressive neighbors in the form of cartoon animals. This was long before *Animal Crossing* single-handedly saved the world at the start of the pandemic. People knew what they were going to get during 2020, but almost two decades earlier, we did not. None of us really knew what *Animal Crossing* even was; we just heard it was fun, and we didn't want something competitive. We only had so many CRT screens to throw.

Four of us made houses on one memory card. The other two made a second save on another memory card. The end result turned us all into the most annoying happy homemakers in the world. We oohed and aahed at each other's furniture and items. And you could find so much in your little digital town! We got jealous when someone else dug up cool fossils and showed them off. Rather than destroying each other

---

48 Wait, let me step back. The localization of the remake of the original Japanese version of *Animal Crossing* came out when I was in college. The game initially came out in Japan on the Nintendo 64, but not here. This addendum exists because at least one person reading this would have been absolutely, positively steaming from the ears if I got that technically incorrect. I know this because I'm also that person.

over someone using Captain Falcon too much in *Smash Bros.*, we were joyfully furnishing homes while we all went to college in one of the biggest metropolitan areas on planet Earth. Maybe as much as we wanted to leave our small towns, we also liked creating a virtual version of them to take with us.

The best part was that all six of us hated Tom Nook. Tom Nook is a landlord, loan shark, grifter, and taxman all rolled into one. He is the worst businessman, the guy who smiles big and talks loud while charging an arm and a leg for housing. I don't mean we got political about capitalism; I mean that Tom Nook was a giant dick. We loved hating him. We loved hating him just as much as we hated each other in *Smash Bros. Melee*. He was as much of a villain to us as our worst professors and terrible exes and dipshits down the dorm hall who'd borrow cups that they'd never return. He was something to focus our young adult anxiety on and someone to make fun of and root against. He's an evil cartoon raccoon. He has no other purpose. But at least complaining about him and his avarice was something that tied us together.

Recently, I reloaded that save on the same GameCube I had then. Our towns were filled with weeds and bugs from the *very long* period of disuse. It was like going to your hometown and finding out that everyone you knew had been aimlessly wandering around for decades, waiting for you to come back. It was a little sad. It made me miss all the good conversations I'd had with my roommates. It made me miss the bad times of getting drunk and falling on a stove and burning my chest, which did happen. Booting up the old neighborhood really made me miss that group of people.

It's the same reason why *Animal Crossing: New Horizons* on

the Nintendo Switch *was* so big during the start of the pandemic. As we all got huddled inside and were terrified that our world would be changed forever, it was nice to have a shared space where you could visit people and show off some fossils. We felt like we had no control over our lives, so we might as well make our virtual ones as happy as possible. The fact that, while trapped inside, we could take a little digital airplane to visit each other only made the game more special. Visiting my town from *New Horizons* now feels similar to visiting the charming fake town from my college days: it was a joyful life for a short time when I needed it most.

Tom Nook still sucks, though, and I would throw a CRT at him if I could.

SATURDAY NIGHT WII

When I was twenty, I made the lifelong mistake of starting to do stand-up comedy. I'd been told by friends I was "funny" and "should just go ahead and try it" for a while, but I'd never actually given it much consideration until the last couple years of college, when I realized I had no idea what I was doing with my life and, worse, had no idea what I *wanted* to do with my life. But comedy had always been something I'd gravitated toward. In school, I was the only person in any of my creative writing courses who ever even approached writing something funny. Oh, there were a lot of barely masked stories about people wanting to fuck the writing professor! But I was the only one who wrote jokes.

I'd always liked jokes, and I'd always liked listening to people like George Carlin, Todd Barry, Maria Bamford, Bernie Mac, Patton Oswalt, Janeane Garofalo, and anyone who'd appear on *Premium Blend* late at night on Comedy Central. I never considered *doing* comedy. It was something I enjoyed. I liked the writing part of it. The connections between two things that poke fun at the brutal, unfiltered reality of living: men *do* drive like this. Women *do* shop like that. Wow, this guy knows what I experience on the daily! That joke is funny because it is true to all hoo-mans. Clap. Clap. Clap. We're all having a great time relating to these unimpeachable life observations.

After hemming and hawing and rehearsing in my dorm room, I did my first open mic at the original New York Comedy Club in what was then called "the small room," a long, thin space that clearly was meant to be a broom closet. Despite bombing on jokes about masturbation and probably more masturbation, I had at least found an activity that I theoretically liked doing: making people laugh. This was *something*. I wasn't terrible at it, and my embarrassment was only at a medium-hot level.

And since I went to college in New York, where there was a lot of television happening, I was lucky enough to get an internship at NBC Casting, and later through that, an internship at *Saturday Night Live*. I was a baby adult, barely halfway through college. I had just started doing stand-up comedy that same year, so naturally I felt that in just a few months, I'd be rich and famous. I just *knew* that they'd soon learn of the genius in their midst and eagerly shake my hand and ask if I needed anything, anything at all, just say the word.

This is not the way the world works. You do not just say the word. At least not for people who aren't a) the most talented person ever born or b) the child of the most talented person ever born.

Like a lot of people, I was a big fan of *Saturday Night Live* growing up, and even more so because of my dad. The original five seasons of *SNL* had been important to him on a critical level. According to the family mythos, he'd left his bachelor party early so he could catch the latest episode. While he'd always liked music and comedy, the show brought those two together in a way that hit every pleasure center in his brain. To my dad, *Saturday Night Live* had been the coolest place somebody could ever work. I truly believe that the fact I interned there raised me in his estimation. Unfortunately, the fact that they took me probably lowered the show in his estimation. He also excitedly asked me if I was going to meet famous people, which is one of the most important things that he believes can happen to someone. If you're already famous he will want to know if you've met someone even more famous than yourself.

SNL was the first place I ever worked that had a solid confidence in its importance and history. Almost every wall had decades of photos from the show going all the way back to year one. A long hallway featured the headshots of every cast member, past and present. Stepping out of the elevator onto the show's offices somehow feels both nerve-racking and calming. It's complete chaos and divine history rolled into one. The place even *smelled* special.

There were dozens of interns spread across multiple departments, not all of which I remember because I'm self-absorbed and this was a while ago. There were interns who worked with the musicians, interns who worked with the bookers, interns who worked with the writers, and so on and so forth. As for my part, I was lucky enough to be in the writers' department, the closest to the comedy action. But regardless of where you were, most of the job consisted of pretty much intern-y things: I answered phones, got coffee in the snow, brought up guests, fetched prescriptions, and transcribed a lot of political news events for cast members. Most of what I did could now be replaced by an app and AI, but I was working at a legendary comedy show in my early twenties: they could've asked me to punch myself in the nuts and I would've eagerly done it. One of them could call me right now and I'd still do it.

Yes, *SNL* was nonstop showbiz, but as interns, a large portion of our week was just hanging around waiting for requests from cast and crew. The most important time for us were the Tuesday-night writing sessions, since we were the ones who got coffee and late-night snacks and grabbed meals from the elevator bank downstairs. Writers and talent would come out and graze, including the show's host for the week; it was the first time I saw celebrities just be regular people. When Catherine Zeta-Jones asked us if she could have a french fry, one of us simply responded, "You're Catherine Zeta-Jones." When Jack Black hosted, he played a game of catch in the middle of the writers' room and generously included interns. These minor interactions that probably took little to no thought from the celebrities meant everything to us ragamuffins.

The greatest part of the job was working with the writers and cast. Seriously, the cast, writers, and crew were super nice to our group. And, Christ, what a time to join. I was an intern when Andy Samberg, Bill Hader, Jason Sudeikis, and Kristen Wiig were all starting on the show. I remember being in the office of the Lonely Island guys (Andy, Jorma Taccone, Akiva Schaffer) as they showed me and a few other interns an early cut of *Lazy Sunday*, which would become one of the show's biggest hits and kick off the popularity of Digital Shorts.

What's crazy is when we first saw the edit, the three of them were nervous that nobody would like it. They were new to the show themselves. They wanted something to make their mark. They were concerned it might be too weird, the editing too intentionally janky. That's not what happened. It was very good. I had nothing to do with making it, but I will say my encouragement of "Guys, this is really great" probably pushed it over the finish line.

I didn't just get to witness show history. Weirdly, I kind of got incorporated *into* it. Amy Poehler, Maya Rudolph, and the legendary writer Emily Spivey had taken a liking to me. I was dorky and needy and earnest and really wanted to help and would do anything, *just anything, Mama!* So for an installment in their Bronx Beat sketch, Amy, Maya, and Emily had host Zach Braff play me, with my name. He dressed like me. He was lovingly awkward like me. He spoke with a thick New York accent, which I don't have, but still. This was my *first* time working for a comedy show, and people were making me—and one or two other interns, such as future TV writer Jess Conrad—feel included as part of the history. That's really something when you're barely out of Florida. Even better, they all loved comedy nerds, and a majority of us wanted to write jokes like the real adults (who were, looking back, maybe six years older than us).

More importantly, I interned at *SNL* in the early 2000s, when the Nintendo Wii came out. This was also around the same time that Nintendo revamped its Pokémon Center near Rockefeller Center into a full-on company flagship store. I spent hours in that store. When I got stressed or was too early to work or nothing was happening, I'd walk over there, listen to the blissful Nintendo music playing over the speakers, and wish I had a job that let me afford everything. I started going every day when they were first showing off the Wii. *The* Wii.

It's easy to forget just how big the Nintendo Wii console was. Everyone remembers it was popular, everyone remembers it sold pretty well. No. It was a fucking tsunami wave. News anchors breathlessly covered the stunning new technology that was wildly swinging your wrist to hit a ball on-screen. Lines to buy the machine twisted around city blocks. Footage from retirement homes showed residents excitedly playing sports around a television screen.

It ultimately sold over 100 million units. That's not as crazy today—and it's still not more than the Nintendo Switch or the current all-time-seller, the PlayStation 2—but was a fucking rocket ship. Hell, Nintendo's previous console, the GameCube, sold about one-fifth of what the Wii sold. Its sequel console, the Wii U, maybe sold a tenth. For a brief moment in gaming history, the Nintendo Wii was all anyone could think about.

Here's how much people wanted the Nintendo Wii. A radio station in California held an unofficial contest in which participants were asked to drink copious amounts of water without using the bathroom ("Hold Your Wee for a Wii," they called it). The person who could last the longest won a Nintendo Wii. A woman died during this contest, and her family later sued the radio station. People were literally dying to get a Nintendo Wii for themselves and their families. That's not a healthy society!

I've been to the New York City Nintendo store about twice as much as I've ever been to any gym, but I have never seen crowds like I did when they were first demoing *Wii Sports*.

I saw an adult cry while playing. There is a man somewhere who definitely remembers holding that Wii remote in his hand. This was his ultimate experience. There would be nothing greater than this. Even the birth of his children would pale in comparison. He wept like Alexander the Great when he realized there were no more worlds to conquer.

Of course, when the Nintendo Wii was released, *Saturday Night Live* also got one. The biggest benefit to being a hugely famous television show is that companies will send you extremely expensive things for free, even though you can afford it more than anyone else. But this delivery was heavily anticipated. The Wii had been so hyped that even adults who'd never played a video game in their life were fascinated. The box was carried into the office like someone was carrying the blessed bones of a legendary saint. In retrospect, the Wii feels like a system that was crushed under a glut of late-stage shovelware and decent, albeit incomplete, ideas. But then? It was like we were about to rub a magic lamp.

It might also be worth mentioning that during my time at *SNL*, I kind of always wore the same red Nintendo sweatshirt. I wouldn't say *every day* I was there, but I would say *too many* of the days I was there. I've never been completely comfortable with my body, and nothing cures that feeling of awkwardness like an oversize, Santa-Claus-ass-looking sweatshirt with a video game logo. So people rightfully assumed I was into video games. The writers for Weekend Update nicknamed me "Nintendo Boy." This also meant people assumed I'd help set up the new console and show everyone how it worked.

To be clear, I absolutely would. To quote Dr. Zoidberg, "Hooray, I'm useful! I'm having a wonderful time!" I'd spent two decades fantasizing that one day famous people would say, "Hey, do you want to show me a video game?" In the second *Jurassic Park* movie, they show this one character being good at gymnastics at the beginning of the movie, and then later on she uses it to defeat velociraptors. This was my gymnastics. Which, I guess, would make putting wires into a television my velociraptor.

Along with an IT guy and a producer who I'm still friends with to this day (shout-out to John MacDonald), I hooked up the Wii and a crowd gathered in the long, narrow hallway. Celebrities from television and movies dropped what they were doing to watch digital bowling. It was like that scene in *The Matrix* in which the little hacker guy grabs everyone because Morpheus is about to fight Neo. Same energy. Running down the hall, banging on doors. "Get out here! They've got *Wii Tennis* going!"

After showing everyone how it worked, I slowly slipped to the back of the crowd and let the grown-ups take over. To be clear, nobody pushed me back. The cast and writers were always nice to me, a sweet but anxious man-child. But I did know my place. I was setting up the system *for* the cast and writers, but I was neither cast nor writer. The barrier between *useful* and *annoyingly eager* is a thin one that I've crossed many times in my life. But not that day, Satan.

So for a while, I watched some of the best improvisers and stand-ups and writers and actors in the world play *Wii Sports*, swinging their arms wildly to bowl or slam a tennis ball. A writer (I forget who, but imagine it's your favorite one) tried to play baseball and almost threw the remote through a wall, so we stuck to tennis and bowling, and I started to be more adamant about using that wrist strap. There's something funny about telling extremely rich and powerful people to please, please keep the plastic toy connected to their hand.

Then I was asked to play. One of the cast members—I believe Jason Sudeikis, but I could be wrong and I'm sorry if so—said I should get a turn because I set it up. They could've let me just sit back and watch like I was an approving father, gently nodding my head whenever someone scored. Instead, they invited me up to play. I felt special. I felt seen. I felt powerful.

I didn't go easy.

True, I was just an intern, the lowest on the ladder of the show. But I also wanted to show off. I needed everyone to see my skills and look at me with awe and respect. The fact that this didn't pan out when I tried to impress various crushes in elementary, middle, and high school slipped out of my mind like dry rice in a colander. All I knew was that if I focused and did well, they would think I was a god. And then I guess they'd hire me on the spot? No flaws in the logic there!

Whoever my opponent was got obliterated. I don't even know who it was, and if I did, I wouldn't say, because I crushed them so hard that any mention of their name would damage any potential future working relationships. I didn't even make it fun. I simply won shot after shot. Completely unfair considering they'd never touched a Wii Remote before and I'd been slipping out to go to the Nintendo store to wait in line and play. I annihilated that fucking wimp (please hire me someday if this is you) and did a whoop that probably made the whole building cringe in secondhand embarrassment.

"Now, that's how you do it!" I said. There were polite head nods and murmurs of *"Congrats"* as we handed over our controllers to the next people in line. My heart was still racing from a combination of excitement and being grotesquely out of shape, and I knew that I'd impressed them. As far as this sort of thing can impress an actor who's probably had sex with more people than just their hand.

After the game, the writers' assistant walked up to me with a cheerful "Hey, man!" I looked up to that dude, so I was ready for a pat on the head. I smiled widely. I asked him if he liked what he saw, which had to be confusing to him because he didn't. He wasn't there to talk about the Nintendo Wii. I asked him why he'd called for me, then. He handed me a list of a dozen orders.

"You got a coffee run."

NEVER HAVE A VIDEO GAME-THEMED WEDDING

In my midtwenties, I was married for about a year. My ex-wife and I had dated for a while, all the way through college. Coincidentally, we were also one of the first couples I knew to meet online. Here's how long ago this shit happened: we met in a chat room. Not a Discord chat or a forum or social media. A chat room back when it was called a chat room. It was for lonely people in our age group, and we began to talk and then talked more and began to date. We shared a common interest in wanting to find someone who shared any common interests.

The majority of our relationship was long-distance; we went to different schools that were far away from each other. Sometimes it was intense. Sometimes it was not. Long-distance relationships are a lot like German board games: you tell yourself it's going to be easy, but the logistics take as much time as the fun.

Yet as it went on, both of our parents seemed eager to see us get on with our lives and marry. So that's what we did. I mea-gerly proposed in a crab restaurant, the other diners watching us to see if she'd make the wise decision to say "No," "Abso-lutely not," or "You're really proposing while wearing a *Star Wars* shirt?" I was excited but also kind of worried? I was at a point in my life when I was somehow still struggling to understand how to live in a society. I realized as I proposed that I was changing two people's lives. This is something I should have respected but that I was not ready to do.

To be fair, planning the wedding was surprisingly easy, and the event itself was actually fantastic. Despite the quick end to the actual marriage, there was very little drama when it came to the special day. Nobody flipped out at someone else. Nobody had a meltdown. We got married at a bucolic, old mansion in New Jersey that had been converted into an event space. The ceremony took place in a massive, lush back-yard. The weather was sunny, not a cloud in the sky. Some of my closest friends were there, who I should probably talk to more, but I'm more of a person who's meant to die alone. She had far, far more friends at the wedding because she also had far, far more friends than me.

And, dear God, I apologize, the wedding was kind of *Super Mario*–themed. We didn't go all out, don't worry. This was my fault; she is a regular person. It was weird, but it wasn't weird-weird. She wore a normal dress and looked lovely. I wore a normal tuxedo and looked like the Penguin. But our exit music as we walked down the aisle was the underwater stage music from *Super Mario Bros.*, so that gives you some idea of the level of nerdiness I was shooting for. I wanted it to be fun without people feeling a vague sense of pity. I bet they shot straight to pity.

We also had two cakes: a traditional one and a *Mario* one. Our little table treats were also *Mario*-themed chocolates molded in the shape of coins and stars, cupcakes decorated to look like mushrooms from the game, question blocks filled with candy. One of our better ideas was setting up stations around the reception room with TVs and different video game systems. Bored kids played *Mario Kart*, which really helped us do well with the under-thirteen demographic. I could not name half of the people who were at my wedding, so there was a lot of calling everyone "buddy." I'm just glad that the people who are usually most bored at events—kids— had something to do.

Eventually, it came time to give speeches. My brother had struggled for days leading up to the wedding. He didn't know what to say. He didn't know how to say it. My family does not express love very well. If this was a speech about what I had done wrong as a brother, that would be easy. But a speech that's supposed to be nice and inspiring? For someone in our family? He asked for my advice.

I could've said "Speak from the heart" or "It doesn't need to be long, just give it your best." Instead, I told my brother to watch some movie speeches. I figured that he could get some inspiration from a dramatic monologue—maybe even from a wedding scene in a movie—and then he could figure out what he wanted to say.

Now, before I continue, let me say that my brother is the funniest person I know. I'm friends with a fair number of co-medians, so this is saying something. My brother might have the most raw comedic talent of anyone I've ever met. Dan, if you've read this far, I've got a message: you did good. You did real good. I've worked on award-winning comedy shows, and I've been honored to meet some of the world's greatest living writers, but nothing tops what my brother did here.

After I gave him some advice, my brother went to work. Little did I know that, over the next few days, Daniel would watch a lot of movie speeches. Especially dramatic sports movie speeches like the one in *Little Giants*. My brother and I still say, "One time!" quoting that speech, so I get where his mind was at when he began planning out what he was going to do.

When it came time for toasts, my ex's maid of honor went first and gave an extremely kind talk about their friendship and the importance of their lifelong connection. It was well thought out, well written, and deeply personal. They were like sisters and had gone through the good and the bad. Tears were shed, and not just by people on her side of the guest list. My ex's best friend gave a great speech. If the wedding had stopped there, everyone would have remembered *that* part.

But then it was my brother's turn. He was my best man. Because he's the best man I've ever known.[49] After taking the microphone, my brother unfolded multiple typed pages. (The maid of honor went straight from memory.) By the smile on his face, I knew that whatever he was about to do would cause a reaction.

---

49 That's not actually true. Sorry, Dan. The best man I've ever known is probably Weird Al. That's not a joke. I would take a bullet for that man, whereas with my family, I'd probably max out at shouting, "Hey, watch out for that bullet!"

He started, "I don't know what to say, really. Three minutes till the biggest wedding of our professional lives all comes down to today. Now, either you marry as a team or you're going to crumble, inch by inch, play by play, till you are finished."

If that sounds a little familiar, it's because that is based on the start of Al Pacino's speech in the football movie *Any Given Sunday*. This is a bit of a monologue where Al Pacino's character reviews how he wasted his life and ruined any chances at happiness while telling his team to focus on what's most important: winning. My brother proceeded to give that entire speech—while mixing in a few elements of *Friday Night Lights*—the whole time replacing the words *football* with *marriage* and *losing* with *divorce*.

Immediately, the table of my comedian friends at the wedding exploded. While I'm not a sports fan, they mostly were, and either way, all of us had seen this movie. They knew exactly what my brother was doing. None of them had witnessed anything like it. The longer my brother read off the pages, the more he committed to the bit, and the more my friends and I howled with laughter. As my ex stared in horror and both my family and hers were radiating fury, my brother stayed the course. He was a hero that day.

A few highlights:

"You find out life's this game of inches. So is marriage. Because in either game, life or marriage, the margin of error is so small."

"Now, I can't do marriage for you. I'm too old." (He was twenty-one.) "I look around. I see these young faces, and I think, I mean, I made every wrong choice a middle-aged man can make."

"I'll tell you this: in any fight, it's the guy who's willing to die who's gonna win that marriage."

You get the idea. He stayed in character the whole time. Never broke or laughed once. As I said, about 10 percent of the people at the wedding were crying-laughing. These were comedians who have gone on to run television shows and star in big Netflix stand-up specials. Up to that point, I had not seen any of them laugh as hard as they did at my brother's speech. It was like we were all watching a rare, precious comedy moment that would never exist again.

And, as I also said, about 90 percent of the people were so, so, so very mad at my brother. After he finished his speech, he received applause and cheers from one and a half tables and dead silence from the rest. I had tears running down my face as I gasped for air. My ex was just happy it was over, her frown turning into relief once it was clear we could move on. And, so you all know, I didn't want her to have a bad time. We just happened to disagree on the quality of my brother's presentation.

I'd later learn that, throughout the rest of the night, comedians approached my brother and told him that it was one of the greatest things they'd ever seen. Meanwhile, relatives and friends of the families approached him and scolded him for giving an inappropriate speech at a solemn occasion. One or two people told me they were sorry about what my brother had done, as if I'd be upset. I had to tell them that, buddy, I wasn't upset, I was thrilled.

Apparently one family friend approached my brother and—

God bless 'em—tried to give him tips on how to give a proper wedding speech. My brother responded, "I don't tell you how to [do your job], don't tell me how to do mine." That family friend later complained to my dad, which is funny because everyone involved was a grown-ass man.

It took me a beat to realize just how shocked by this a lot of people were. They probably saw it as an inauspicious start to the marriage. Which I suppose it was. But my brother's fucking speech didn't cause that. My own immaturity and lack of direction caused that. I made family members fly to New Jersey and rent a hotel so they could see me cut a Mario cake and hear my brother talking about "pissing away" his life in a speech. Our registry had been for a honeymoon. At best, they probably felt like they got swindled into paying for a trip to London.

Either way, my ex and I got divorced a little more than a year later. We didn't live together immediately, which itself caused friction. Neither of us were financially sound or ready, and I don't think I was even mature enough to be in that type of relationship. Our honeymoon should have been a sign of things to come: we fought as often as not. I remember seeing *Wicked* in the West End, and I remember vehement arguments over where to get lunch, and that's it. When we got back, the fighting continued, often followed by bouts of isolation.

I still hadn't figured out what I wanted from life, and here I was, punishing another human being by locking them into it with me. I resented myself. To make a long story short (because this part has nothing to do with games and because I'm garbage), I fell in love with someone else and confessed this fact to my ex. We tried to make it work anyway and finally moved in together when I got a job across the country. By that point, our relationship was already broken. We barely talked. I was doing a speed run at failing in life. In Washington State, you could file for divorce by mail if it's not contested. We didn't have kids or land or a shared account; there was nothing to contest. The most expensive thing we supposedly joint-owned was her car, and I didn't drive, nor would any judge have handed me the keys. After we filled out and notarized the final paperwork, I simply left the apartment for two weeks, she moved out, we had a pancake breakfast at a nice diner, and we never spoke again. From what I understand, she's since remarried and to a much, much better person.

Still, hey, I can't deny it was a great wedding! I'll remember seeing my ex in her dress. I'll remember hearing the *Super Mario Bros.* theme music as we entered the reception hall. But without a doubt, what will always stick with me the most is my brother's speech. It was one of the funniest moments of my life. I just fucking wish someone had recorded it. When I'm dying, hopefully one day very soon, of all the things I think about, of all the memories I'll treasure, that speech is going to be at the top of the list.

On the other hand, please take one word of advice. If you have any doubts about your relationship, any doubts at all, please talk about it with your partner before getting married. It can save you both a lot of heartache. Actually, two words of advice: if you have any doubts about your relationship, *do not give your wedding a video game theme.* This is your one shot! You cannot do two video game–themed weddings if the first one doesn't work. If I get married again, I can't do blue *Sonic the Hedgehog* cakes. I just can't.

But my brother can give any speech he wants.

THE FORMER NINTENDO EMPLOYEE

I did not take my first job interview with Nintendo seriously.

Around the late 2000s, a friend of mine named Ed left New York and moved to Seattle to work at Nintendo of America. They'd been looking for writers, and since he had been a comedian and playwright with lots of experience, he got the job. I was so jealous. Why couldn't I be someone who worked at Nintendo, the land of dreams, the home of joy? I didn't even know Ed liked video games until he got the gig, and now he was living a life meant for me. I'm the center of reality, Mom!

So naturally, when that same friend recommended me for a writing gig at Nintendo, I had absolutely no idea what to do. A couple years after my internship, I had scored a full-time job returning to *Saturday Night Live* as a photo researcher/assistant. I'd basically find all the elements of the graphics for Weekend Update, and then artists would put them together. It was a stepping-stone gig, and a great one at that. However, I wanted to be a comedy writer. Being there kept me close to the action—and I was able to write some jokes for Weekend Update—but I wanted to *just* be a writer and a comedian. This was my shot.

SNL was between seasons, so most of my income was coming in from freelance writing and the occasional paid stand-up gig. And, honey, it was *not* a lot of money. I filled out the Nintendo application online and sent a writing sample. Did I have a writing sample? Yes, I did! Did I have the ability to fill out job applications? Yes, I did! Did I think there was a chance I'd ever get hired? Absolutely not.

Then I got the job interview.

My first interview was with Nate Bihldorff, then one of Nintendo's top English-language writers and now a higher-up at the company. Nate Bihldorff handled the English writing side of the localization for the early games in the *Paper Mario* series, starting with the original on Nintendo 64. If you don't know about *Paper Mario* games—and God help you if you don't—they have far more text, dialogue, and story than most *Mario* games. While each one has a different plot, they're all role-playing game comedies, and every character is written better than they have any right to be. Nate Bihldorff didn't just help localize it to English, he put *Paper Mario* on the map as one of the funniest games ever made. Obviously, it was already funny in the original Japanese version. But, as someone with experience, it ain't always easy translating humor. Nate was truly a king among men. He's also extremely handsome. I became a writer because I look like a large baby made of raspberry jam and you can hide behind words, but Nate has cheekbones that could cut glass. Yet he wasn't the *most* handsome man at Nintendo while I was there. That guy now works on the *Destiny* series and knows exactly who he is.

I'll be honest: I was so nervous that I was shaking before the call. I was certain that I was going to embarrass myself and that there was no chance in hell I'd get this position. I was young, didn't speak any Japanese, and, despite being a fan, I had zero experience working for a game company. In my mind, there were older, far more experienced people who were ripe for the picking. It was cool that I'd get to talk to them, but I believed they were doing it out of courtesy to my friend. Nintendo was a special place, and I was as fucking far from special as you could get.

Now, just because I didn't think I'd get it didn't mean I was going to blow off the interview. Even if I failed, I still thought it would be fun to get to talk to someone from Nintendo. Especially someone whose name I'd seen in video game credits like Nate. He was and still is a celebrity in my mind. I'm almost certain he'd hate reading this, so I'm leaving it in!

When it actually came time to talk, I was suddenly, surprisingly calm. If I had no chance, why worry? We discussed my history with games and Nintendo. He talked about what the job would be. I talked about my writing process and comedy background. For the first time, having an MA in English literature at least seemed worth more than the student debt I owed on it. At the end of the call, Nate told me that I'd learn more soon. I figured that basically meant a polite we'll-let-you-know rejection. I said (and I'm not sure why I did), "I really appreciate the interview. I'm sure whoever you choose is gonna do great." I genuinely told him that when they picked someone else, they'd do a good job of it. There would be no second date, so I wished them the best.

What I learned later was that by not going apeshit on the

phone, I had put myself nearer to the top of the pile. Apparently, that happens. A lot. People love Nintendo, I get it. But it's pretty funny to me that one of my advantages was that I didn't scream in excitement or ask for *Zelda* spoilers. As someone who lacks even an ounce of chill, I was lucky that this was the one moment in my life I shut the fuck up and acted cool.

The second interview was in Seattle, which made no sense to me. That had to have been a mistake. They flew me in (!), put me up in a nice hotel (!!), and took me into Nintendo of America's headquarters (!!!). This headquarters was in a brand-new building. It had just opened a handful of weeks before I got there for the interview. The previous building—the one I'd seen in photos in old game magazines—was abandoned nearby and set to be demolished. They'd soon put in a soccer pitch for employees called, God bless them, Hyrule Field.

Nintendo's American headquarters was and still is dazzling. Every surface seemed to be metal, glass, or wood, all polished to a shine. You know how good it feels to peel that clear plastic sheet off new electronics? That's what it was like walking into that building, both the first time and every time after that. My whole body experienced a shiver of joy. Plus, I saw a silhouette of *Donkey Kong* on the wall and felt nice about that.

Now that it seemed like I actually might get hired, I was more focused with the second interview. I wasn't freaked out, but I knew they'd spent money to fly me out and put me up in a hotel. It terrified me, but I knew that I had a shot. I could actually work at Nintendo.

I met with more people, including Leslie Swan, a longtime Nintendo writer and manager who was actually the original voice of Princess Peach in *Mario 64*. I spoke with department directors and HR representatives. They asked me the same questions Nate did but also ones clearly to test if I was an asshole, which they probably did not want. They asked if I was comfortable working on secret projects and especially comfortable *not telling* people about secret projects. They made the job sound like I was going to become a spy. Meanwhile, I wore a weird suit with cringey gold buttons that I'd bought off the rack at Men's Wearhouse specifically for this interview. I did not own a suit before this interview. I'm a fucking child. It's a miracle I didn't sweat straight through it.

I don't remember flying home from the interview. I don't remember getting home. I don't remember doing anything between the interview and when I got the phone call with a job offer. It was more money than I'd ever made working freelance and doing assistant work at television shows. It felt like a trick. It was real. I let my bosses at *SNL* know I wouldn't be coming back next season. I was bound for the Mushroom Kingdom! I wish I'd said that last part just to see if they'd have put me on a psychiatric hold. I expected some of my bosses to be surprised or sad, but mostly the reaction was "Nintendo? That's *perfect* for you!"

So I moved my life from New York City to Seattle. That wasn't easy. I was at the start of an already-crumbling marriage and had to navigate us finally moving in together but across the country. I also had established an entire social life in New York City around comedy. Finding friends isn't easy for me. Do you think someone who writes a book like this has a big hangout group? I'm begging anyone who reads this to invite me to a text thread. Just one. I'm begging you.

I did a big dorky last show in New York at The Creek and

The Cave, a venue that has since moved to Texas. But in 2010 it was near my apartment in Queens and, even better, willing to let comedians do whatever they wanted as long as we didn't break anything. So for this show, I actually gave away things from my apartment to anyone who wanted it. It was a combination stand-up show and charity event (I was too lazy to do a garage sale). I gave away an old laptop, a TV, a bunch of toys, basically anything that I felt wasn't worth taking across the United States.

Stand-up friends like Sean Patton got onstage and talked about me as if I was dying and not just moving for a dream job. As they did sets and roasted me, I felt a chapter in my life coming to a close. Plus, it was a nice opportunity to see which friends *really* wanted a small television with a built-in DVD player. I probably should've charged people. My friend Mike Lawrence, a beyond-brilliant comedy mind and a lifelong comics fan, gave me his Incredible Hulk toy. He told me it'd kept him sane during his early years of stand-up, and now he was giving it to me for my new trip. People cried. Those people being mostly me.

And then, an airplane ride later, I was there. At Nintendo. I was an English-language localization writer and editor. What that means is I was paired with a Japanese-language translator, and we'd work together to ensure text and dialogue made sense in American English. This could vary from simply translating a few lines to fixing jokes to naming new characters to really whatever the developers in Japan needed. But the job itself was largely going through a game's script line by line, discussing the literal translation with my project partners, and trying to find something that retained the spirit of the meaning. For certain games with a lot of dialogue and jokes, like *Kid Icarus: Uprising*, we were given a bit more freedom to get creative. Regardless, we always wanted to make the developers happy. Nothing scared me more than disappointing the heroes who made my childhood bearable.

After the American English-language team finished their pass, we'd hand our text off to the Latin American Spanish and Canadian French localization teams in our office, who still worked directly with us and the Japanese developers. After *they* were done, Nintendo of America would then pass our text to the European teams who'd do their own work for their territories. Even British English got a pass so they could add a *u* to every word possible.

The misconception of this job is that localization teams are handed a finished project and some dolt with a Japanese to English dictionary ruins the one, true text without the team in Japan ever knowing. That might have been the way some games worked, but even when I was at Nintendo years ago, that wasn't really the way we did it. We'd check in with the Japanese developers every day. They'd ask us questions about our translations. That's another odd misconception: Japanese developers very, very often understand English. They might not always be completely fluent in certain phrases, idioms, and cultural touchstones, but many could understand and communicate in the language just fine. We weren't making changes behind their backs. The point was that we specialized in making the game click for our players just as much as it did for theirs in Japan.

Again, it's all about ensuring the widest-possible audience understands what's happening without losing the *spirit* of the original. The reason companies don't usually do literal one-to-one translations is because they often make no fucking sense if you don't have a solid understanding of a culture and the idiomatic way the people in it talk. Characters have dialects and accents and modes of speech that, if you understand the Japanese language and culture, denote certain things. But if you just directly translate those phrases into English—especially as unspoken prose text—they can ironically lose their intended impact and meaning. It's a balancing act.

I was lucky enough to be in an elite department called the Treehouse. In my office, three of the four walls were floor-to-ceiling windows. I could see deep into Pacific Northwest evergreen forests from my desk. God, what a time.

The first day I got there, I was so excited. Ed greeted me at the door and gave me a big hug and told me that I was about to have the time of my life. Side note: I'm still happy whenever I see Ed. When we met, the man was five years older than me, but somehow in the present day he looks like he's twenty years younger than me. Either way, he made me feel right at home. This was it. I was going to work at Nintendo forever. No turning back now. There would be no problems.

And then I got lightly hazed by a few writers and translators who began shooting me with Nerf darts. Like, a lot of them all at once. In my face until it knocked off my glasses and spilled my little coffee. This was not a big deal, and it's not like it was a company-condoned event. I know for a fact that they meant it as a small prank to welcome me to the group, but, as you've likely gathered, I'm easily shaken. It completely fucked any sense of joy I had for about two weeks. Or rather, it pissed me off for two weeks and made me certain I'd just made a big mistake. Wah! I was going through a lot of emotional shit around then; this was definitely one of those it's-more-about-something-else situations.

And it wasn't that serious! It didn't even hurt. They were foam darts. I don't know why it made me angry and such a baby. Maybe it was just that I felt like maybe I'd hoped I'd found an environment where mean shit *didn't* happen? There's a chance I felt like I deserved it? Or perhaps it was inevitable that *something* was going to knock this job off the pedestal and this just happened to be the first negative feeling to come along. I wasn't going to quit over it—and I *do know there was absolutely no harm or hurt intended*—but the microscopic hazing definitely made my first day a real one. I was being ridiculous.

The incident made me more eager to try way too hard. If I couldn't make friends at Nintendo (not true), I could at least work harder than everyone else at Nintendo (extremely not true). I focused on my job, went to every optional office gathering. I was going to be the perfect, indispensable employee so they'd love me forever and gnash their teeth if I ever left. It's always fun being a people pleaser who's bad at people.

Fortunately, all of that minor emotional pain was soon replaced with major *actual* pain.

You remember how I mentioned Nintendo had just moved into new headquarters? Well, a few days into my time at the company, they announced there was going to be a huge paintball game inside their old building before it was demolished.[50] This was literally my only chance to ever see the inside of the old Nintendo of America in person. They weren't letting

---

50 You already see where this is going, but stick with me.

anyone in otherwise. It was done. You either came in with body armor and a paintball gun or you didn't come in at all.

I'd never played paintball before, but I had played *a lot* of video games that featured shooting something. How hard could it be? You just point and press the trigger!

It turns out, real hard!

We were all given loose-fitting plastic armor and paintball guns without much instruction. Half of us watched the others as they put on their armor, imitating them and hoping someone knew what they were doing. Employees were then divided into random teams and sent into the dark, empty headquarters with a few loose Nintendo 64 signs still hanging in corners. We all got into position. Hands squeezed guns tight. Plastic vests squeaked as people knelt down.

Ready? Set? Go!

I got shot in the nuts immediately. Now, this part wasn't hazing. The coworkers who'd ruined my week with the world's lightest-touch gag were on a different team in a different area of the building. Plus, I was wearing a mask. Nobody knew it was me. Someone—no idea who—had just aimed, fired, and got lucky hitting one of the few spots that my armor wasn't covering. You know in a *John Wick* film when he shoots someone in the tiny crack between their armor plates? That's what happened to my balls. My balls got *John Wick*ed.[51]

And if I didn't take pillow-soft Nerf darts with a smile on my face, I definitely didn't take a high-velocity shot to my nads like a champ. I slammed into the floor in the fetal position. A few people helped drag me to a corner like I was a wounded soldier in Vietnam. There was absolutely no way

---

51 Forget *The Sims*, this is probably why I'll never have children.

to get out of the building without being shot again, so I went full *Metal Gear Solid*. That is, I literally hid in a cardboard box until the round ended. You know in a war movie when a character begins rocking back and forth, saying they want to go home? That was basically me while people were having fun.

Eventually, the game ended, and I limped to the changing area, limped to the bus stop, and limped into my apartment. The lower half of my body felt like it was ready to put in its two weeks' notice.

But at least it helped snap me out of my navel-gazing bullshit.[52] I had been so self-involved, first as an excited Nintendo employee and then as a sad Nintendo employee, that I forgot that I was here to do a job and be a person. This wasn't an extended trip to a theme park. This wasn't my birthday party. Annoying little things were going to happen. Not every coworker was going to be a shining white knight welcoming me back to the stage of history. I needed to grow a pair. Especially after the last pair was obliterated by paint.

Thankfully, after the first couple weeks of watching in wonder as real adults localized games, I was given an assignment: writing the English version of the box and manual for the Nintendo Wii *Super Mario All-Stars* rerelease. Since it was just a Super Nintendo game collection slapped on a Wii disc, there wasn't much in the way of actual localizing to do. In fact, it took about two days to finish the text for the manual and the box, and that was it. But it was still related to *Mario*, it was still me working on it, and it was still a fucking delight.

After working on *Super Mario All-Stars*, I got my first big as-

---

52 He wrote in a book about himself.

signment. I'd be writing on a revival of a dormant D-list Nintendo franchise called *Kid Icarus*. There had only been two previous games. The second one came out when I was about seven, and I remember that because it got my Game Boy taken away by a teacher in elementary school. I was working on the third one at the age of twenty-six. Unlike almost every other Nintendo franchise, *Kid Icarus*'s lore wasn't really that well-known at the time. This wasn't *Zelda*, where decades of games had created a vast matrix of very specific themes, stories, and characters that had to be kept in some vague sense of continuity. You played a little angel boy named Pit who fired arrows and worked for a goddess named Palutena. The only other content we had to go off were a few weapon and enemy names (shout-out to my boy, Eggplant Wizard).

I was to be the secondary writer under an experienced, talented writer named Ann Lin. The fact that she put up with my bullshit questions and minor freak-outs every four minutes is a testament to her ability. Without her, I probably would've melted down whenever we got an email from the lead on the project, Masahiro Sakurai, the genius behind *Super Smash Bros.* The dude who created *Kirby* and directed his first game at nineteen. He was a mad scientist of a man, and he was rebooting the *Kid Icarus* series in his own image.

The good news was what he wanted, in addition to it being fun, was for the game to be *funny*. He wanted jokes. He believed that his Japanese one-liners weren't going to translate perfectly into other languages. He wanted all audiences to experience the same level of humor, which meant that the gags might have to vary up a little between cultures.

So we were given a lot of leeway. When I wrote the descriptions of different "idols" in the game (think trophies you could earn), I got the ability to slot in jokes and references without worrying I was going to cause someone to get death threats because I accidentally violated canon. We took Mr. Sakurai's jokes and self-referential humor and did our best to match it. One line I was weirdly proud of pitching was when Pit, in danger, shouts, "I never learned how to read!" It's a childish nonsense joke, and I couldn't believe it was in the final game. That was part of the joy: we really laughed hard and tried to one-up (no pun intended) each other with silly, goofy bits and ideas for lines in the game. It's the same feeling I'd get when I'd later write for TV.

Long after I was gone from Nintendo, that same line I pitched made it into a later version of *Super Smash Bros.*, in which Pit was now a playable character. When I heard that, my entire ass popped off my body and slapped the floor like a wet Butterball turkey. Weirdly, there are YouTube videos in which people earnestly discuss Pit, saying he doesn't know how to read as if it's an important topic to human civilization. Folks, it was a joke. Or it's vital canon. Don't ask me— I'm outta the company!

The other great thing about working on *Kid Icarus: Uprising* was that we were localizing it while it was being developed, writing step by step as Mr. Sakurai himself was making it. He could see what we were writing just as we could see what he was adding. We were able to have conversations about the story and the game and what might be ahead. It was, in the most humble, meager sense, a collaboration between translators, writers, and one of the greatest game designers who ever lived. Every morning was a little like emailing Santa Claus.

Thanks to Mr. Sakurai, I officially got to write jokes for a Nintendo game. I felt like my entire life had brought me to that one moment. It was like Eminem in *8 Mile* except not that serious and not that similar at all. Nobody threw up spaghetti.

But people in the Treehouse didn't just work on one project the whole time. While there were dedicated teams for every game, we'd also occasionally have meetings with a room full of writers and translators. These were usually to name something, whether it be a character, a monster, an object, or a concept. This is how I named a character in the *Legend of Zelda* franchise, the only real notable accomplishment of my life.

The Legend of Zelda: Skyward Sword was in mid-development in 2010. Around this point, some games started having naming sessions to flesh out their worlds. I loved doing this. These meetings were some of the most fun you could have in the Treehouse. You basically went through a slideshow of funny pictures and were like, "I wanna call that one Cloudzilla!" and someone at the whiteboard would be like, "Why, that certainly is a name! I'll write it down, but maybe let's keep going!"

I was in the brainstorming room with people whose only job was writing and naming things in some of the most famous games on Earth. Many of them had named more items, monsters, lands, and characters than I could've ever even imagined. It's like what happens in a hockey game when every goalie is injured and they have to bring in the Zamboni guy for a period. It ain't much, but it's more than most get. This was my one period.[53]

In one specific *Skyward Sword* session, we were pitching names for a few characters. A lot of *Skyward Sword* takes place (spoiler alert) in the sky, so one of our main parameters was that new characters should have bird-themed names. This seemed easy enough. But the names also had to convey character qualities so players could quickly get a grasp on their personality. "Bird-themed and helpful," or "bird-themed and mysterious." It's weirdly difficult, especially when you have decades' worth of games in the franchise you're trying not to bump against.

At one point, we were shown an image of an arrogant-looking guy with broad shoulders and big red hair. The parameters were basically "bird-themed and a jerk." And, as I said, these meetings were always fun: there was no jockeying to get your idea on the board. We were goofing off for money while trying to please extremely serious businessmen in Kyoto.

"Bird-themed and a jerk. Bird-themed and a jerk. Bird-themed and a jerk…"

I thought about asshole bird species. Growing up near bodies of water, I knew that geese were (and still are) the shittiest animals alive. They are jerks that just poop everywhere. They'd chase you to your death if they could. They would fire Nerf guns at you on your first day of work if they could.

---

53 Side note to my side note: the only thing more fun than naming sessions were sessions where we had to come up with anything and everything that would go into a game's swearing filter. You know, so kids couldn't call each other *"motherfuckers."*

Geese are big, wretched creatures that think they are better than anyone else. That part seemed to fit.

The character we were naming looked like someone who was completely full of himself. I ran through men's names in my head. What was a masculine name that simultaneously carried an air of silliness? I needed something that could sound like the name of a confident dummy while combining it with the name of a giant dipshit bird. *Goose. Bruce.*

Groose.

And, baby, it stuck! Groose became Link's bully-turned-friend in the game. He's a fan favorite. Not because of the name. I'm not that delusional. I didn't do anything. I had the most surface-level involvement possible for this character. He's just a fun guy that's designed and written well in every language, literally none of which I had a hand in. But I fucking named him in English. I've never had a one-night stand with a world-famous celebrity, but I imagine the sense of accomplishment is pretty much the same. You dine on that story for years, no matter how small that feat might have been.

I don't care! My name for a character is official! Books about the series feature him. And, again, I had nothing to do with this man outside of a name—and I'm sure everyone I worked with at Nintendo thinks it's slightly pathetic that I'm so proud of this, but look, that's what I got, and that's what I'm holding on to.

My time at Nintendo was limited. I was getting more and more paid comedy work. As a stand-up, I was featuring and headlining around the Seattle area at clubs like the Comedy Underground. I took two weeks off from Nintendo to write for the ESPYs when they were hosted by Seth Meyers. I almost missed work when I was late coming back from road gigs. And while I'd left *SNL*, I was still freelancing jokes for Weekend Update and getting some on the air. I had just become a full-time writer and now I was becoming an actual *comedy* writer. When I was there, Nintendo wasn't against moonlighting, but they weren't particularly encouraging it either. Apparently they expected you to focus on your job while you had a job. Weird.

So when I got offered a position writing comedy about video games—and more money with it—I broke the glass and took the job. I loved and still love Nintendo. It's the only place on Earth in which I could have had the honor of meeting legends like Shigeru Miyamoto and Satoru Iwata. It's also the only place on Earth in which I could have had the horror of playing pickup basketball with Reggie Fils-Aimé and passing the ball to the wrong team.[54]

But I had to choose between the opportunities in front of me or the ones behind me. I had to choose between a life making people laugh or a life working for my favorite childhood brand.

Like a fool, I chose comedy.

On my last day at Nintendo, I tried to capture everything in my mind. They didn't let you take photos in the department where secret projects were being developed. But I wanted to remember. I wanted to remember the bookshelf of the full run of *Nintendo Power*. I wanted to remember all the incredible people I'd worked with, even if I'd never find out who shot me in the nuts. I tearfully said goodbye to folks like Nate and my coworkers and Ed, the guy who'd hooked

---

54 Reggie is very, very nice but very, very tall and thus very, very intimidating.

me up with the job. I even hugged the guys who blasted me with Nerf darts, because it had been years, all was forgiven, and also one of them had saved our team in that basketball game with Reggie. I gave away some of the old Nintendo memorabilia I'd bought on eBay and put on my desk. It turns out when I move, I find it easier to give things away than take them with me.

After two short years of (*Super Mario*) wonder, I walked out those doors and left behind the luxurious new-game smell of the castle that Mario built.

And I've regretted it every day of my life since.

HOW TO PREPARE FOR A SOLO PEN-AND-PAPER ROLE-PLAYING NIGHT

In today's culture of instant gratification, it can be hard to organize a group for a tabletop role-playing game night. People are busy, and not everyone has the space in their lives to create little gnome wizards for RPGs like Dungeons & Dragons. Whether it's because they have children, obligations, or were there the last time you had people over for a game night and ended up screaming at everyone for not being more serious about *Vampire: The Masquerade*, it's tough to gather a group of adult friends. It's even tougher to convince them to play a pen-and-paper role-playing game when you're known for turning beet red if someone seems like they're not having a good time. Or even bursting into tears just because!

But that doesn't mean you need to give up on pen-and-paper role-playing games. There are dozens, if not hundreds, of amazing solo RPGs that are available for *your* entertainment. Take it from me, a person who made up names and personalities for condiments during the pandemic lockdown: you can have a lot of fun by yourself with the power of imagination! And solo role-playing can be an amazing experience. Dungeons are designed to be isolating places. Dragons are lonely creatures. The real treasure isn't the friends you make along the way. The real treasure is treasure.

Fortunately, you won't need to go on your solo role-playing game journey alone. Well, I mean, technically you *will* ultimately have to go through it alone. That's the entire point of it being solo. Let me start over. Fortunately, I've spent a lot of my life in abject solitude, so I think I know *a little something* about pretending to be a paladin while sitting in a dark basement apartment in Queens.

If I was going to tell you a sentence you'd immediately believe, it would be that I own dozens of solo tabletop role-playing game books and supplements. I especially recommend *Thousand Year Old Vampire*, *Star Trek Adventures: Captain's Log*, and *Quill*. Regardless of any jokes coming around the bend, I've had a lot of fun with those. One is a horror journaling game, one is a sci-fi journaling game, and one you write some very fancy letters. I'm not doing these games justice: they're great. And there is one quality to playing a tabletop game by yourself that's actually very fun: you get to play at your own pace. You get to make all the decisions. There's no arguments outside your own head. It gives you complete freedom to use your imagination any way you want, something that wasn't possible before people added dice, math, and rules.

That said, if you're going to play a solo tabletop role-playing game, there are a few steps you should follow to ensure you have the greatest experience possible. And if people on Reddit can post unhinged diatribes about the *secret unspoken rules* of games like Dungeons & Dragons, I can do it for people who play solo RPGs, too. There are many of us. We just don't really know it because we tend to keep to ourselves.

1) Do Not Tell Anybody You're About to Do This

Trust me. It's not because of the shame. You felt shame long before you decided to go full solo RPG. You're here because you're built of shame and need to feed it every day lest it take control. You've crossed many rubicons of low self-esteem before you got to these shores, and I personally salute your journey into self-destruction. Or you've got some spare time, and you want a fun activity. Life contains all kinds.

The real reason you can't tell anybody is simple: follow-up questions. Follow-up questions are bad enough in this world, let alone when you're just trying to put your head down and fight as an intergalactic bounty hunter in the (blessedly solo) game *Notorious*. *Naturally*, telling someone you're playing a physical, nonelectronic role-playing game by yourself will make them curious. First, they'll tell you they didn't know it was a thing. You'll say, "Yeah." Then they'll ask what it's like. You'll say, "It's like a role-playing game but alone." Then they'll ask if it's still fun. You'll say, "Fun is objective, and most of us are just trying to make our way through the universe while doing the least amount of harm."

And so on and so forth.

You can tell someone that you already played a solo game. At least you'll have a few details to make it sound more like an adventure and less like an exercise in randomized cartography. But if they find out beforehand that you're about to play solo, they're going to want to learn more and they're going to want in. There's a line of games in a series called *Micro Chapbook RPG* that allows solo play in countless different settings, from horror to sci-fi. I lent a friend my entire stack of books from the series. Do you know what he did? He got a job in another state and moved. That's what happens when you let people know about solo role-playing.

2) Don't Let Anyone Join Your Solo Game

If you're not telling people about the game, you better not be letting people tag along. You are here because you are *so very alone.* You've already gone too far, cowboy. You bought the books. You got the conversion guide for taking a character from D&D into another, slightly more confusing system. You even have a random encounters guide that lets you roll to see what happens next. Hell, maybe you went the full distance and bought one of those handy solo adventures for *Call of Cthulhu.* It's so much fun, but...wouldn't it be more fun to share with other people?

No. It wouldn't! Too fucking bad! Solo role-playing games are for solo people. You want friends? You want family? Go hang out with the social butterflies at your local board game café. You want to learn the depths of your own madness? Go solo. I didn't write this list for tourists. I wrote this list for people who want to pump their fist in victory after a critical hit and then make eye contact with their pets for validation.

3) Set the Mood

You know how women in movies will light candles that look like they came from a basilica and line their bathtub with thirty of them to set a mood? Then they luxuriously lean back in the tub, sip from a glass of wine, and open a book while you keep thinking to yourself, "How does that book not get ruined by the water?" Anyway, *that* is what you have to do with your solo RPG.

After all, you're alone. Nobody cares if you go full cringe. Who gives a shit? This is all for you, baby. Go ahead and light that candle. Put on a little music to match the theme of the game. I once ran a solo campaign in a sci-fi universe where, for some reason, I decided I wanted to start a space restaurant. Because the rules didn't mention how to do that, I just made up some shit and had the time of my life. I made a playlist of songs that switched between sci-fi club music and 1950s diner hits. Was it corny? Yeah, it was. Did it set the mood? Yeah, it did. I'm jealous of my past self even thinking about it.

4) Make Your Character

The good news is making a character in a solo RPG is often much easier than in something like Dungeons & Dragons or the cybernetic Hell that is the rules of *Shadowrun*. Folks, I wanna love *Shadowrun*, but it feels like I can only make a character by filling out exams for law school. Fortunately, solo role-playing games tend to have fewer stats to track and items to pack. You should be able to have a character up and running within minutes, even though you've got hours of alone time ahead of you. Feel free to make them look like you. No! *Better* than you! Make 'em the hottest version of you possible. Or, if you're extremely hot, the absolute worst version of you possible so you can see how the rest of us live. Then draw a little portrait of who they are and come up with a backstory!

The best part? You can do anything here. Nobody at the table is going to complain you're overpowered or whatever because you are literally the only person at the table. There are enough empty chairs set aside for Elijah and his whole crew to sit down. Do whatever you want. This is hermit time. Live your darkest desires (within reason, and don't tell me what they are). Make yourself the strongest person on Earth. Swear all you want without getting in trouble with Mom. Nothing will stop you now because you're both the player *and* the dungeon master.

5) Okay, Actually the Rule Books Are the Dungeon Master

While they vary, many solo role-playing games rely on checking tables in their rule books to determine everything from what trap is behind a door to which boss monster faces you at the end of the dungeon. Or spaceship. Or castle. Or whatever setting you choose to go with. The point being, you roll your cute little dice, flip to the back of the book, and realize that Dracula is hiding out in your high school gym. This actually happened to me in a game. Obviously. It would be both the best and worst day ever if it occurred in real life.

Without a human to tell you what's going on or to generate conflicts for you (or a machine programmed to do so), that little solo RPG rule book is your daddy. It's not your father. But it is your daddy.

6) Actually, the Book Isn't Sentient, So Fuck It

I feel like every time I read a Dungeons & Dragons book, there's a little subsection that says if the rules conflict with what your characters and DM want to happen, it's okay to bend and break those rules a little for the sake of the game. However, you'll still usually have at least one player that complains anytime anyone even remotely strays from the calculus required by the player's manual.

Here, that does not matter. That's because this is all 100 percent entirely imaginary bullshit. Yes, you're pretending to be someone else with goals, but—not to belabor the point— who cares? Nobody is going to catch you out if you ignore the rules. You could throw the book in the trash and still have a good time.

If the book says a boss killed you and you don't want to take that loss…don't? Nobody will know. It's not cheating. It's all fake. During one game, I completed a whole run through a ghost-infested psychiatric ward, and when I suddenly died, I wasn't going to pack up my pencils and papers and dice and be like, "We did our best."

I simply lied to myself and told the story I wanted to be true, the same thing I do every time I fall asleep.

7) Just Write a Novel

I just got off the phone with God, and it turns out that there's little to no difference between making up a story using predetermined rules and making up a story entirely by yourself using your imagination. Don't let the rules tell you what to do! Just make something up and go on an adventure in your precious mind's eye. Unless the rules are cool, in which case, definitely do what they tell you.[55]

With these helpful tips in mind, you're sure to have a great time, until you look in the mirror and take a quiet shower and stare at the ceiling as the pillow next to you stays as cold as it's been since the divorce.

Enjoy!

---

55 I really do recommend *Quill*.

DUNGEONS & DRAGONS & DOOFUSES

As I emphasized in the previous chapter, there's no wrong way to play a tabletop role-playing game. You can play it at home with friends or you can play it on camera if you're attractive. You can run a game with devilish monsters and dramatic stories. You can act out your fantasies and be part of an adventure. Or you can be the most annoying person on Earth and yell at everyone whenever the Dungeon Master (or Game Master, if you're feeling freaky) accidentally lets an arrow fly one square too far.

That's to say, I'm more of the act-it-out-and-make-a-fun-story type, because to me the main appeal of playing a game like Dungeons & Dragons with friends is that the rules are loose. You can make wild decisions and—fuck it!—maybe they'll pan out! While there are electronic role-playing games that did this for years, and especially recent ones like *Baldur's Gate 3*, it's only in a pen-and-paper game where there are literally no limits. Unless one person in the group endlessly complains about other players' choices, in which case everyone reaches their limit very fast.

The best tabletop RPGs I've played are the ones where the DM (or GM or whatever) uses the rules as *suggestions* rather than boundaries. Saying "Your character can't do that" is far less fun than saying "Let's see if your character dies trying it. Roll that twenty-sided die, nerd!" This all seems like obvious improv shit, but I've learned over the years that some people think RPG rule books are Holy Bibles that will burst into flames if a player tries to, I dunno, throw a cat at a goblin. "There isn't a specific rule for it!" Who gives a shit? It's called imagination! Let the cat rip up that goblin like Garfield on lasagna.

With this in mind, I consider myself lucky that most of my postcollege role-playing games have been with writers, comedians, and video game developers. This isn't because I'm fancy. I just don't know a lot of people outside of places I go to earn money. But the upside is these are people who usually understand committing to the bit. They're creative!

During one game I played with a group of comedians (with Jared Logan as our Dungeon Master), we came across a kingdom in the Underdark. If you're not familiar with D&D, the Underdark is a vast underground world filled with putrid creatures, deadly terrain, and the most disgusting villains you can imagine. It's basically Florida without sunlight. Anyway, a king in this little charming corner of the Underdark was in a bit of a pickle: his forces were at war with mushroom people.[56] Therefore, he needed us to brave a dangerous cave to retrieve a MacGuffin of some sort that would turn the tide

---

56 Ironically but hilariously unrelated to the Mushroom Kingdom.

of the conflict. We were obviously being prepped to start a dungeon crawl. Cave. Treasure. Go.

Except that one player, who we'll call "Tim" because he has power in my industry, had an idea! He said, "I want my character to use a charisma roll to convince the king to send in his own guards first to help clear the way for us." Our DM groaned. "Really? You want someone else to go into the dungeon? Okay." Jared asked him to roll a die to see if it worked. The player rolled a natural 20: automatic success. In fact, with a grin on his face, Jared said that Tim's idea was *so* successful that the king's guards totally cleared the dungeon themselves and got the treasure without the players' help. He said, "They all had a great time in there without you and talk about how glad they were that you weren't there with them." He then had the king refuse to help us escape the Underdark because we basically told the dude to solve his problems by himself.

Jared Logan's Dungeons & Dragons groups were so good because he is an incredible comedian, extremely fast on his feet, and seemed to have an encyclopedic knowledge of every rule book. Playing D&D with him was probably the closest I've come to playing it with a trained professional running the game. Which is fun, because later on, he would actually *become* a professional who runs role-playing games. The man is *good*.

But tied for first with Jared's D&D game is the one I had with a few friends in Seattle. Some of the folks in the group—including my translation partner—were also Nintendo employees. You know that super handsome coworker I mentioned who now works on *Destiny*? That dude was there, too, humbling us all with his radiance.[57] Other players had

---

57 Now, that's a man who should be playing D&D on camera.

even cooler jobs than us. One guy worked at Valve (he got every game on Steam for free and would answer absolutely zero questions about *Half-Life 3*). Another player designed robots that built other robots. There definitely could've been more women or, you know, *any*, but hindsight is 20/20, and we were a bunch of dorks.

Rather than have one specific leader in this group, our Dungeon Masters tended to switch up every so often. We all had characters that popped in and out of different stories. My character was a tiefling bard named "Linda Mattos." A tiefling is a type of species you can play in Dungeons & Dragons that get much of their power from the demon blood running through their veins. A bard is a type of character class you can play in Dungeons & Dragons that get much of their power from constantly annoying the other players at the table by singing.

My character came by her name after I decided my bard was going to play an instrument. So I went to Goodwill and bought the cheapest, worst Casio keyboard I could find. A little keyboard that cost $5 had the name "Linda Mattos" on it. Since I hadn't named my little demon spawn anything yet, it felt right to have her name match the one on her keyboard. It fits with all great demonic names: Satan. Lucifer. Beelzebub. Linda.

In the game itself, I pretended she played a melodica,[58] which only made it stupider. Fortunately, we were doofuses who loved weird ideas and big swings. By the way, I should mention that I could not and cannot play the piano in any way. I have literally no musical ability. None. I have a rudi-

---

58 You know those little handheld musical keyboards with a hose you blow into? That's a melodica!

mentary sense of *rhythm* that has been useful for music games, but anytime I've picked up an instrument, it's been a lesson in the chaos of cacophony. The DM told me that I could only subject the group to the musical pain of me hitting random keys if, and only if, I role-played the entire thing. I had to sing. I had to give it my all. I gotta sing, Mama!

But whether we were in a battle or hanging out at an inn looking for our next big score, Linda Mattos was ready to tickle those ivories and make things happen. She was a high-charisma, medium-intelligence goofball, and I absolutely loved it. The DM (at this point, my translator!) started leaning into it. Monsters and enemies were confused by Linda. Not because she'd play some sort of *confusion* spell type of song, but just because everything that Linda did was bonkers. Imagine negotiating with an undead wizard to convince him to turn over the keys to his cursed crypt, and then one of your teammates comes in playing "Chopsticks," singing, "Give us your keys / We're saying please! / Give us your keys! / That's what we needs." (Yes, that is another actual quote and, yes, this was after I'd taken improv classes seven years prior.)

As you might expect, Linda Mattos died fairly quickly. It turns out that a tiefling bard who is screech-singing while smashing her hands on piano keys isn't everyone's favorite. I'm not saying my translator made it a point to kill me, but I don't think he *didn't* make it a point to kill me. In one of our biggest quests of the campaign, we were supposed to pull off a heist. Break into an evil rich dude fortress, get another MacGuffin of some sort, and get out. My plan, which I was asked by the other players not to do, was to distract the enemies using the emotional power of music. I'd walk up to the front gates, put on an impromptu concert, pull the guards' focus, and allow my team a better chance at sneaking inside. This would have been a foolproof plan if not for the dummy trying to execute the plan.

I had Linda approach the guards and begin singing. Our DM asked me to roll to see how the performance went. Did I distract the guards a lot? Did I distract them a little? No! I rolled a one. Critical miss. Automatic failure. The smile that crept across my translator's face was chilling. Usually he was pretty easygoing about critical misses. He's a nice dude! We carpooled to work! Unlike a lot of DMs, he used bad rolls to have fun with us and create new challenges we weren't expecting, challenges that could be overcome and won if you just put your mind to it. He wasn't the type of jerk to kill your character and humiliate them in the process.

He killed Linda and humiliated her in the process. Her melodica exploded, doing severe damage to her hands and face. The explosion broke the spell. Instead of being lulled into a stupor, they suddenly noticed a bright red tiefling with her hair blown back like a Looney Tunes character after holding a bomb. The enemies swarmed Linda Mattos, and soon she, one of the best imaginary musicians of all time in this one specific game, was no more. The rest of the team *could've* helped, but I think they also really wanted to see Linda die.

I made a new character. My friend felt a bit bad about what had happened. Not bad enough to allow Linda Mattos to come back to life or, as I suggested, have her twin sister, Binda Battos, show up with an identical melodica. Since those ideas didn't really take the group by storm, I asked if I could play a changeling character. A lot of groups don't allow changelings because they're racist. (No, that's not true, but what if?) They don't like changelings because having the ability to shape-shift can break the game. It's an incredible power to have, especially at lower levels, when your entire party could be killed by a strong breeze. Plus, once one person gets to be a changeling, *everybody* wants to be a changeling. And then it would all be everybody changing into everybody else while rolling around on the ground screaming, "I'm the real one! Take the shot!"

Like Linda, I boosted up the charisma of my new change-ling, Ted. I'll always prefer a character who can talk their way out of a situation as opposed to fighting. This stems less from a pacifist desire for love in our world and more from the fact that battles in Dungeons & Dragons take *forever*. I understand and respect that, for a lot of people, these battles are what make D&D fun. People spend days, weeks, months, and even years getting their role-playing characters godlike powers to crush their foes. Cool. Not for me. Don't get me wrong: I love a good battle to cap off a heist into some leg-endary vault. But I always feel like tricking a dragon into just getting up and leaving their treasure behind is much funnier.

In this new quest, Ted and the rest of the adventurers were facing off against an evil magical cult. As with a lot of evil cults, their plan was to use their labyrinthian underground base to summon an ancient dead god to devour the souls of the living. Or, at the very least, give them some modicum of authority over the local municipalities. Honest question: Where does someone even *meet* a dead god to worship?

Like the best moments in a tabletop RPG, I can remem-ber this one like it actually happened. I don't remember most of the rolls or which apartment we played in. I do, however, remember all of us, as our characters, meeting at the damp stairs leading down into the cult's chambers and making a plan to infiltrate. I can close my eyes and still see the texture of the stones in the walls and the slipperiness of the steps as we walked down. Everything was described in detail; it felt so real in my mind.

Once we got down a level, we could see the cult beneath us. There those dumbass cultists were in robes standing around a massive flame, conjuring some sort of evil and whatnot. The leader of the cult stood on a raised stone platform, dressed in far more regal garb. Sort of your classic, popular Aleister Crowley cult leader: long, pointy beard; wide, insane eyes. Ra's al Ghul meets Lovecraft (which, I guess, is just Ra's al Ghul, but that's not important). When you're standing higher than the rest of the cult and you look like a *Flash Gordon* villain, it's pretty easy to go, "Yes, that is probably the leader." As we all learned in school as children, if you take out the leader of a cult, you take out the cult itself. The only downside of an imaginary scenario in which anything is possible is that the cult is completely correct about their god being able to return and devour the world.

At one point in the ritual, the cult's big boss stepped away. He whispered something in another cultist's ear and walked down the steps as everyone else kept working those chant muscles. As he departed, our jolly group of adventurers turned to each other and began arguing about what to do. The real-life engineer in our group, who played a barbarian, suggested we run down and kill everyone. He always suggested that, though, so it didn't get as much consideration as it maybe should've. "Smash now, questions later" is pretty effective in Dungeons & Dragons if you enjoy the battles. Not me, buddy! Ol' Mike Drucker works overtime to skip those pesky battles. I pitched that I, as the changeling, should take on the form of the cult leader and march downstairs.

The rest of the group was against this for a couple reasons. One, my solution was essentially "Sit back and watch me handle it," which isn't that fun for other players to do in most games. Two, more importantly, I had just recently failed a similar task as Linda and ended up being completely obliterated. Nobody wanted another Linda Mattos situation, whether it be her horrid death or even worse music. I assured them that this time would be different. This time, we'd *succeed*!

During this conversation, I was asked what I planned on doing once I got down there. I told them I'd wing it. Everyone thought it was an even worse idea, because it was. Another player pitched having his thief sneak into position and shoot a carefully aimed arrow at the cult leader's neck. Unfortunately, the angles weren't great. Our paladin player wanted to call on his character's god for help. His god did the equivalent of leaving him on read. We got a few more suggestions that we run into battle with our axes and crush the bones of our enemies underfoot. Obviously, only the barbarian had footwear that could make said crushing safe to do.

So I had Ted shape-shift into the form of the cult leader, clothes and all. I asked a few times, and the other characters assured me that I looked "so cool." I also asked if this was a bad idea and was met with a resounding "yes." But bad ideas are fun in tabletop role-playing games. It's always more fun to have everything go wrong than everything go right.

I rolled a successful acrobatics check to safely get my character down to the platform. No injuries or sprained ankles. Good. I made a successful stealth check to ensure nobody saw me. No *Metal Gear Solid*–style exclamation points over anyone's heads. Still good. I casually approached a cult member who looked especially meek. I love a good meek nonplayer character. They're easy to persuade to tell you secrets! So I sidled up.

"Minion!" I shouted a bit too loud. I could hear the rest of my party groan. The cult member turned around and looked at me, cowering in the presence of who he thought was the boss at his part-time cult job.

"Yes, my lord?"

This was as far as I'd thought ahead. I don't know what people expected. I was pretty busy convincing everyone that this was a good plan to actually come up with a good plan.

"There is a grave issue with the ritual," I said, raising my voice to trick the other worshippers into thinking I was more commanding, like my dad's friends did when I was a kid. "We are…" I looked back at my group "…summoning the wrong god! If we open up this portal, it will bring destruction." I licked my lips. "But not the kind of destruction we'd want! Trust me, this is a bad situation, my man. Minion. My minion. Right." A lot of DMs would've responded by this point, rolling a twenty-sided die to see how the cult NPCs would react. Instead, our DM just let me keep talking.

"So. We gotta stop it. Like, now. Guys. Okay? If we don't cut it out…big… Boom?"

Our DM grinned like the Cheshire cat just did ecstasy. The cult member said, "Oh my! That *is* very serious! Everyone, gather around! Our lord has something to say! Lord, please! Tell everybody what you just told me!"

"Oh! Hi, everyone. Good afternoon... Or bad afternoon? Um. So. I checked a grimoire and, darn it, we gotta stop this ritual. I'm as disappointed as anybody else."

The cult surrounded me. They were quietly speaking with each other. To demonstrate this, our DM said, "Murmur, murmur, murmur."

The cultist spoke up again. "My lord, speak! Tell them all why we must stop the ritual!"

I cleared my throat.

"Thank you, um..." My character froze.

"Terrence. You don't recognize your own son?"

The DM was throwing some curveballs. I had to keep it together.

"Yes. I know. I was preparing to speak, Terry! I mean Terrence! Or Terry? Don't interrupt me. So. Everyone. We need to shut down this whole thing before we summon the wrong god. Which, I've told *my son* here, would be, you know, not great for us. The cult."

The crowd murmur-murmur-murmured more.

"What shall we do?" asked one cult member.

"We shall take a break! And we shall rethink this whole thing! Maybe leave this place for a bit and take our time to figure out what's going on with these kooky chthonic gods. Crack open some books and look up what we're doing wrong..."

Quiet at the real table. Quiet in the fictional ceremony chamber.

"And then start the ritual over and get it right this time!"

Polite, if confused, applause from the cultists.

"Then we will conquer the world! We will devour the souls of the nonbelievers! Just, it won't be today! Soon! Soon it'll happen, my friends!"

The DM asked me to make a roll. This was to see whether or not they believed it was me. 14. Just *one* above the number I needed to beat. Since it was a very small success, the cultists seemed *pretty* sure I was who I said I was. A little confused by my change of heart, but not too suspicious. Except for one, who seemed less convinced by my completely unconvincing act. My friend running the game was going to screw with me even more. As the other members of this small but industrious religion of doom walked away, the lone skeptic asked me a follow-up question.

"My lord, forgive my impertinence, but could you tell me where we keep our artifacts?" The DM chuckled, performing the words as if this character already knew I was full of shit. "We seemed to have lost track and need your guidance to find them."

I decided to have my character Ted intimidate him. I accused the skeptic of being incompetent and not knowing his place. I'd seen this in movies, and it seemed to always work. You yell at someone, they snap to attention, and you send them on their way. After you rob the place, they probably get super fired from their job. Then they have to go home and tell their spouse they got tricked by adventurers and so the boss—who's been on one this week—says that was the last straw and fires them. How are they going to face their children now?

Anyway, to see if this second attempt at chicanery worked, I had to make yet another roll. Persuasion. Thank God. I had a lot of points in Charisma, so that was easier. I could roll pretty shitty numbers and still come out on top. There's only one number I absolutely did not want to roll: a 1. And as you might expect, I absolutely rolled another automatic critical failure. As that twenty-sided die tumbled and stopped, our Dungeon Master looked straight into my eyes.

"You lose your concentration and your mustache and beard fall off."

I didn't even know a changeling could just lose hair like that! My character panicked. That is to say, I panicked. The cultist was about to run to get the authorities when I asked if my character could knock him out before he got help. I failed that roll and screamed to the rest of my group, "Boys, the jig is up!"

At this point, in the real world, we couldn't stop laughing. This was the funniest, most nonsense failure I'd ever had in a game. Our DM's response was perfect. My plan, which I was told was a bad idea, once again proved to be a bad idea. I love Charisma characters, but apparently I can't talk my way through shit without getting myself murdered.

And wouldn't you know it? The cult murdered me. Murdered me a lot. And thus another annoying character fell by the wayside. To their credit, I don't think the other players betrayed me this time. I do think they purposely took some extra time to come down the cyclopean stairs to see what would happen. After I died painfully, the group defeated the cult, and I made another character: a quiet Cleric who shut up and did what he was told.

EVERY STEAM REVIEW EVER

Not Recommended
975.2 hours on record

I have been excited about *War-Fight: The Hardening* since it was announced five years ago. As a fan of the original *War-Fight*, I wanted this game to be both a completely original take on the series and also not change anything at all. And after spending more time with this game than I have my own family, I have to say I'm disappointed. I expected an action adventure role-playing survival game, but what I got was a survival role-playing adventure action game, which, as we all know, is completely different.

I tried to keep my expectations low during early access, when the company making this game charged me full price to play a complete mess. I cannot believe that a game would be released in this broken state after years of development, despite the fact that this happens all the time to me (see my other reviews).

My biggest problem is that after spending more hours playing this game than there are in a month, I worry it doesn't have any depth. And then there's the graphics! Talk about an asset swap! I hate asset swaps! Don't ask me what an asset swap is, because I only have the barest understanding that I picked up from a friend on Discord. Although the developers of this game are two teenagers working in a hut powered by a bicycle, I really expected them to put more time into designing the individual blades of grass. It breaks my heart when I see trees in the game that look too similar to each other. The fact that this bothers me definitely does not say more about me than it does the game itself.

Around my four-hundredth hour of the game, I began to worry it wasn't for me. I had completed it five times, unlocked every achievement, and seen all the endings, including the joke one. I had played completely through the Boss Rush and New Game+ mode. I had taken computer programming classes to mod the game and include an entirely new quest written, designed, and voice acted by me. But was I enjoying myself all this time? You'd think yes, but I'm going to keep talking about this game like it repulsed me to my core. It's just not fun!

My only hope is that the developers of *War-Fight: The Hardening* release years of free patches that improve the experience for me. I can't imagine putting another five hundred hours into this game if it doesn't change. Two hundred and fifty hours maybe! But five hundred? That time is better spent on different games I hate. Hopefully, every expansion for *War-Fight* will be free or I'll be right back here mad at that, too. I also won't tell you what I specifically want fixed or added, but if you don't do it, batten down the hatches!

I'm not sure I'd recommend *War-Fight: The Hardening* to other users. I wish I could get a refund, but they cut you off at two hours, and I played nearly a thousand. Yet there was never once a pop-up from Valve saying "Do you actually enjoy this?" because then I could've clicked *"No!"* I simply kept playing it until the heat death of the universe to make sure I didn't like it. And I don't! Hence how much time I'm even spending talking about it!

War-Fight: The Hardening overpromises things they never promised and underdelivers on things I just kinda decided to expect. There's some fun in there, but I wish I'd waited for a sale so I could leave the same review anyway. Thank you for reading this, and I look forward to the developer's furious response in which we become personal enemies.

7 Likes.

THE *IMAGINE GAMES NETWORK*

I only worked at *IGN* for one year. But getting hired by them in 2012 at twenty-seven years old wasn't my first interaction with the company. Since *IGN* was, and still is, one of the biggest entertainment news platforms on planet fucking Earth, it was hard to avoid their presence. I have been in and out of *IGN*'s life like an ex who moved far, far away (or shingles).

I'd been reading *IGN* since middle school, when they were still calling themselves the *Imagine Games Network*. The internet was young, and outside of physical gaming magazines, getting accurate video game news back in the mid- to late '90s was difficult. Unlike now, in which getting accurate video game news is impossible. Either way, my school friends and I were relying on the reporting from very important, very adult people who were probably, at best, a few years our senior. Now there are a thousand social media feeds and official Discord chats and surprise press conferences and influencers, including ones with *very* strong opinions on *IGN*!

While being a games journalist seems like a deceptively hard, often thankless job that mostly pays in free branded tote bags, what we all *really* thought would be cool when we were younger was to review the games. Or movies. Or anything! My high school wasn't packed with rich kids: we all lusted after the idea of making money off getting things for free. It's the American way.

This is also how I got conned into my first so-called writing job in my freshman year of college. Because the man who scammed me is a trained lawyer, and because I genuinely don't feel like looking up his name, I'm going to call him "Frank Ass." Frank Ass was a little embarrassed to be a lawyer, for some reason. Instead, he proudly talked about his real passion: being a movie reviewer. Or at least he was *theoretically* a movie reviewer. You see, he conducted these little "internships" in which he'd have young college students go to the movie screenings and write the reviews for him, which would then go into newspapers across the country under his byline. I didn't even get exposure. The joy of getting to see new movies for free quickly washed away. I was fucking writing reviews under another dude's name. The only two good experiences I got from that was watching *Spirited Away* with an entire American audience seeing it for the first time and sitting next to Joy Behar in a screening for *The Matrix Reloaded*. Now that I think about it, the whole thing was almost worth it to see Joy Behar watching speculative science fiction.

Fortunately, I got wise to Frank's scheme relatively fast. I asked if we could share credit, and he said, "It doesn't really work that way," which is a funny thing to say when you're the only one deciding the way things work. I slowly ghosted him. His emails went unreturned. Frank seemed actually hurt that

I wasn't responding to him. Maybe that was immature of me, but I was fucking nineteen, and he was making money with my work and getting all the credit. He didn't get to feel bad.

By this point, *IGN* had grown past video game news and moved into general pop culture. They had a burgeoning DVD review section, and by chance, I saw an editor (I believe it was Todd Gilchrist, who now works for *Variety*) mention they were looking for freelancers. Great. I reached out, sending samples of the reviews I'd done for Frank Ass while emphasizing that I myself was *not* Frank Ass. Somehow they believed me.

The good news was that my name would be on every review and I'd get to keep every DVD that I reviewed. The bad news was that, again, it wasn't paid. Looking back, I should've been paid—and if you do similar work, *you* should be paid—but you have to realize that working for an international video game site and actually getting my name on my work felt like a cold breeze in a hot hell after dealing with Frank Ass.

So while in college, I reviewed DVDs for *IGN*. Of course, I had no real critical authority to do this. I didn't know anything other than what a movie was. And some of my reviews are outright bad. Just super embarrassing stuff. Let me give you a little something to wet your beak a little bit.

"But now that it's finally on DVD, is *High School Musical* worth all the cheers, or should it sit in the cafeteria by itself?"

Oh my God, you can still find that online. This was written in 2006. I had recently finished my undergrad degree at NYU and was just starting a one-year graduate school program in English literature. So, yeah, I was all over the map. I also gave the DVD of *High School Musical* a 5/10. That's malpractice. I was wrong. If you or someone you love were involved with *High School Musical*, it's good. It's a musical that gets your, gets your, gets your head in the game. I was wrong to think otherwise. I should post this apology online as a screenshot from the Notes app on my phone.

And while I wasn't paid for my DVD reviews, having my name on them *did* get me places. I began to write small articles about movies and video games for other entertainment magazines and websites, most of which are long dead like *GameSpy*. The first time I was paid for writing was in an issue of *FHM* with Paris Hilton on the cover. *FHM* (or *For Him Magazine*) was part of a brief trend of publications for pubescent millennial boys who weren't allowed to use the internet. Most of the articles were like "Which Mountain Dew Would Get YOU Laid?!" Fortunately, my article for them was about a local *Halo 2* tournament in New York City. The piece paid $250, which was more money than I'd ever received at once in my life. As checks from other paid assignments began flowing in, my interest in working for freebies waned. I politely told my movie editor at *IGN* that I needed to focus more on getting paid work. It was easier to break up with them than Frank Ass because they'd always been 100 percent honest about the working terms.

About a year before my groundbreaking *High School Musical* review, I had started doing stand-up. Over the course of that year, I slowly moved from "sucking so bad" to "kind of sucking so bad" to "at least he didn't embarrass himself and rush offstage this time." My comedy career hadn't taken off quite yet, but at the very least I was beginning to earn enough making people laugh to buy dinner after a show. I also began to meet people who encouraged me to submit to places like *The Onion* and *McSweeney's*. *The Onion* was an especially big win for me. I'd been reading *The Onion* since our middle school got an internet connection. One of my favorite jokes of all time comes from an *Onion* headline: "Archaeological Dig Uncovers Ancient Race of Skeleton People." I was proud that I'd made it into the newspaper with headlines like "Twisted Sister Now Willing to Take It" and "There's Nothing to Fear but Fear Itself, and Also Me, the Ghost of Franklin Delano Roosevelt."

When I discovered a website called *The Minus World* writing fake joke articles about games, I reached out to them and asked if I could do it for free. *The Minus World* preceded *Hard Drive*, a satire video game site with fake news, by at least a decade.[59] It was simply two guys named Brian—Altano and Miggels—trying to make some jokes.

Anyway, I reached out and became an unpaid freelancer for them. Getting paid for your work as a writer is the most important thing you can do and was, again, the first thing I sacrificed. But this time it wasn't an "it's for exposure!" situation. Nobody was bullshitted. They were honestly a little confused why I'd be willing to help for nothing. I don't even think *they* were making any money. But to me, this was the same as joining a sketch team or putting on a stand-up show. I just wanted to make something fun for myself.[60]

Despite *The Minus World*'s meager beginnings, it got noticed. Brian and Brian were presented with an incredible opportu-

---

59   By sheer coincidence, *Hard Drive* later added a section called *The Minus World* that was ironically genuine gaming news.

60   I recognize there's some cognitive dissonance between my love of this memory and my only-chumps-work-for-free philosophy. But hey, I was a happy chump!

nity: taking their sense of humor to the biggest gaming site on the internet, *IGN*. As I would later do, they took the gig.

Even better for me, the most important person, they kept me on as a writer and, more importantly, a *paid* one at that.[61] That's all I wanted out of life. And it was a good time, man. Folks, I hate to say this, but the window has closed for the "good times" in games media. I'm friends with plenty of video game journalists and critics, and they're the most dedicated, brilliant people I know who still have to scramble to get proper housing. This has far less to do with poor editorial decisions and far more to do with business affairs departments across media companies asking why every reporter needs their own bed in a convention hotel room. One criticism some people have of *IGN*'s parent company is that it seems to buy up successful websites, lay off anyone who has a family to support, and then drown that site in a bathtub. But the people on camera talking about whether *Lego Batman* is better than *Arkham Batman* don't usually make those decisions. They're the ones who get yelled at online, but most of the time they're not the ones who control mergers and acquisitions.

Most of the articles I was writing were ostensibly little goofy opinion pieces—not too dissimilar to what I do now as a good reason to write off video games on my taxes. For a man baby who wasn't earning very much money, those freelance checks were paying the bills and keeping alive my dream of a life entirely controlled and ruined by games. If you're looking to copy what I did, it's not hard. Just time travel back to 2005 and kill the worst-looking guy you see at a New York Comedy Club open mic and then take his place. As the per-

---

61   As opposed to getting free DVDs to malign *High School Musical*.

son you'd be killing, I can assure you that you have both my encouragement and my consent. Please kill me.

The crazy part is those articles *did* help me and my career. Even after I finished grad school and got jobs, I kept freelancing jokes about games. When Nintendo was looking for English-language writers who could handle comedy, a large portfolio of video game–adjacent bits *definitely* helped. Although, ironically, taking on that job at Nintendo also required me to stop writing those articles. Like an asshole, I asked if I could keep writing jokes under a fake name. Like professionals, they said, "Of course not, you complete idiot." I wasn't trying to be *that* shady! I didn't want to leak stuff! I just wanted to keep writing half-baked jokes about Sonic the Hedgehog's dirty ass. With their very proper denial of my extremely poor suggestion, I stopped writing for *IGN*. Again.

Luckily, I loved being at Nintendo. Unluckily, my comedy was starting to take off, and I was getting more and more opportunities. In Seattle's comedy scene I was a medium-small fish in a medium-small pond. I was able to book plenty of stand-up work featuring and headlining because there were just fewer experienced people willing to work for peanuts. I was traveling to gigs across the country and worked with people who are still some of my best friends. And by "best friends" I mean "only friends."

It also meant that I was beginning to see more over the horizon. While I wasn't writing for *IGN*, I had still been freelancing for *The Onion* and Weekend Update and making a decent amount from both in the process. After years of throwing myself at the door, the door was budging. I'd also remained friends with some of the folks at *IGN*, and when I'd see them at events or conventions, we'd have a drink and

laugh about this silly industry. To any Nintendo people reading this, I never told them anything… Other than how handsome Nate Bihldorff is.

Around this time, in parallel with my comedy, *IGN* received
an investment from YouTube to create new, professional-level
gaming content. Editors and executives at the site had a few
ideas for it, but the one that they were really excited about was
a video game late-night show. *IGN* asked if I'd ever consider
leaving Nintendo for the gig. Which is insane because, for *a
lot* of people in the video game media, one of the biggest brass
rings you can get is transitioning from writing about games
to working for a company that makes them. Here I was being
offered the opposite.

I'd be a goddamn moron to leave the job I'd dreamed of
having since I was a child. I made scrapbooks and cardboard
Nintendo toys when I couldn't afford games. I still own Nintendo Power posters that have little pinholes from when I
hung them on my wall in the third grade. I was the exact type
of person who should have spent the rest of his life working for
the only place on Earth where you can buy first-party Nintendo games at a discount. Losing my coworkers and friends
was hard. Losing that employee discount was a tragedy.

IGN flew me into San Francisco. Instead of a taxi, they had
me use a new app called something like "Uber." I met with
them on Friday, December 30, and there were still Christmas
decorations on everyone's desk. Someone had a little Jabba's
Palace playset with a tiny Christmas tree in it and little gar-
lands strung across the diorama. Employees were relaxed and
festive. Most of the end-of-the-year coverage had wrapped
up. The last *Game of the Year* video was in captivity; the galaxy was at peace.

Whereas Nintendo's headquarters had an air of humble pride, *IGN*'s offices were packed with giant statues of game characters and had walls covered in signatures from famous developers. Conference rooms themselves were designed to feel like you were inside different video games, including one that looked like a vault from *Fallout*. If Nintendo had a culture of restraint, *IGN* had a culture of "this cardboard cutout of Lara Croft was free, so we took it and now it lives here." I'm being a bit unfair. *IGN*'s staff just loves video games. And since the place wasn't beholden to any specific video game company, an entire floor could look like GameStop became a human and vomited all over the walls.[62]

I should also mention how nice everyone was there. They told me how excited they were to have me come in for an interview. They introduced me to a ton of the staff. They made me waffles (I'm not joking). There was a point in this process that I realized I wasn't interviewing for a job, I was being courted by a company. And didn't that just turn me into blushes and smiles? I was suddenly the prettiest boy at the ball. I mean, seriously, waffles! A few folks earnestly and politely questioned why someone would even consider leaving Nintendo.

I also finally got to meet Brian Altano in person. We'd been friends through email forever and only then got to shake hands. I also met Greg Miller, a couple years before he founded his own gaming media empire with Kinda Funny. Brian and Greg were two of their best writers and on-camera talent. Both are good friends to me, to each other, and to people I care less about. Both were probably constantly annoyed with

---

62   This is a compliment.

me while I worked with them, but it was nice to put a face to the people who'd been paying me.

Then, at the end of this daylong "interview," one of the business executives took me into a room. He asked me what I thought of the place. I mumbled something like "Oh, it's amazing. I love the *Fallout* room." It was amazing. I did love the *Fallout* room. But even now talking to this executive, I was certain at some point they'd realize that this was a mistake. The executive reiterated how thrilled they were at the prospect of me joining the team, and then, without fanfare, he offered me the job with a number of dollars that I'd never even come close to making before.

Now, people who give job advice might say that you should take time to think over an offer. Sleep on it. Compare and contrast. Maybe even—if you've been raised with confidence—counter with what you think you deserve! You'll begin the job on solid ground and prove your worth.

I did none of that. I just went, "Sure!" in a high octave and that was the end of my career at Nintendo.

True, a 50 percent salary increase was nice before I realized that living in San Francisco was infinitely more expensive than any place on Earth. More importantly, I was being offered the chance to help develop and head a ridiculous comedy project featuring ridiculous people doing ridiculous bits about games. Again, I know the order of operations was usually reversed: people work in game media and *then* transition to game companies. But now comedy would be my full-time job. (Because nothing makes you love your passion more than turning it into required work.)

Of course, that also meant telling people at Nintendo. They were very understanding about it, albeit somewhat confused by the move. But they just wanted me to be happy. They said they looked forward to still seeing me around at events and hoped we'd keep in touch. Then they banned me from working on anything for my last two weeks and made me give back my free Nintendo 3DS, which I bravely did. I'm sure there was at least one closed-door meeting about the absurd asshole who was somehow leaving them for the site that reported on them.

So I moved from Seattle, the best place that I have ever lived, to San Francisco, a place that I have lived. I emptied my entire savings account to pay the deposit on a new apartment. My home was at the very edge of San Francisco. If there was an old map of the city, my one-bedroom shoebox would've been in the corner where they wrote "here be dragons." It cost twice as much as I was paying in Seattle for half the space.

My lucky break was actually working with the people at *IGN*. Their team was far more professional than me. Their video producers, editors, and camera crew were all able to make it seem like I knew what the fuck I was doing with this project. We had no specific format, a small studio space, and a shoestring budget. We'd figure it out ourselves.

What emerged was *Up at Noon*, a weekly show hosted by Greg Miller, with Brian Altano and the amazing Naomi Kyle starring in some of the sketches and interviews. I was also on camera here and there, usually to furiously complain about shit that didn't matter, like the look of the Michael Bay *Ninja Turtles* movie. I could've put all that effort into helping the world. Instead, I spent my time on "Turtle Talk," a completely avoidable media juggernaut.

While I had worked on television shows before as an intern and a researcher, as well as writing jokes where I could, I had never produced a full project before. Making television is an incredibly complex process that takes "what you want to do" and replaces it with "what you have time to do" and *then* replaces *that* with "what you have money to do." I had to share producers, editors, artists, camera crew, and hosts with other *IGN* departments. Which makes sense because those people were there first. I was the new dork sucking up resources.

I want to say that *Up at Noon* was the fire that vulcanized me into an unstoppable force of production. But, as I've tried to demonstrate in this book, I'm incredibly stoppable. Putting the show together every week broke my brain. But at least *IGN* allowed Greg, Brian, and me to spend hours hiding in a corner room and pitching the moronic ideas. Most of them we would never have the ability to do. I seem to remember one idea about a teenager in the *Grand Theft Auto* universe having to survive their driving exam. There was no way we were going to do that.

For a year that was my life. Reading gaming news. Writing bits about gaming news. Taping bits about gaming news. Checking comments and feeling sad about our show's bits about gaming news. We didn't do terribly, I just only believe negative comments on anything I have a hand in making. One weirdo on YouTube watched literally every episode and left a comment on each one about how much he *didn't* like it. His criticism was specific enough that he wasn't just trolling, he was watching each video as it came out just for the sake of being mad.

On the bright side, there were a lot of people who loved our show, including the studio audience when we allowed fans to come see it being taped. As much as we were accused of faking a laugh track, we did actually have people in that room laughing. The live studio audience was great, including a man named Greg (not Miller) who showed up for every episode, even when we didn't know what we were doing. Greg was a delight. He was a built man who wore a *Naruto* headband every day and could break your body in half like a twig.

The one problem we did run into (outside of having no time or budget) was that we kept being told by our bosses that some video game companies didn't necessarily want to be mocked. And because *IGN* relied on good relationships with these game companies for access and advertising, we initially hit a lot of walls. We were never censored, but the people in charge of us *strongly* believed that *Electronic Arts* wasn't going to enjoy jokes about the recently released *Mass Effect 3*'s less-than-popular-bordering-on-hated ending. Was this true? I don't know. It was weird, but I got why.[63] We were also warned that Rockstar didn't like jokes about their games, so we were asked to do nothing about *Grand Theft Auto*. This made less sense to me, since *GTA* did extremely well and the series usually leaned heavily into comedy. Who knows if Rockstar would have actually cared, but a few managers at *IGN very much* cared. I'm sure every new episode we made was a unique heart attack for them.

Luckily, we flew under the radar enough that it never became a bigger issue. It also helped our case that we often had game developers in our sketches. I always think about a bit we did with Keiji Inafune, one of the original designers behind *Mega Man*, where we eagerly pitched bad robot-villain ideas with the underlying theme of us really wanting to just

---

63 And we made fun of it anyway.

be his friend. I'm not sure how much his *team* loved it. But he seemed to enjoy that he wasn't just being asked the same ten questions he'd get in every interview. When dealing with big names in any medium, you usually have layer upon layer of PR people you need to get past with an idea. Their job is to protect their client at all costs; our job is to make a client say something silly into the camera. Depending on what you want someone to say, the two can sometimes conflict.

At the same time, I got in a bit *too* deep in the show. This was my first project in a leadership role. I wanted it to go well, and I wanted it to be respected, and I had literally no self-esteem. One time, Greg very lightly quipped on camera that one of my jokes didn't work. I decided to get big, giant mad at him and confront him about it. How *dare* he light-heartedly goof on my brilliance? In front of the whole world, no less! I was humiliated the moment I brought it up. I really told an educated adult man that he shouldn't make fun of a floppy joke that itself made fun of toys. Greg, for his part, apologized for it. Me, for my part, apologized eight or nine times after that for making a furious godlike volcano out of a molehill. My body may be best described as "porcine," but I needed thicker skin. It was foam darts all over again. Sensitive!

But we also really, really cared about each other. It was a small team working on *Up at Noon*. It's silly, but it was personal for us. When Greg got cancer, we used the show to update fans on his progress. *Borderlands* producer Randy Pitchford shaved Greg's head on camera. Fans reached out with love and care and appreciation for Greg's vulnerability. Some of them were going through similar issues. Somehow on this show we fit in jokes about *Transformers* as a form of contraceptive *and* went through one of the scariest moments in our host's life.

Outside of *Up at Noon*, the best project I got to do at *IGN* was their 2012 April Fools' video. Usually *IGN*'s April 1st videos are fake trailers for things like movies based on popular brands. Unlike the old magazine pranks that pissed people off, most fans knew these trailers weren't real. They were just a fun way for *IGN*'s video team to create a what-if scenario while trying to make it look as official as possible. But *Mass Effect 3* was released that year, and the sci-fi series always felt like a Saturday morning cartoon to me. I pitched that we should make a fake 1980s cartoon called *Mass Effect: The Animated Series*. It was a parody of every weird Hanna-Barbera show in which the members of a musical group solve a mystery together. (Both my proudest and least proud moment is making a pun on guitar amps and *Mass Effect*'s biotic amps.) It might not have been a massive undertaking, but it was so much fun to write.

What ultimately sealed my fate at *IGN* wasn't the pressure or the low resources or the potential for angry companies. It was the fact that, like at Nintendo, I was suddenly being offered chances that I couldn't turn down. *IGN* was nice enough to let me take time off to attend the Montreal Just for Laughs comedy festival, where I was one of that year's New Faces. When a writing spot opened up at *Late Night with Jimmy Fallon*, I was recommended by a couple people, including folks at Weekend Update and someone who saw me at the festival. I could write jokes extremely fast, which was exactly what they needed. I did a writing sample packet, interviewed, and got the job at the very end of December, literally one year after I'd accepted the job at *IGN*.

Everyone very much got why I was leaving. It was television, and once again, I'd be making more money than I ever thought possible since my dreams were always very low to the ground. I still miss making nonsense videos for *IGN* and the people I worked with.[64] I know the place can have a mixed reputation for various reasons (fans have never forgiven *IGN* for giving *Mario Kart: Double Dash* a cruel 7.9/10[65]). But it's a giant media site made up of a lot of people. There are going to be some bad takes here or there. In fact, if you want to know about one of the worst takes *IGN* has ever had, I once more refer you to my *High School Musical* review. I have also never reviewed a video game in my life, so please don't yell at me.

Some of those *Up at Noon* videos are still online, including when the series continued for a while without me. Watching them again, I'm reminded of how loose everything was. We felt so restricted by budget and time and bosses, but that tension didn't show on camera. We were just buffoons playing dress-up showbiz.

---

64   If anything, I wish I'd had more appreciation for the people there at the time, like Jeremy Parish: I never worked with him, and I was intimidated by how well he dressed. We simply worked under completely different parts of the umbrella. Now he's a friend that I'd call one of the best video game historians of all time. I coulda had that friend the whole time!

65   I think we can all agree that, at the very least, it was an 8.0.

SECTION 4:

NIER AND FAR

THE LEGEND OF LATE NIGHT

In the early days of Jimmy Fallon's run on *Late Night*, producers allowed me—and a couple other comedy writers—to submit freelance monologue jokes (and get paid when they got on). A few late-night shows used to do this, but most don't anymore for a variety of reasons. I do think it kind of bent Writers Guild union rules? I didn't know that, of course. I just wanted to break in. So I was allowed to submit jokes and actually got some on the show. Not many, but enough that at the very least they'd heard of me and knew I could do the job in some capacity.

My time being a weird, eager nerd at *SNL* had actually made me some, well, I want to say "friends," but really more like "people who took pity on me." Seth Meyers was the first person to ever hire me to write for a television event, the ESPYs. Unfortunately, everything I knew about sports circled around Miami, Florida, from 1984 to 2002. I didn't tell Seth this when he asked because I desperately wanted this job. I didn't *lie*, but he also didn't *ask* what I knew about football. Plus, I got material in the show; whether by luck or by skill, I didn't screw up. He brought me back a second time.

I was also getting a little traction in the industry. People at comedy shows were starting to know my name in a context other than "guy in the red sweatshirt who gets coffee" and more in the context of "guy in the red sweatshirt who once said something clever, so let's see if it can happen twice." Opportunity was knocking, and for another brief period of my life, I had the emotional energy to open the door.

I had not met Jimmy Fallon before my interview at *Late Night*. I'd seen his work at *SNL* and people at *SNL* spoke fondly of him, but he was already gone by the time I was an intern. Which might be a good thing, since it took looking past *a lot* of red flags to enjoy having me around when I was twenty-one. At the moment, you still have to look past some red flags, but at least it's less like a boreal forest and more like a small grove. The good news was that I was being recommended by a couple people from the *SNL* world. The bad news was that I am an extremely awkward person whose conversational skills beyond two or three subjects are mostly me nodding and going, "That's so crazy. Say more." And while not thinking that I had a shot is what *helped* me get a job at Nintendo, there's far less confidence when you actually think you have things on the line.

But I knew Jimmy loved video games. Even before the job was up for grabs, I had seen an interview where he talked about playing *King's Quest* back in the day. I was *very* ready to have a conversation about that. I had also read that his favorite series was *The Legend of Zelda*, so we were having Groose for dinner. Hell, I'd even seen that Jimmy had a cameo in the

Nintendo DSiWare game *Dark Void Zero*, a retro spin-off of
Dark Void.[66] I did my research and took note of our overlap
on the only topic I could discuss while properly modulating
my voice.

Before this, of course, was the packet. What's a packet? Oh,
God. I'm sorry I brought this up. Hoo boy. When a late-night
show has a spot open, they often give a set of instructions for
a writing sample that you do at home. Usually this is a couple
pages of jokes or sketches or ideas. Because each show is different, each show has a different packet, and even within one
show different writing positions might have different packet
instructions, which I know is confusing. Let me start over.
You know how tech companies will give computer program-
mers tests? It's sort of like that, except you should probably
have at least one good commercial parody. Fortunately, I'd
spent years desperately writing jokes almost every morning,
so I was able to finally push past this stage.

Despite being prepared, I was still panicking. It probably
would've been weirder if I wasn't. I knew I could talk about
my joke process. I also knew that I needed to mention *something* that got my foot in the game door. Luckily, while I was
at Nintendo, I happened to snag one of the last *The Legend of
Zelda: Spirit Tracks* track jackets. Yes, it's a track jacket. Yes,
it's from *Spirit Tracks*. Yes, it's a *Spirit Tracks* track jacket. It has
since been worn to shreds over the years, but at that point it
was fresh and bright and had a big old *Zelda* logo right over
my man boob. I know that me dressing up with gaming wear

---

66 I know *Dark Void* sounds like a fake game you'd make up as a joke, but I
promise that it really existed and there was a spin-off that you no longer
can buy anywhere.

hasn't always panned out in my life, but at least I wasn't show-ing up looking for love in a homemade *Mario 3* costume.

This time, it panned out. You do better in your life when you don't wear a piece of a sock as a video game mustache.

I feel like the interview would've been fine anyway, but walking in and having Jimmy Fallon say "Oh, *Spirit Tracks*! Sweet!" was the greatest relief possible. Because that's a bit of a risk to wear a bright green track jacket to a job interview. When I rode up the elevator and looked down at myself, I had a moment where I was like, "Buddy, what are you doing? Why can't you just dress like a businessman in a commer-cial?" That said, it could have been worse: my manager had specifically instructed me not to wear a suit, especially the one I owned, which looked like it had been rented for a se-ries of funerals that got progressively sadder.

We broke into a conversation about video games. I felt like we slowly lost the other people in the room as we talked about old Sierra On-Line games and which *Zelda* was our favorite. I snuck in my little Groose story like the needy worm I am. And while working on any late-night show can be a lot of pressure, that might've been the most pleasant job interview I'd ever had up to that point. If I had the opportunity, I'd talk about *King's Quest* for hours with anyone. I once dated someone in part because of our shared love of that adventure series. I bought her a sealed copy of *King's Quest IV: The Per-ils of Rosella*. We lasted a few months.

Then the interview ended. They told me I'd find out soon. This isn't the brush-off you'd think: in the always-efficient world of entertainment, if there was a job offer, it would first go to my reps, who'd then discuss it with my other reps, who might talk to the lawyers, and then they'd let me know. You very rarely get hired on the spot, which can definitely be nerve-racking when you've flown into New York City for a job interview in a famous building for a life-changing gig. For someone who catastrophizes everything, I actually felt pretty good when it was over.

In reality, like Nintendo, half of the interview was intended to make sure I wasn't going to break windows and steal art off the walls. There are *a lot* of weird people in comedy. Sometimes you look in the mirror of a comedy club bathroom and realize you're becoming one. You'll smile in the mirror and wonder what happened to the person you used to be. But you get to make people *laugh*! Now, get out there!

Then I flew back to San Francisco and went to work again at *IGN*. I didn't tell many people there I had interviewed at *Late Night*, just a few folks on my team who might've needed to make adjustments if I got the job. I didn't want to embarrass myself if it didn't happen, and worse, I was afraid others would see it as a bit of a betrayal. The company had just hired me a year before. But when one of my reps texted asking if I could talk *immediately*, I knew I was in. The call itself was anticlimactic. I was at work. I couldn't celebrate in the middle of the workplace I was about to leave. Instead, my brain skipped to logistics. What would my girlfriend think? How much did I have saved up for a move? My rep asked me if I was still there, and I was like, "Yeah," and he told me that they wanted me to start immediately at the beginning of the year. In other words, that would be my last week at *IGN*.

I love working in late-night television. I've written on multiple shows with live audiences, and there really is something to that reaction in the moment. The studios may be freezing, but it's electric when the audience enjoys a sketch or a song or a bit.[67]

One of the funniest parts of being at *Late Night*, later *The Tonight Show*, was that I *did* have a connection to Nintendo. I'd met Reggie Fils-Aimé at my old job. I'd even humiliated myself playing basketball with him! So when I saw him in the hallway to be a guest on the show, it was with great pleasure that I surprised the hell out of him by yelling, "Mr. Fils-Aimé!" Nintendo really drills in that professional language, and that dude is both a literal and metaphorical giant. He smiled wide and shook my hand in his massive paw and asked how I was. Thank God he didn't remember how fucking bad I was at basketball.

During my time on *Late Night* and *The Tonight Show*, I was also occasionally invited to play video games in Jimmy's office and, later, on an *NBA Jam* arcade machine in the writers' room. While we shared a love of story-based games, he was also into sports games like my brother. *This* made me more nervous than the job interview. I could talk about video games all day, but I couldn't necessarily do well in *FIFA* or *Madden*. The scientific phrase I'd use is "absolutely awful." One lesson I took away is that you should know all the rules of a sport before you try to play it with your boss.

When I got asked to play, it was with Jimmy and a couple longtime writers and producers. This was their regular

---

67   Although, the best people to make laugh during the show is the band. Their job isn't easy. They have to pay attention to the show for any sudden music cues, and they've seen thousands of episodes and heard millions of jokes over and over and over again. So when you crack the musicians with something, it's like making the coolest kids in school laugh.

game they'd been playing since the start of *Late Night*, long before I got there. My being invited in was extremely nice, even though I was absolutely dead weight on anyone's *NBA 2K* team. They could write off having me around as charity and the IRS would allow it. Still, I didn't want to look bad, so I'd try so hard that I'd break out into a sweat, thus literally causing me to look bad. I didn't make things worse, but I probably did not impress with my football, soccer, basketball, tennis, or baseball video game abilities.

I was pretty good at *Rocket League* and *Mario Kart 8*, though. That's something.

A LIST OF STRUCTURES I'VE BUILT IN *MINECRAFT*

Square Shack

Square Shack (Two rooms)

Square Shack (Bigger two rooms)

Hole in the Ground

Cave

Square Shack in a Cave Made from a Hole in the Ground

Funeral Parlor (Square Shack I died in because I didn't realize there was a gap in the walls)

Basketball Court with No Hoops

Outdoor Dance Stage (Renamed the basketball court)

Two-Story Square Shack

Roller Coaster (Copied off YouTube. Extremely unsuccessful.)

The Neighborhood I Grew Up in Replicated in Square Shacks

My Office Replicated in Square Shacks

Stack of Square Shacks

Stack of Square Shack Stacks

Shake Shack Made of Stack of Square Shack Stacks

Square Shack Skyscraper That's Almost All Stairs

Nice, Geometrically Pleasing House (Was drunk; do not remember how)

Square Shack Death Star

CONFESSIONS OF A GAMING HOARDER

As of writing this, I have 2,710 games in my Steam library, and over 200 games for the Nintendo Switch. Services like Xbox Game Pass and PlayStation Plus have pretty much eliminated compulsive buying on those consoles, so there are fewer *owned* games there. These are companies that realized people would probably enjoy playing games like, I dunno, *Farming Simulator 22* more if they were nominally free. That said, if you included everything I've downloaded off those services—including *Farming Simulator 22*—I'm sure you'd find hundreds of games in those virtual libraries, too. Most of which are eternally sitting in virtual shrink-wrap, installed but never played.

It brings to mind what it must feel like for the toys in *Toy Story* that never get opened. Silently staring forward, sentient enough to suffer, hoping one day they might fulfill their cruel purpose until obsolescence. These libraries of games are basically digital licenses that a company could revoke at any moment and (in a sad twist) I'd probably barely notice until some random day three years down the line when I want to replay *Far Cry 12: Another Wacky Cult Leader Strikes Again.*[68]

While owning this many games might seem like a humble brag, I can assure you it is not. It's a sorrow brag. It's not healthy that I have more video games in my Steam library than I do people I've ever met in my life. I should not have more than one version of *Skyrim*, let alone six, including two—that's right, two—different versions of it in *virtual reality.* And I'm starting to worry that knifing my bank account Steam sale after Steam sale isn't going to fill that deep void within my heart. You could have watched the hair fall from my head and the lines crease on my face as the seasons changed and I went from owning ten to fifty to a thousand to over two thousand Steam games. And if you tried to stop me, I would've asked who you were because you were suddenly in my room. There's just no fixing it.

It's hard to control digital hoarding because you get the game immediately! I don't have to wait for some game to ship in a physical medium that's both more valuable and longer-lasting. I can buy some old-ass *King of Fighters* or an artsy indie adventure about a depressed ghost, download it, and play it instantly. Will that fix my life? No. Will it make up for all these financially terrible decisions that no person should make? Absolutely not. And I probably won't even play it right now!

The second reason it's hard to control digital hoarding is that these games take up no shelf space. Space has never been

---

68 Note to my editor: this is not a real game: please don't fact-check it. Note to my editor of the 11th edition of this book: this has somehow become a real game. Note to my original editor: I know there'd be no reason for an 11th edition of this book.

freely available in my life. As a kid, I shared a room with my little brother. Then, later, my bedroom also became the family computer room—because every little boy in middle school loves waking up to see his dad in his underwear doing spreadsheets at six in the morning. That Excel doc needs to be done while the inspiration is piping hot!

There was very little space for cartridges, let alone full game boxes. I'm jealous of every single person who was able to keep their older games and their boxes in good condition. Did your house have more than one floor? Did your garage have space for a car? I congratulate you on all your successes. Rooms in my childhood home were filled with bins of school papers and Christmas decorations and sports memorabilia and old, stained Halloween costumes and spatulas that were on sale and a pile of magazines charting every election back to 1988.

As a kid, my parents' messes seemed normal to me. You don't always learn which parts of your childhood were weird until someone else looks at you with dismay when you talk about it. My dad had boxes filled with VHS tapes. My mom had a lot of Beanie Babies. Both would obviously be worth millions of dollars one day very, very soon. Just you wait.

If I hadn't moved to New York City for college, I might've picked up those same habits. Okay, clearly I've picked up on *some* of those habits, but at least it's confined to the digital world. My dorm at NYU was tiny—and it was one of the biggest spaces I would live in for maybe seven years after that. I had room for some books, some personal items, some posters for things that are now either cringey and/or regrettable. And a laptop. Between that and, later, a GameCube, I just needed a CD book filled with game discs. Everything was compact.

My world could be contained without towering boxes that I live in fear will fall and crush one of my parents to death.

Then *Half-Life 2* dropped and Steam with it. Fans all thought it was just a little service to organize games that we'd still buy on disc forever. Instead, we were getting a Trojan horse containing the future of obsessive shopping. Everyone I knew that played games wanted *Half-Life 2*. The first *Half-Life* is remembered as a classic. It felt like someone had cracked the code on making a shooter feel deeper and more narratively satisfying than ever before. Sure, other shooters like *Dark Forces 2: Jedi Knight* did great work, but *Half-Life* ushered in an entirely new age of immersion.

Plus, *Half-Life* pulled off a magic trick that *always* works for *every* video game: they made the hero some random nerd. I remember experiencing the horror of *Silent Hill* in high school and my friends and I were amazed that Harry Mason wasn't a cop or a super soldier or magic. He was just some guy who got tired when he ran too much. And you know who else got tired when they ran too much? Me. After exercise, I sound like a fifteen-year-old dog who swallowed a whistle.

Half-Life's hero, Gordon Freeman, was a simple scientist with a wrench. He was just there to do his job but, *nooooo*, interdimensional alien monsters had to crawl their way through a veil of reality opened by some hapless PhDs. Helping Gordon Freeman get the approval of the thin, mysterious, *X-Files*–inspired G-Man[69] meant everything to us.

I was thus quite excited for *Half-Life 2* and that it was releasing on a new application called Steam! That's all we knew! Of

---

69　Part of me wishes Gordon also called himself "The G-Man."

course, Steam eventually kicked open the door and allowed me *to have as many video games as I ever wanted*!

So, yeah, digital stores have caused me to fall into my family's hoarding habits, but at least there's no threat of finding a dead lizard in a packed closet. Yet it remains a little embarrassing. And sometimes I'll read about a game that sounds incredible, go to buy it, and find out I already own it from some long-ago preorder or Kickstarter campaign or whatever. Occasionally I get codes for free games, but that's still relatively rare. If you're reading this: oh my God, I'd love the code for your game, and ignore everything else you've read here. I *will* play it! It's at the very top of my to-do list after "Get life together."

It's easier to continue having a problem when there are few visual reminders of your problem. The damage is done to my bank account, but nobody sees that except me, and I've already told my siblings I don't need a funeral when I die. I'm clearly justifying self-destructive behaviors, but I'm also taking comfort in the fact that it'll give my landlord an interesting story to tell his friends when he finds my dead body three weeks after I have a stroke trying to finally beat *Shadow of the Erdtree*.

I own so many games that I'll never end up playing and definitely never finish. But you don't have to take my word for it. Instead, you can take even more of my words for it! Here are just a few games in my Steam library that I've paid for but never touched, as well as my guesses on what they may be about. I know that some of these may be very good games—and I hope to try them all someday! But for now, I can only work off assumptions.

King Arthur II: The Role-Playing Wargame: You thought you knew the story of King Arthur? Well, think again, morons, because King Arthur is back in *King Arthur II*! This time it's personal and back in the habit. He's still mad about Lancelot hooking up with his wife and he's ready to start a war against the evil forces of someone else. For centuries, humanity has asked itself, "What else happened to King Arthur after that one story?" Now you will know. *King Arthur II Fast II Furious.*

Legend of Dungeon: There once was a dungeon. This is the legend of it. There were walls. There were passageways. It was a good dungeon. We wish we were still friends with this dungeon, but people and their caverns drift apart after high school.

Z1 Battle Royale: Without looking, I'm going to guess this is a multiplayer zombie shooter that has either been shut down for three years or is the most popular video game ever made. Regardless, according to my list, I own this game.

Tybot Invasion: The Typing Runner: This must be an endless runner where you just type words. In fact, it sounds cool as hell! I'm going to download this one right now! Great job, past me!

Winter Voices: Okay, I can do this one. I'm going to assume that *Winter Voices* is an indie survival game with some sort of story element. The "winter" part—oh, that's gonna be harsh! Bundle up, everyone! But there will be "voices," too! Maybe spooky ghost ones? I'm pretty certain I'm spot-on with this. I'll even review it right now: "47 hours. Recommended. *Win-*

ter Voices broke my heart with its hard-hitting storytelling set against the backdrop of a very cold time of year."

Haimrik: Hallmark tried to release a game, but their intern died while typing the title into the database.

Hexceed: Being a witch isn't easy. Caring for magic plants and accidentally killing your lover can be disheartening and depressing. So here's a visual novel where you play a motivational speaker for wizards and witches. "Don't just hex! Go out there and hex-ceed!"

Inunaki Tunnel: This is either a cozy farming sim like *Harvest Moon* or a terrifying horror game that lasts forty-five minutes. There is no in-between.

Golf Gang: Think fast, hotshot: you're on a golf course and there's a group behind you. Do you speed it along? Step out of the way? Or just hope this isn't the Golf Gang that's been murdering country-club members across the country? (To be fair, everyone is pretty cool with Golf Gang doing this.)

Hydrophobia: The Prophecy: Someone warned you that you were afraid of water! But did you listen? Noooo! You had to wait for the prophecy to come true! And now look at you: afraid of water. Maybe it's a survival horror game in which a virus turns people into liquid? That's pretty scary! I'd be phobic of that!

Pinstripe: You spend money on an expensive suit but still feel like a phony because the person inside the expensive clothes hasn't changed. It's easier if you also get some sunglasses so they don't see the emptiness in your eyes.

Reveal the Deep: Come on, man! Do it! Reveal the deep already! Just show us a little deep! Nobody even needs to know we saw the deep!

I know many of these are genuinely great products made by loving, dedicated teams! I'm not trying to diminish anyone's work. And I do want to play these games. I very well recognize the pain of "I'll be sure to check that out sometime!" I probably will enjoy these games at some point! I already paid for them! I will download them! I will finish them! At least, that's what I tell myself the same way my mom tells me that her off-brand Captain Jack Sparrow painting is going to be worth something someday.

NIER AND FAR

I met my friend Sara in late December 2019 when she DMed me about a video game I had tweeted about, a sentence that has already aged like a parent during the Great Depression. I think the post was something about *Final Fantasy VII*, and she was a dedicated fan. I might have already been a full-time television writer who'd won awards, but I was still *very, very* sad. In fact, I'd been going through what you could generously call a small mental health crisis at the time. And while I have a lot of friends in the video game world, I don't always have people I can just gush with about a game, let alone reach out to in times of duress. This is an ongoing problem that hopefully this book will help solve, but probably not.

Sara was a stand-up living out in Los Angeles, which also gave us some common ground, common friends, and common enemies. She also did voice work for *Robot Chicken* and often streamed with other comedians. But none of that really mattered as much as the fact that we were into the exact same games in the exact same way. We both enjoyed role-playing games made in Japan and all the melodramatic trappings that went along with them. We talked about them with the same furious wonder. Many of you probably have *lots* of friends with encyclopedic knowledge of *Dragon Quest*; I did not at this point in my life.

The thing was, despite Sara loving *Final Fantasy VII* and owning a large, somewhat questionable statue of Tifa Lockhart, her favorite game of all time was *Nier: Automata*. She *loved* that depressing, sad-ass game. She read all the spin-off books filled with tragic side stories. She went to a live concert of the soundtrack from the game. *Nier: Automata* was important to her, and at that point, I'd never finished it. I liked it, but I didn't give it enough time and attention for the real brilliance to start kicking in.

If you don't know what *Nier: Automata* is, the story focuses on a group of robots in space defending humanity from a different group of robots on Earth. That sounds incredibly simple, but there's a reason that designer Yoko Taro—a man who wears a giant mask of a character from the games in public— is a genius. He took a simple sci-fi game plot and turned it into a story about what it means to be self-aware and how we often refuse to see the internal life in others. But it's still also about robots fighting robots, because that's just cool.

Sara and I became friends right before the pandemic hit, and our only shared interests were comedy and games, so the distance wasn't an issue. When we weren't going through personal meltdowns over the tragedies engulfing our families and the world, we'd talk about role-playing games, especially *Nier* and soon-to-be-released *Final Fantasy* games. The world may have felt like it was ending, but at least there was some decent content coming up!

I took another try at *Nier*, and this time, it got me. Probably because Sara carefully explained each thing she wanted me to *specifically* pay attention to. There's one scene in the game where your character 2B (yes, as in "to be or not to be") enters an abandoned amusement park swarming with enemy robots. The thing is, as you work your way through the game, these robot enemies become more and more emotionally real. Rather than just being evil for the sake of the elaborate costumes (the main motivator of villains in RPGs), these other robots turn out to have their own beliefs and fears. At one point, you find out you couldn't save a group of child robots from self-destructing because they believed they were about to be killed anyway. That messed me up. It got under my skin and, after my friend Sara died, stayed there forever.

For her part, Sara was just happy that she finally had someone to talk to about *Nier*. Like me, she wasn't exactly great at making friends. She'd also suffered *a lot* throughout her life. She had been in college for video game design when she and her boyfriend were in a deeply horrible car crash that killed him and savagely injured her. She talked about him a lot. She missed him. She blamed herself for the crash. She wished she could've been the one who died instead. She was full of misplaced guilt. Because of one bad day, she lost her future and the man she wanted to spend it with. We know this sort of thing happens every day; we often forget that it fucks people up forever. She was on a trajectory that excited her, and it was ripped from her hands.

The crash itself caused additional issues. Because of the reconstructive surgery, Sara often had trouble walking without stumbling or bumping into walls and tables. She was in constant pain, which itself led to addiction issues. And mentally she was in a state of constant, everlasting anguish. That also didn't help with addiction issues, by the way. I don't know if I'd be any fucking different if I went through something like that. After the death of her boyfriend, she lost interest in designing games. He had been a partner, both romantic and creative, in that ambition. They were going to make role-playing games together. Without him, it seemed pointless to her.

This isn't the deepest observation or newest sci-fi trope, but *Nier: Automata*, a game about robots and more robots, is essentially about humanity. Rather than shout "Kill" or "Destroy" or "I'm gonna get you, here I come, I'm-a coming," the robotic characters question their own existence. They want to know why they suffer. Why they have to die. And why they exist if they have to die eventually anyway. Maybe that's a bit of high school nihilism and maybe it's just catnip for sad people like me (and, I'd learn, Sara). The Venn diagram of *Nier* and depression is a circle. These are tragic figures going about their lives while constantly suffering, and they don't really know *why*. Learning more about themselves doesn't help. It just causes them more pain. Every time the character 9S figures out that humanity is long extinct and the entire robot war is bullshit, 2B has to kill him and then start the whole charade over.

Yes, the game is a deep dive into sorrow, but making a video game friend *just* as the world shut down was a nice thing. Rather than discussing our massive anxieties and fears, we talked our way through replays of *Final Fantasy VII*, *Para-*

site Eve, and *Super Mario RPG*. We eagerly awaited the first in a series of *Final Fantasy VII* remakes, with the first one having the innovative and original name *Final Fantasy VII Remake*. Neither of us had watched the trailers because neither of us wanted anything spoiled. I will also forever love Square Enix and the franchises they created, but we had worries: the company is like an aging circus performer who used to be able to juggle chain saws and now can barely juggle tennis balls.

Final Fantasy VII Remake—and its since-released sequel, *Final Fantasy VII Rebirth*—didn't quite follow the average video game remake model. Most game remakes update the graphics and change the gameplay for modern audiences, which, to be fair, also happens here. However, *Final Fantasy VII Remake* is secretly a sequel to the original.

Fortunately, Sara and I both understood the assignment. We played the new *Final Fantasy VII* and then replayed the old *Final Fantasy VII*. We talked about Midgar, the expanded roles of Biggs and Wedge, and the expansion of the Honey Bee Inn. In the original game, the Honey Bee Inn is a brothel that Cloud Strife can visit while cross-dressing to sneak into a villain's hideout. As you can probably guess, this is a segment in the original that doesn't hold up *great*. And we, as well as most fans, wondered if and how they'd actually make that work.

But to Square Enix's credit, they juggled the shit out of the chain saws this time. Rather than cut it, they *expanded* the scene. In the remake, the Honey Bee Inn is more of a nightclub than a brothel, and you work with a fashionable character named Andrea Rhodea to help Cloud dress as a woman. The climax of the segment is a massive rhythm game dance bit that only happens once. I respect that, both for the scene being rhythm-based and for the confidence to only give it to us one time in an eighty-hour game. It's like bringing out the most delicious key lime pie ever made and going, "No. Just one bite so you think about it forever." That takes a self-esteem I'll never have. The Honey Bee Inn expansion was one of the highlights of our conversations about additions and changes to the game. I replayed the dance scene a dozen times. Rhythm games for life, baby.

But as the pandemic went on, Sara became sicker. Not with COVID, nor with something she could simply push through or rest away. Her body had already been a nexus of pain and emotional torment, but new conditions were taking over, and she was finding her ability to walk and move and hold a controller harder than before. She had trouble working a job and had to move back home with some of her family. From what she told me, this was not a good, healthy situation for her to be in. I feel like being forced to move away from the life she'd built was what finally crushed her.

Nier: Automata is sadder the more you play it—which is really saying something since it doesn't *start* in a happy place. The game has twenty-six different endings, from early failure in the game (basically a glorified Game Over screen) to hidden shit you basically need a guide to find. The most "happy" one, Ending E, occurs only after you've already beaten the game once before. This is the ending that fans consider canon, where it revives and restores the memories of all the major characters who died (which is good), allows you to play a minigame fight against the credits (which is cool), and asks you to delete your save (which is insane). Even the best ending of *Nier: Automata* requires sacrifice and letting go of the past.

As Sara got sicker, we talked less, which I regret now. She struggled to type messages, and even using speech-to-text wasn't easy for her. Sometimes we would go a week or two without talking. She was busy with doctors and family, and I was busy with work. When we did talk or text, we discussed the ending of *Final Fantasy VII Remake*, how it changed everything, how we couldn't wait until *Final Fantasy VII Rebirth* came out to see where it went. Sara seemed more resigned, though. Looking back, I think she knew she couldn't last much longer.

Our final phone call was a surprise. Neither of us were big phone people; we mostly communicated by texting each other links to gaming news. But that day she called me out of the blue. While my usual instinct is to ignore literally any phone call I'm not expecting, this time, for some reason, something told me I should answer. We had a fifteen-, maybe twenty-minute conversation before she became too tired. Sara talked about how some of her older family members weren't treating her great. She was sad she hadn't been able to play a new video game in over a month: her hands wouldn't cooperate. I meekly offered to buy her an adaptive game pad to make it easier. She politely declined while sounding hollowed-out.

And then, just a few weeks later, she was dead. I didn't even find out for almost a day. Most of her friends slowly learned about it on social media after her siblings posted about it. Comedians checked in with each other: "Wait, what the fuck happened?" I texted her to tell me it wasn't true. She had been suffering beyond anything I could understand, but I wanted it to all be a misunderstanding. I kept texting her, demanding that she respond, even though I knew all those blue bubbles only meant that the phone was on but the person was gone.

That night, I went for a walk for hours listening to the *Final Fantasy* and *Nier* soundtracks. Somehow the glasses on my face fell off, and I've got no memory and no idea of where they went. Maybe I took them off to cry. It's a blur.

Sara wasn't religious, but she constantly talked about hoping she'd see her boyfriend again when she died. I really hope she has. When friends die—and more than a few have died before their time lately—I sometimes find myself imagining them in the afterlife. Regardless of who it is, I'll take a long shower in the dark and just sit on the floor and think and talk to myself as if I were talking to them. It's macabre, but what kind of mourning isn't? For Sara, I imagined that she reunited with her boyfriend and they finally got to make that role-playing game they had planned. I threw in an imaginary comedy special for her just to round out the experience. Silly.

I also played *Final Fantasy VII* again. And *Final Fantasy VII Remake*. And, eventually, *Final Fantasy VII Rebirth*. I really wish she'd lived to see that one. She would've loved the minigame *Queen's Blood*. Seeing Red XIII put his doggy paws on a Segway scooter would've made her fall down laughing. She would've had a good time. Maybe if we live in a benevolent universe, she has been able to look down from heaven and watch people play it, too. That may not seem like a great use of the afterlife, but it's what I imagine her doing. And I'm sure she's disappointed with how many times I've checked a guide for help.

Anyway, Sara would hate this whole thing with its seriousness and lack of jokes. I miss you, dude. You were a good egg who got shafted by life. *Final Fantasy* is less fun without you. *Nier* is less fun without you. Games are less fun without you.

ANDREW RYAN'S HELPFUL Q&A FOR MOVING TO RAPTURE

Hello, and thank you for your interest in moving to Rapture!

I am Andrew Ryan, and I'm here to ask you a question: Is a person not entitled to the sweat of their brow? Because if you think so, you're going to *love* buying a home in Rapture, the sparkling new city from Ryan Industries! Rapture is a completely regulation-free town made for hardworking people who want to taste success without greedy parasites asking for a handout! And the only way you can avoid the parasites of society is by living in a city built entirely out of glass at the bottom of the ocean, where the water pressure alone could crush a bus.

Rapture will free you from the boundaries that restrict lesser people with their laws and safety regulations and teams of engineers warning you that constructing a full metropolis under miles of water is a bad idea. Here you can thrive as you watch whales swim past your studio apartment that's a world away from anyone who's ever loved you.

But you're not here to get *told* what to do! You're the one in charge! You probably have questions about our moist little town. That's why our team has created this helpful Q&A guide for you, a potential resident. And by *potential*, I mean *potential for greatness*! We pride ourselves on only allowing the best and the brightest citizens into Rapture, so if you've got this brochure in your hands, you're on your way to a beautiful paradise under the sea where no rescue subs could ever reach you in time!

Q: What is Rapture?
A: Rapture is a vast underwater city miles beneath the surface of the Atlantic Ocean. Our location is completely hidden and unknown by others, which will not cause problems if something goes wrong. But don't worry, you'll easily get to your new home with the help of our ship captains or a plane crash set up by Andrew Ryan. The second is only in case of emergency.

Q: Who will be living in Rapture?
A: Hopefully you and many other brilliant thinkers, artists, and titans of industry! Whether you've proved yourself to be wealthy, well-off, or rich, there is a place for everyone in Art Deco skyscrapers mere inches away from abyssal darkness and deadly ice-cold water.

Q: Why build Rapture underwater?
A: Andrew Ryan's vision of a complete libertarian paradise

would be impossible to create in a preexisting country. Politicians and their pointless rules limit free trade. Hence putting Rapture miles beneath the surface of the ocean! It makes free trade *that much easier!* What, do you think we'd build our city in the *clouds*, like idiots?

Q: Is living underwater safe?
A: Absolutely! Our contractors that made the lowest bid have worked hard to ensure every pipe is completely safe within a minimal budget. They left as soon as they finished, probably because they were too impressed by the floor of a deep-sea tomb shaking whenever a Big Daddy walks by.

Q: What's a Big Daddy?
A: An all-important figure around Rapture, that's what! Big Daddies handle everything from repairing cracks on windows to repairing leaks on ceilings to brutally murdering anyone who gets even within one inch of a Little Sister.

Q: What's a Little Sister?
A: An even more important figure around Rapture, that's what! Little Sisters are adorable helpers that harvest a substance called ADAM that can be used to give yourself superpowers like shooting fireballs or launching bees from your hands. Don't worry, everyone gets these powers, so you'll be completely safe inside this confined space that's too deep for radio transmissions to reach the surface.

Q: Is there a way to protect myself if I accidentally anger a Big Daddy?

A: Yes! We've already told you about shooting bees from your hands, but that's not all! We have installed an easy-to-use gun dispenser in nearly every room of the city. There are also plenty of bullets and rockets that can be used to defend yourself and/or break the glass separating you from Davy Jones's locker.

Q: How are Big Daddies made?
A: We break someone's mind and mutate their body until they're an unthinking monstrosity.

Q: How are Little Sisters made?
A: Next question!

Q: Will there be security?
A: Yes! We feared that hiring human security guards might lead to unions, so we've designed flying robots that will fire machine guns at anything that crosses their path. We recommend not being near a window when security arrives.

Q: What happens if I'm standing near a window when security arrives?
A: The water will kill you if the shattered glass doesn't.

Q: What if I'm unhappy with my Rapture experience?
A: If you're unhappy within ninety days of purchasing your home, we'll be happy to refund you the money! If you're unhappy after that ninety-day grace period, we will break your mind and mutate your body until it's an unthinking monstrosity.

THE RETURN OF BIGFOOT'S ARCADE

I collect little arcade machines. And not just any little arcade machines. We're talking working, theoretically playable little arcade machines. Some of these are so small it basically feels like I'm making fun of myself. Playing *Pac-Man* on a two-inch-tall keychain arcade machine is really a lesson in "trying to prove to yourself you didn't waste as much money as you did."

But the slightly healthy reason I collect these arcade machines is that they remind me of the wonder I felt in Bigfoot's Arcade. Or literally any place that had an arcade machine. Pizza Hut and Fuddruckers both had those magical NeoGeo machines with a handful of games in them. I was afraid of *Metal Slug* because of the violence. I was afraid of *Neo Turf Masters* because it was a golf game. Fun fact: *Neo Turf Masters*? I found out later it's pretty great! That's the way golf should be!

Having little arcade machines on my desk at work gave me a microdose of wonder. And since I certainly don't have photos of family or friends or loved ones to get me through the day, the next best thing are the inanimate objects that would be found covering me when I die because a box of toys and game cartridges fell on my head. So I began putting them on my desk with little GI Joe figures standing at them as if playing the game. It was the cutest, most divorced-man thing I'd ever done.

Originally, I had just a couple tiny machines. A novelty. People would stop by and say, "Oh, those are great!" and I'd let them play them, and then after maybe forty-five seconds, they'd put them back down. The machines were less fun than the promise of fun, a reminder of fun.

This collection quickly grew. In addition to the tiny arcade machines came bigger (still small) ones, a foot tall and larger. To this day, I still don't have any full-size arcade machines. I know they're both readily available and affordable now, but I live in a one-bedroom New York City apartment: if I had a real arcade machine, it would take up more space than my kitchen. My living room would be a television, a couch, and a *Robotron: 2084* machine that gets played twice a year when I'm drunk.

While I had a few little arcade games on my shelves at home, most of them were on my desk for all to judge. First at *The President Show* and then at *Full Frontal with Samantha Bee*. I'm not going to say which show's staff judged me for it or dunked on me, but I'll give you a hint: it was definitely both.

By this point, I had a *Street Fighter 2* machine, a *Centipede* machine, a *Space Invaders* machine, a massive (still smaller than usual) *Pac-Man* machine, a Japanese *Taito* arcade collection that you could put on a little plastic stand to make it look more arcade-y—and that's just the shit off the top of my head. Whereas some people spent their money on their children or their retirement, here I was, buying slightly worse versions of games I had emulated both legally and illegally on fifteen different systems.

But I'll say this: those games are a fun little distraction at work.

I'll also say this: none of that fucking mattered after COVID hit.

Everyone had been warned about COVID for months, but I feel like none of us knew it was going to shut down our entire planet. While the news talked about the coronavirus, Kristen Bartlett and I had *just* been promoted to cohead writers. We were still discussing which couch we wanted for our shared office. (Said couch arrived two days before we shut down. I don't even think anyone got to fart into it.) At work, we were washing our hands and keeping a small distance, hoping for the best. Masks weren't even a thing yet. We hadn't come to the desperation to find masks, the requirement to wear masks, the backlash against wearing the masks, the backlash to the backlash against wearing masks, and now a world in which I feel like I'm doing it wrong whether or not I'm wearing one.

At *Full Frontal*, Mondays and Tuesdays were usually dedicated to writing the topical part of the show and putting the scripts together. Between Tuesday night and Wednesday afternoon, we'd review the scripts, do a read through, and fact-check them, and then shoot the show. On Thursdays and Fridays, we'd prep for upcoming episodes and work on writing more evergreen pieces for future episodes. More or less, that was our schedule.

The day we shut down was a Wednesday—that is, show day at *Full Frontal*. We had a whole episode written and ready to go. As I said, Kristen and I had just been promoted to be the new head writers, so we were still processing the role. Fortunately, we'd already worked well together in the past. Before we were head writers, we called ourselves the Bash Brothers because we were often the dorks on the show who'd get asked to add a ton of dumb jokes at the last second if needed. Kristen Bartlett is one of the funniest people on Earth and writes scripts with the same speed that most people write text messages. For the entire run of my time as head writer on that show, I was eternally grateful I had Kristen there saving all our asses.

Early that Wednesday, an executive producer came into our new office and told us that, due to growing safety concerns, we'd be shooting the show without a studio audience. That seemed fair. Nobody knew much at this point, but "giant groups of people" seemed to be a contributing factor to the issue. We asked what we should do. The producer told us it would be okay with an expression that told me she was also thinking: "Oh my God, *is* this going to be okay?"

Losing the studio audience alone was a big shift. I mean, I'd definitely done comedy in front of silent audiences before. But if you think performing for people glaring at you is hard, try doing it in a vast, freezing, empty room to a crew of terrified people who would love to wrap this shit up and get out immediately. So we prepared to do the show without an audience. We continued about our day, preparing the script, checking show graphics, and ultimately having our Wednesday afternoon rewrite meeting.

Rewrite could be a bit stressful in the best of times. Writers and producers were all stuffed into Sam's dressing room for hours reading a script and changing it line by line to fix, add, and fact-check jokes. During this particular rewrite Kristen and I received the same message on Slack at the same time. It was from the executive producer. She said that she had just learned there was a reported COVID infection in the building—nobody from our show, but somebody on *some* show in the vicinity had it.

In the message the producer asked us to quickly wrap things up and gently get everyone to leave as fast as they could without causing any panic. That in itself is kind of funny, because nobody wanted to leave more than everyone in that rewrite room.

Kristen and I calmly flew through the rest of the rewrite. We finished two hours of work in about five minutes and then told our staff they needed to split, like, right away. Everyone left except Sam, Kristen, me, some producers, and a few crew members who volunteered to stick around. Nobody was forced to stay. We were then told that the building itself was about to go into lockdown, so we had just one hour to shoot the episode if there was going to be one. It's silly to think this was so important to us, but it was our job, and we cared about it. Plus, we didn't know when we'd even get to do another show. Maybe this was it?

Kristen and I huddled together and rewrote an opening to reflect why everything was so weird. Sam herself was nervous, both of what was happening in the building and of doing the show without an audience. Kristen and I strategized. We decided to write Sam jokes she'd never seen before and put them in the prompter. All we told her was that there would be new jokes, but not what those jokes would be. It worked. When she hit those lines, she was completely surprised and broke down laughing. It was an absurd situation, and it was absurd to make a television episode during it. It was also our very last time in that studio.

From that point on, the rest of my time at the show was remote. Six large boxes arrived at my little apartment, packed to the brim with my workplace toys and games and—of course—the mini arcade machines. Way too many arcade machines collected by a man who never dreamed they would return home to haunt him.

I had no place to put everything, so I left them in the boxes in my combination foyer/kitchen/living room for a couple weeks. I was busy trying to navigate my new life being the head writer of a show that no longer had an office while figuring out if I'd need to learn how to make my own toilet paper from newspaper pulp. I spent three months using rough industrial toilet paper I found on a website that sells to businesses in bulk, and *I liked it*.

In a way, I was lucky. Outside of work, the pandemic didn't drastically change my day-to-day life the way it did for others. I was fortunate to have a job that could go remote. Meanwhile, I didn't have a spouse that I suddenly had to share a workplace with or kids that were using the same computer for school as I was for my job. I could exclusively eat ramen for a month (which I did) and nobody else was affected by my idiocy. That's what I'd love to have on my tombstone: "Nobody Was Affected by His Idiocy." Either that or my name.

Some comedians and entertainment folks set up alternate ways of doing comedy. The amazing Jenny Yang and the brilliant Gary Whitta both used *Animal Crossing: New Horizons* to create their own comedy shows. My in-game character "visited" their islands to do talk show interviews and stand-up sets, which were streamed online. Other comics spent months on Twitch playing games like *Quiplash* that were basically digital joke-writing prompts with a score at the end. Because if anything makes comedians more pleasant, it's putting them in direct competition with each other joke by joke.

My apartment building has a weird horseshoe shape that's resulted in my windows being mostly blocked by tall brick walls on every side. It does have its moments, though. Between 1:00 and 1:15 p.m., it's almost bright enough to read a book. Fortunately, the fact I rent an apartment for vampires does kick the price down quite a bit. I was fine with being in the dark for a while. These were the early days of 2020 when everyone ran on fear and adrenaline. Bars and restaurants weren't back to serving customers yet. GameStops weren't open to briefly look in and then feel bad as an employee watches you with pleading eyes. Even outside hangouts were rare, and when they did happen, nobody wanted to take the subway to get there. *Germs!*

Around May, two-ish months after the start of lockdown, I snapped. My brain felt cramped and small and sad. After a few weeks, even my lights annoyed the shit out of me. Like everyone else, I noticed every scuff on the floor, every minor chip in the counter. I yelled at a bottle of mustard for not having the cap on tight. I literally said, "You always do this," to a condiment.

I was stuck in my space, so I decided to change my space. I decided to bring back Bigfoot's Arcade.

The first move was to adjust the lighting. I switched lamps

around. To get that neon arcade look, I took a smart bulb that changed colors and put it in the ceiling. I found a small travel projector I'd bought for a trip that I never went on. I then dug through old boxes to find another projector, this one ancient and much larger, and put it on my bed facing the wall above my headboard. I connected a Dreamcast to the projector, with *Marvel vs. Capcom 2* blasting on the wall. That was going to be the secondary arcade room. There wasn't much space to work with, so I felt using a big wall was best.

I set up the smaller, newer projector to play a video game movie on my front door: *The Wizard* starring Fred Savage. There were newer, more recent video game movies, but since I was re-creating my childhood arcade, I felt like I could lean into that. I didn't have the Power Glove anymore, but at least I could watch a movie where it actually works. I also had the original *Super Mario Bros.* movie in the queue, followed by *Mortal Kombat*, followed by *Detective Pikachu*. I turned the volume down so it was only just audible. The arcade games would be the star.

In my main living space, I set the smart bulb to the darkest purple, nearly approaching a black light. I cleared everything off my counters and coffee table. Anything that didn't fit in a cabinet was put in the bathtub. I wouldn't need the bathtub for the time being. However, to give the bathroom a little ambience, I turned on a home planetarium to project stars onto the ceiling and used a cheap Bluetooth speaker to play light, relaxing music.

Once I was able to clear all that space, I set up all the arcade machines I had. The big ones—meaning the ones that were a foot tall—went on the kitchen counter. I lined them up side by side, making a U shape. To keep the machines charged, I had a

USB hub that looked like an old arcade quarter-dispensing machine. In the center of the counter I set up a tiny laptop connected to a full-size fighting game–style arcade stick. On that laptop was MAME, an arcade emulator. There were more games loaded onto that one machine than were ever in the real Bigfoot's Arcade.

I set up the even smaller six-inch arcade machines on my coffee table. Because they were so small, the quality of the emulation wasn't as good, and playing them for longer periods was a bit more frustrating. So of course I had dozens of them. In between these I put a toy Skee-Ball table and a small off-brand version of Whac-A-Mole. And—Jesus—a smaller, this time on-brand version of Whac-A-Mole.

On strips of paper, I wrote prices for each game. Fifty cents for a fighting game. Twenty-five cents for an arcade classic. A whole dollar to play *Mario Kart 8* on my TV using a cardboard Nintendo Labo wheel. Three dollars to ride a roller coaster in my virtual reality headset. For years I'd been slowly amassing a large jar of quarters, so it felt like a way to add some physicality to the experience. There was absolutely no reason to set prices on the games, but there was also absolutely no reason to do any of this. I just wanted to be somewhere else that wasn't my apartment, and in May of 2020, this was the only way for me to make it happen.

There are a few YouTube channels that offer ambient arcade sounds. I played one of those videos on my living room speaker. Like the movies, the volume was just low enough to layer in a little more atmosphere. On yet another speaker, I played a very crappy '90s playlist that I more or less picked at random on Spotify. Weirdly, the effect worked. I was approximating an arcade of some sort. A horrifying, mutant bastard child of an arcade, but it would exist for that night. I was giddy. It was the silliest thing I'd ever done for myself.

I turned on all the machines, adding even more bleeps and bloops and hadoukens to my apartment. I flipped all the other lights off except the smart bulb. One bulb and a television screen was enough to illuminate everything. I checked all the prices. I made funfetti cake from a mix that had been sitting in my cabinet for six months, as well as a frozen pizza that I intentionally burned a little so it had that bad, roller rink feel.

Then I grabbed that quarter jar, and I began playing games at the newly reopened, for one night only, Bigfoot's Arcade.

I'm not so absurd that I wasn't aware I was being absurd. I know it sounds somewhere in the range of crazy to very sad. But it gave me a sense of place I couldn't find anywhere else at that moment. Over the few hours of playing, the space of my apartment expanded. My bedroom wall with *Marvel vs. Capcom 2* felt like it was the size of a movie theater. My living room/ kitchen turned into multiple play areas. Even the bathroom, with its spacey spa ambience, was a little nicer. I spent my quarters, placing them next to each machine as I played. *Space Invaders* and *Super Street Fighter 2 Turbo* had the biggest stacks. I gave myself three dollars and rode a roller coaster in VR and almost threw up. I accidentally tore the cardboard wheel playing *Mario Kart* and had to briefly break the illusion to find some tape.

It was wonderful. If you had shown childhood me that night, I'd have been impressed. If you had shown childhood me anything else about my life, I'd have been devastated.

After it was all over, I cleaned up the solo party. Light bulbs were moved back to their proper lamps. I placed the old projector back into a plastic bin under a loose birth certificate and some copies of *Kid Icarus: Uprising*. The arcade games returned to bookshelves and boxes, once more to be observed rather than played. I washed the dishes. I cleaned the pans. I lit a Yankee candle to get the burned-pizza smell out of the place.

I've set up the arcade a few more times over the years. They were fun, but none matched that first night. And the more I did it, the harder it was to keep up the illusion. A fun idea becomes less fun when you have to set up equipment by yourself over and over. Perhaps I noticed how silly it was or that I only wanted to play a few of the games, so it wasn't worth setting up everything. But I enjoyed myself each time—and even invited a date over once humanity resumed. I did warn them it was going to be pretty fucking weird. And then when they showed up, they said, "Holy shit, this is pretty fucking weird."

The distinction between my DIY arcade and a Steam library doesn't make sense when you think about it. We all own *Pac-Man* collections and *Street Fighter* collections. We all have access to hundreds of classic arcade games for free or near free online. Hell, even Game Pass and PlayStation Plus can feel like a virtual arcade where you browse around before finding something fun. Maybe the difference is just joysticks versus controllers. Maybe the difference is a vibe.

I could play every single game from Bigfoot's Arcade on my crappy laptop alone. But on that first night, for a few imaginative minutes, I had my own miniature arcade. The world was mine.

★ ★ ★ ★ ★

ACKNOWLEDGMENTS

This book wouldn't exist without so many people, so if you're upset about anything, please blame them. I'm kidding. Any mistakes or oversights or opinions you hate are my fault entirely. While I know I do the whole self-deprecating routine, I recognize that I am extremely lucky in my life and I've been even luckier to be surrounded by great people who I don't appreciate until it's too late.

I value every hour my parents worked to keep our family fed. I'm grateful for every time my sister canceled plans to babysit us. I'm thankful for my brother being the funniest person I know and always playing games, although that had no effect on my childhood survival. Christmas is my favorite holiday because of all of you, and I definitely wouldn't have this life without your influence and love and shoe throwing.

Also, thank you to the staffs and crews at *Late Night*, *The Tonight Show*, *Saturday Night Live*, *Full Frontal with Samantha Bee*, *Adam Ruins Everything*, *The President Show*, Nintendo, *IGN*, and other places that have been nice enough to hire me, work with me, and allow me to read my phone in your bathrooms. This also goes to the students and teachers at Maplewood, Parkway, Dillard, and NYU who kept my love of gaming alive and confirmed it is the one bare thread of social connection I've got left.

I also want to give a shout-out to my agents at United Talent Agency, Dan Milaschewski and Jon Levy, as well as their assistants, Franck Germain and Sophia Westover. Same for my managers at Independent Artists Media, Kara Welker, John Dunne, and Dave Rath, along with his assistant, Florida's own Veronica Contreras. Do you guys want to set up a call soon? I'll start an email.

All of this writing would make no sense without my editors John Glynn and Eden Railsback. Their input and feedback got me out of my head, helped me clarify my thoughts, and stopped me from repeating the same phrase thirty times. And without the copyediting of Vanessa Wells, this thing would have absolutely zero consistency and read like the serial killer's notebooks in *Se7en*. I only look relatively competent because of them.

Almost done. Thanks to all the people in my life who put up with so many annoying conversations. Maxine Kaplan, Evan Waite, Sarah Arellano, and Lane Moore have been vital at every stage with advice. They're all better writers than me and have great books, shows, and games to prove it. Adam Conover has always been a font of knowledge, and my conversations with him about Nintendo to avoid work at his show genuinely helped kick up some childhood memories. The same goes for all the times I've bothered Rich, Sydney, Ben, Gerry, Brian, Patton, Blaine, Dana, non-agent Chicago Jon,

Chloe, Alisha, Mitch, Zoe, Kaylie, Xalavier, Tamara, Devon, and Derek about the books and the bleep bloops.

And finally, to paraphrase games, thank you for reading.